PELICAN BOOKS

A424

MEDIEVAL THOUGHT

GORDON LEFF

GORDON LEFF

MEDIEVAL THOUGHT

St Augustine to Ockham

PENGUIN BOOKS

Penguin Books Ltd, Harmondsworth, Middlesex

U. S. A.: Penguin Books Inc., 3300 Clipper Mill Road, Baltimore 11, Md

AUSTRALIA: Penguin Books Pty Ltd, 762 Whitehorse Road,
Mitcham, Victoria

—

First published 1958

—

Made and printed in Great Britain
by The Campfield Press
St Albans

To Kate

Contents

PREFACE   ix

INTRODUCTORY   11

PART I

THE AFTERMATH OF ROME
(*c.* 400–1000)

1. *Introduction to the Period*   23
2. *St Augustine and his Successors*   32
3. *The Carolingian Renaissance and its Effects*   55

PART II

THE TRIUMPH OF SCHOLASTICISM
(*c.* 1000–1300)

4. *Introduction to the Period*   77
5. *The Renewal of Letters and Speculative Thought in the
   Eleventh and Twelfth Centuries*   87
6. *The Philosophy of Islam*   141
7. *The Thirteenth Century: the Age of Syntheses*   168

PART III

SCEPTICISM
(*c.* 1300–1350)

8. *Introduction to the Period*   255
9. *The Fourteenth Century: Scepticism versus Authority*   262

BIBLIOGRAPHY   305

INDEX   309

Preface

MY treatment of this subject calls for two comments. The first is that attention has been directed primarily to philosophical, rather than political, thinking: that is to say, to those ideas concerned with the nature of man and the universe – in medieval terms, God's relation to His creatures – as opposed to the nature of human society: man's relation to man. The second is that my approach has been historical. I have sought to place medieval ideas, not to pass judgement upon their validity. It is only possible to assess a thinker justly when we have considered his circumstances: his aims, assumptions, the knowledge at his disposal, his impact upon the prevailing modes of thought. Questions of the truth or falsity of his ideas do not here arise; for beyond providing this understanding the historian does not attempt to go. In order to further such comprehension, I have attempted to depict the more important developments in medieval society, as well as to keep abreast of the changes in education and learning. Inevitably, these sketches contain many generalizations which have had to stand unqualified. Similarly, in attempting to compass a thousand years of intellectual development within the space available, much has had to be sacrificed.

In writing this book I have throughout been only too aware of my dependence upon previous scholarship; although the emphases are mine, I make no claim to novelty in what I have written, except on certain aspects of fourteenth century thought. My debt is at once too general and too vast to be acknowledged individually. I must, however, express my deep obligation to Miss Beryl Smalley, of St Hilda's College, Oxford, for her criticisms, and also to my wife for reading the proofs; both have saved me from many more errors. Finally, I wish to thank Miss M. Norquoy for typing the manuscript.

Manchester
9 December 1957

Introductory

THE term medieval thought is in many ways as loose as the term modern thought. Far from referring to a single outlook to which every thinker, from St Augustine to the Renaissance, subscribed, it covers a diversity of phases, systems, and attitudes. It would be no more just to pick out any one thinker, like Augustine or Thomas Aquinas, as the representative of medieval thinking than to choose Descartes or Kant or Hegel to represent more recent times. On the other hand, this is not to deny the common framework within which nearly all medieval thinking was carried on; and it is here that the thought of the middle ages must be sharply distinguished both from the classical thought of Greece and Rome and from modern, post-Renaissance thought. This framework was provided by the Christian faith; it was regulated by Church authority; and it was largely sustained by ecclesiastics.

The hegemony of Christianity was the distinctive trait of medieval thought. It has been largely responsible for conflicting views over the meaning of a Christian philosophy. At one extreme, it is held that Christian thinking has as much claim to be an independent philosophy in its own right as any other method of speculation; at the other, it has been regarded as little more than the enumeration of dogma. Neither view seems to be justified. Clearly an outlook which is founded upon a guiding set of assumptions cannot claim to be unconcerned with where the argument leads or uncommitted to certain fundamental propositions; at the same time, it is quite possible to apply those beliefs to matters of practical experience and by a process of reasoning to adduce arguments in their favour. This is very largely what all medieval thinkers did: they sought to explain the natural and the human by reference to such tenets of faith as God, creation, the Incarnation, using philosophical and logical argument to do so.

This dependence of reasoning upon the dictates of faith is central to the whole of medieval thinking. It meant that there was an ultimate yardstick by which to judge the validity of an argument. However impeccable its reasoning might be, it had to conform to the tenets of revelation. Thus to deny God's existence, or the creation of the world, or the necessity of grace, was to fly in the face of Christian authority; it was to make philosophical error into heresy. This in turn meant that the last word on any question rested with the Church as the final arbiter. If a view conflicted with accepted doctrine it was condemned and had to be withdrawn. Inevitably, therefore, there had to be a degree of conformity which no one could overstep with impunity: hence the medieval preoccupation with heresy, for it offered a threat to the established order; hence, also, the periodic outbursts of heretical ideas whenever either thought or society was in a ferment: Arianism and Pelagianism in the fourth and fifth centuries, Manicheism in the eleventh and twelfth, extreme apocalyptic views like Joachism in the thirteen and fourteenth as well as the recurrence of a kind of Pelagianism; and all the time there were the infidels like the Jews and the Moslems to be combated. As a result, some of the most elaborate works on Christian thought, including much of St Augustine's output and St Thomas's *Summa against the Gentiles*, were those directed to refuting heresy and defending the faith.

This exclusive allegiance to a defined body of dogma did not, however, mean a uniformity of thought either in type or in time. As soon as there is a desire to supplement belief by reasoning, personal judgement comes into play, and, with it, the search for convincing arguments and concepts. That is to say, a philosophy, a system of knowledge regulated by reason, will emerge in contra-distinction to theology, a body of revealed truth held on faith. From the juxtaposition of faith and reason, Christian philosophy was born; and there is no need why the relationship of reason to faith should be uniform. It can vary in the methods of reasoning, the concepts employed, the definitions accepted, the scope which it is given in support of faith. All these different considerations determined the course and nature of medieval thought.

Firstly, there were the main sources of medieval thought: these were, in addition to the Bible and the early Fathers, the philosophy of Greece, more especially Plato and Aristotle; Neoplatonism, as it developed in the third and fourth centuries A.D.; the systems of the Arabian and Jewish thinkers of the tenth, eleventh, and twelfth centuries A.D., especially those of Alfarabi, Avicenna, Averroes, Avicebrol, Maimonides; and a general smattering of Greek and Arabian science, such as Euclid's mathematics and Alacens's astronomy. None of these was taken over *en bloc* in its pure state; they mingled together to form a multitude of different concepts which sometimes jostled one another uncomfortably. Nor did they all reach the West at the same time or in equal proportions.

Consequently, we have to distinguish both their guiding ideas and their point of impact.

As far as Christian belief is concerned, it revolved round the simple tenets of a God who by His love and freely of His own will had brought into being His creatures and who, as a result of Adam's transgression, had sent His only-begotten son Jesus Christ to redeem mankind from its fallen state. It therefore recognized a supreme being whose providence guided and directed all His creatures. Now philosophically, as we shall see, this view of creation as the free act of a God who was the supreme being, the fount of all love and goodness, was a very different one from the pagan philosophies of Greece. These had all been preoccupied with the discrepancy between the order and constancy of the world of ideas, and the flux and change of the world of the senses. How to relate the stable unchanging concepts of goodness, whiteness, heat, with good things, white things, and hot things, all of which were in a continual process of coming into being and going out of being, had led to a variety of explanations.

Both Plato and Aristotle in their different ways had attempted to escape from the stark alternatives of Heraclitus, who said reality was change, and Parmenides who said it was stability. For Plato there was an ultimate reality of pure unchanging forms or Ideas and there was the sensible world where everything was transitory. The latter was a pale reflection, a manifestation of the true unchanging structure of the ideal, and the object of knowledge was to penetrate to the universal principles which lay beyond the particular objects. The forms or Ideas alone provided certainty; they existed in their own right and their first principle was the Good, the source of all other forms and the means by which they were known. So far as man was concerned, his soul had originally pre-existed as a spiritual substance, in which state it had been able to grasp the intelligible directly. Now, however, it could only reach the truth by means of disengaging it from its material setting in individual things. Accordingly the way to truth lay in contemplation of the ideal by which the soul could recover the knowledge that it used to possess.

Although Plato went a good part of the way in seeing an immaterial source of reality, it was far from approaching the Christian position: he accorded no place to a creator; there was no explanation of the way the forms came into being or whither they led; there was no sense of movement or development, but simply a timeless process without *raison d'être*; there was no eschatology: the soul itself pre-existed and migrated to different bodies, but it never met a last judgement or an eternal life. Thus the most distinctive aspect of Platonism for Christian thought was its approach to reality: its acceptance of the need to transcend this world to reach the ideal and the eternal.

Aristotle, on the other hand, took an essentially empirical view of the nature of existence. He was the first to devote himself to metaphysics as a separate study. He defined this, 'the first philosophy', as he called it, as 'a science of what is simply in its character of Being and the properties which it has as such'. He was therefore concerned with the constitution of Being: its nature, its modes, its properties; in short, that which things needed in order that they might be. His analysis, unlike Plato's, was in terms of things, not ideas. Thus he accounted for change and movement in themselves, as opposed to dismissing them as idle uncertainties. The means by which he did so was to divide all being into matter and form. Matter of itself was pure nothingness, what Aristotle called potentiality; it depended upon a form to make it actual. Thus a stone could only be a stone in virtue of the form by which it became a stone, and it is by its form that we are enabled to recognize it as a stone. Accordingly Aristotle saw the whole process of growth in the progressive realization of matter into the actuality of its form. Once the realization is completed the process is at an end: the acorn has become an oak and cannot then enter a process of becoming a beech.

This view that everything has a natural end or purpose dominates Aristotle's doctrine, and by it he explains the existence of the universe. For the existence of each thing, four causes are needed: the matter or stuff to be realized (the material cause), the form into which it has to be realized, e.g. an oak tree (the formal cause), the agent by which it can be realized (the efficient cause), and the end to which it strives (the final cause). Ultimately, then, the final and formal causes are two aspects of the influence of the form which governs the movement from becoming to being; while the efficient cause presupposes the impulse to set the process in motion. Now there must, Aristotle holds, be a first cause, an unmoved mover which starts this train of development, and this is God. He, again, is not a personal creator: indeed He has no interest in His creatures, for to know what is imperfect would be to demean Himself. But His very presence makes all beings strive to reach Him, and, though they never succeed, He is at once the cause of their movement and the cause of their order.

Aristotle, then, provided a cosmology within which to explain existence, but it was not a Christian one. His God is not a creator, but self-contemplating being, pure actuality, the 'thought of thought'; He plays no providential rôle; He is not responsible for matter, any more than Plato's God; and the process of being is an eternal movement without beginning or end. Although Aristotle had approached the problem from the opposite end to Plato, and had criticized the latter for giving an independent existence to forms, they had reached many of the same cosmological conclusions: the first and final causes did for Aristotle what the forms did for Plato.

With the Neoplatonists, above all Plotinus and Proclus, we come closest to a Christian outlook. They developed Plato's hierarchy of forms into a more cohesive structure, and if they did not reach a theory of creation they at least saw a procession of being from the One to the lowest spiritual being, the human soul. The Neoplatonists translated Plato's Good into the One; it was the principle of all existence, though itself above being, immaterial and indefinable. From the One's self-knowledge emanated the first Intelligence (the Logos or the Word) containing the immaterial Ideas (Plato's forms) of all beings. The Logos in turn gave rise to a second Intelligence, the World Soul, from which the individual intelligences derived, passing down in a hierarchy from intelligence to intelligence until the moon and the sub-lunar world was reached. The human soul was last in the hierarchy of spiritual beings.

Christian thought was from the first greatly influenced by at least four fundamental Neoplatonic concepts: the hierarchy of spiritual beings or Intelligences (which in Christian thinking were usually regarded as angels), with God at the summit; the spiritual nature of reality which was accessible to the human soul; the return of the soul to the One through contemplation, which enabled it to regain the state it had formerly possessed as an Idea in the Logos; and the belief in the goodness and fullness of being. It came from God or the One, and therefore that which had it in the fullest measure was participating most fully in the One; conversely, a privation of being was the cause of sin as a negative quality. Yet here, again, Neoplatonism could not be directly interchangeable with Christian belief: its triad of One, Logos, and World Soul was not the Christian Trinity; its emphasis upon the transmission of being from the One to the individual Intelligences was not an act of creation, but an eternal procession; the soul, despite the emphasis put upon contemplation, was still, as with Plato, imprisoned in a body and so cut off from its true source; its knowledge was regarded as reminiscence, the recapturing of what it had known in its previous state; there was no explanation of matter or sensible being.

The Arabian and Jewish philosophies that reached the West in the later twelfth and thirteenth centuries were an admixture of all these different concepts. They largely constituted systems which tried to combine Plato and Aristotle (who was frequently confused with Plotinus and Proclus) in an attempt to explain the universe.

Now these various sources did not reach the West at the same time, nor were they equally influential. In the period of the early Church Fathers, from the second to the fifth century, when the full heritage of the Greek world was still accessible to both East and West, there was a marked preference for Platonism and Neoplatonism, though this was far from being exclusive. So far as the West is concerned (the thought of which is our subject), St Augustine was the first to make a fusion of Neoplatonic and Christian concepts; and Augustinianism was always one of the dominant streams in medieval thought. With the fifth century came the break-up of the Roman Empire and gradual separation of its Western and Eastern halves. Thenceforth, there is no real knowledge of Plato himself until the end of the middle ages: only fragments of his *Timaeus*, and later two other dialogues (the *Meno* and the *Phaedo*) were available to the Latin world. Neoplatonism itself was largely rediscovered first through the fragments which came with the translations from the Arabic in the later twelfth and thirteenth centuries, and more particularly the translations of Proclus's works in the 1280s by William of Moerbeke. With Aristotle, the case is rather different: certain of his logical works were known throughout the middle ages, largely through commentaries and translations by Boethius; but it was not until the second third of the twelfth century that the rest of his logic was recovered together with an increasing flow of his metaphysical scientific, and ethical writings.

We can say, therefore, that, so far as the West was concerned, it had no direct knowledge of the main body of Aristotle's works, Neoplatonism, or Arabian thought until the twelfth century; that its heritage in the previous centuries was largely made up of St Augustine's writings and those of the Fathers, together with a smattering of Aristotle and Neoplatonism; and that it was only with the thirteenth century that a series of full-fledged systems based upon a coherent body of metaphysics emerged.

The effect of these developments was that, far from being static, medieval thinking was continually undergoing change: the years from the sixth to the eleventh centuries, except for John the Scot, were barren of any important intellectual development, after the achievement of St Augustine and Boethius; but the Carolingian reforms played an important part in putting learning upon a permanent footing. The later eleventh, the twelfth, and the thirteenth centuries were a period of mounting intellectual ferment, until with the fourteenth century the lines of development began to be reversed and the edifice of faith and reason crumbled. Throughout the thousand years which we shall examine, these changes in the components of thought, together with changes in society and innovations like the universities, gave rise to a diversity of problems which prevented any uniform state of development.

The greatest problem that Christian thinkers had to face was the antinomy between their own body of doctrine and the philosophical concepts drawn from pagan outlooks. The application of Plato, Aristotle, Proclus, Plotinus, Avicenna, to Christian revelation was fraught with difficulties, and yet their notions in fact largely made a Christian philosophy possible. The differences between Christianity on the one hand, and the different non-Christian philosophies on the other, were great. Starting from a conception of a personal God, the creator of the universe, Christian thinkers had to take into account a number of fundamental considerations that were not to be found in the pagan systems.

The first was the view that God was Being above all: before He was good or wise or just, He existed. Nearly all medieval thinkers took as their text God's reply to Moses to describe Himself: 'I AM THAT I AM' (Exod. 3: 14). It coloured their entire vision of the world: it made God a being in His own right rather than a nebulous assembly of qualities (Plato and Neoplatonism) or a mere self-contemplating cause (Aristotle); it demarcated His existence from that of His creatures while at the same time making their being the result of a participation in His own; it provided a means of explaining God's triune nature as three Persons subsisting in a common essence, where Neoplatonism saw three separate Intelligences and the Jews and Moslems saw but one Person; it made God's will the direct cause of creation, since His own being, infinite and yet completely realized, had no inherent need to multiply beyond itself – unlike Neoplatonism; above all, as Being, God provided an ultimate reference, in His own essence, to all creation: and man was created in His image.

Secondly, it made Christian philosophy a philosophy of creation. Not only was it the result of a free act by God, contingent and from nothing, as opposed to an eternal and necessary process; it also made the nature of creation different. For the first time, there was an active providence regulating all creation, matter as well as form, the brutes as well as the angels. It made the whole of existence God's province, and so, where all previous philosophers had confined themselves to the intelligible or at least had ruled out, as of no account, the material and the corruptible, sin and the body, Christianity had equally to consider the latter. Christianity, therefore, differed in dealing with the totality of being and in relating it to God as its principle; it sought to explain that before which the pagans had stopped. All existence was germane to enquiry because it was germane to God; it was also, in its nature, good because it came from God. The difference between this outlook and the Greek philosophies hardly needs stressing. Not only did it demand new standards of judgement; it judged everything. With the *minutiae* of existence thrown open to its scrutiny and explanation, new preoccupations arose which the pagans had been largely able to dismiss: the cause of sin in a world which was in itself good; the place of the human body not as the soul's prison, but as the way in which man had been created; the place of the senses, not as a distortion of reality, but as part of creation; the relation of God's providence to free will. Christian thinking, therefore, introduced a new framework.

Thirdly, it also introduced a conception of time and history and movement. Where the Greek world had been a timeless necessary procession of existence, without any visible culmination, Christianity saw a beginning, a middle, and an end. Its beginning was creation; its middle was, for man, the journey through this world as a voyager (*viator*), when, with death and the Last Judgement, he would reach his end in eternal salvation or in eternal reprobation. This teleology was of a very different order from Aristotle's: it was providential and personal at the same time; it made for a dynamic outlook, and amongst most thinkers for an optimism, in their belief in a final consummation. It also made the whole of human history revolve around Adam's fall and Christ's Incarnation; and ultimately all power in this world and reward in the next rested upon them.

Finally, with the infinite gulf between God's necessary being and the contingency of all creation, one of the greatest problems for medieval Christian thinking was the means by which the created could reach the divine. It recognized two levels where the

Greeks had tended to see only a progressive separation of the image from its source. For Christians there could be no single union by means of contemplation; for this itself demanded a supernaturalizing of natural powers, if the latter were to transcend their own limits. Such a change was achieved by grace, a divine gift awarded to a rational creature for its salvation. Its infusion had a variety of forms, but, in essence, its function was to heal man's infirmity which had resulted from the fall, and to elevate him to God, enabling him to know Him and to do His will. The need for grace, therefore, was the measure of the disparity between the created and the divine. In the last analysis truth was a supernatural awareness belonging only to the believer in grace.

For these reasons philosophy had a very different part to play in Christian thought as compared with ancient Greece. Reason of itself could never directly reach the truth; it acted in the light of faith; and was essentially an accompaniment to man in his transitory state as voyager in this world, to be sloughed off when he reached the next. This allowed of no easy relationship between faith and reason. It is not surprising that it knew a state of equilibrium only for a fleeting passage of time with St Thomas Aquinas's system; and St Thomas himself was the calm before the storm which engulfed the later thirteenth and the fourteenth centuries.

The effort to harmonize reason and faith was the motive force of medieval Christian thought; it determined the different attitudes adopted and systems evolved. Throughout, the attempt was beset by two overriding difficulties which very largely governed its course of development. One, internal to thought itself, was the paradox that while there could be no philosophy without a body of metaphysics, logic, and natural knowledge, so soon as these reached a degree of self-sufficiency they challenged theology; that is, they offered a rival interpretation based upon natural considerations to that which theology held by dogma. The widespread dispute over the eternity of the world, man's soul, and many other topics were evidence of this clash during the thirteenth and fourteenth centuries, when philosophy had once more reached maturity. The other obstacle was that the very process of study and teaching, to which profane knowledge gave rise, tended to negate its ultimate end: instead of being a means to a theological end – the better comprehension of faith – it became an end in itself, carried on by specialists whose job it was to teach it. This, too, led to a clash between those who took theology as their guide and those who followed philosophy as far as it would lead. The battle-ground for these rival outlooks was to be mainly the arts faculty in the University of Paris during the later thirteenth century. With the fourteenth century the fabric of scholasticism could no longer contain these rival pressures, and faith and reason began to fall apart. When they did so, the authority that faith had so long exercised over reason was rejected and with it medieval Christian thought.

PART I

THE AFTERMATH OF ROME

(*c.* 400–1000)

CHAPTER I

Introduction to the Period

THE six centuries following the breakdown of the Roman Empire appear, at first sight, to present a paradox. On the one hand all seems confusion: a succession of invasions and transitory kingdoms; the replacement of Roman law and order by instability and unrest; the casting into oblivion of Roman civilization. On the other hand, there were positive achievements and imposing names; and the sudden flowering of society from the eleventh century onwards forces us to acknowledge these. We have to recognize that the earlier middle ages were a formative period and that, though they were in many ways dark, their darkness was not from a sudden plunge into the abyss but far more from passing through a tunnel which itself led to light.

The collapse of the Roman Empire was neither sudden nor primarily the work of external agents. It resulted from a process of internal decline and barbarization. Internally, it could not support its own weight: its government, bureaucracy, and military machine were top-heavy, a constant drain upon its resources; its economy was largely driven by slave-labour, incurring great wastage. The centre of the Empire, in Italy, was largely a parasite upon the provinces. Inevitably, as the Empire became more and more unwieldy, power passed into local hands; as it outstripped its resources, central authority broke down. Already in the third century the Emperor Diocletian had recognized this and had attempted to redistribute the load. Amongst other measures, he had divided the Empire itself into a Western region based on Rome and an Eastern region with Constantinople for its centre. This division was a sign of its impending dissolution; and the Empire was never really again united.

One of the most important consequences of Rome's over-expansion was barbarization: the dilution of the Roman

23

element by barbarians and non-Romans until the Empire became dependent upon the latter for its functioning. This, in a sense, had long been foreshadowed in the development of the provinces, where mercenaries had been recruited into the army from the tribesmen. By the third century, however, whole tribes had been settled within the imperial frontiers as allies (*foederati*); and barbarians came increasingly to dominate the army, the Empire's main instrument of preservation. Rome could not survive without them, but neither could it remain the same with them. They began to clamour for rewards and recognition until they helped to destroy the Empire by internecine strife. The turning-point came in the late fourth and fifth centuries when, impelled by attacks from the Huns, there was a series of movements by the Germanic tribes, the Vandals, Visigoths, and Ostrogoths, into the heart of the Roman Empire in the West.

This was not a sudden cataclysm, nor was there any wholesale destruction by the barbarians. Often fighting resulted, as with Alaric's sacking of Rome in 410 and the Vandals in North Africa; but, primarily, this was a migration of peoples who had long regarded themselves as members of the Empire and who sought protection within its borders.

In their settlements they followed the accepted pattern adopted for *foederati*, and they continued to observe the practices of the Empire. Barbarians like Stilicho, Odovacar, and Theodoric acted as representatives of the Emperor and not as independent rulers; indeed Theodoric went as far as any man could to preserve the authority of the Roman Senate and Roman law. Conditions were naturally not uniform, but even the variations were in keeping with the past. Thus in the more highly Romanized provinces, such as North Africa, Gaul, Spain, and Italy itself, there was no immediate break with Roman ways. In the more remote regions, along the Rhine and in north-western Europe generally, where tribalism had always predominated, there was simply a reversion to type. Provinces like Germany and Britain retained little or nothing of Roman life, and in Britain what traces remained were soon effaced by the Anglo-Saxon invasions shortly after

A.D. 450. The stark contrast between the silence into which Britain was plunged and the continuity of life in, say, Gaul, which we can gather from Sidonius Apollinaris's letters, is the measure of the prevailing diversity.

Yet, if the change was not sudden or immediately destructive, it was none the less real. These barbarian incursions marked the end of the Roman Empire in the West, destroying the common framework within which the different provinces had existed. For the all-embracing authority of the Empire they substituted a series of independent kingdoms, all unstable and for the most part ephemeral. This involved a twofold division. The West became divorced from the Empire in the East; although contact was retained until the seventh century, they henceforth followed separate paths. The West remained cut off from the main sources of culture until intercourse was renewed in the eleventh century; only then could it begin to vie with the higher civilization of Byzantium. Similarly, within the West itself, there was a marked divergence between the countries north of the Alps and Italy. The Mediterranean was no longer the focus of a Europe whose centre had shifted to the North West. The great Mediterranean cities which had been *foci* of trade with the East had little part to play in the life of a predominantly agrarian society. Once sundered from the common Imperial authority there was little in common between the Franks and the Romans.

Inevitably, therefore, the character of society underwent great changes during the fifth and sixth centuries. The uniformity of Roman law gave place to a mosaic of local custom, varying from region to region; its influence was confined to Italy, Gaul, and Spain (until overrun by Islam). The universal monetary system of the Romans fell into disuse. Towns, for so long the centres of wealth and power, lost their pre-eminence and declined, together with the long-distance trade in spices and luxuries from the East. Life reverted to the localities; the landed estate or the family was the basic unit of society; government from the centre was replaced by the private authority of the local ruler. Only the Church retained a central organization and a universal character. Modelled on the lines of the Imperial administration, with its dioceses and provinces, corresponding to Roman divisions, it was able to maintain its cohesion while the Empire crumbled. It was therefore the main bastion of order and administration, able to take charge of cities and regions. This ability, together with its unique spiritual authority, was to make the Church the most influential power in preserving the past and in re-fashioning the future.

These changes should not, however, be exaggerated. Although they signalized a reversion to a more primitive existence, it must not be imagined that the whole of the West suffered a sudden lapse from civilization. As we have said, most of the areas beyond those fringing the Mediterranean had always been more barbarian than Roman. The Empire had been largely an artificial creation without firm foundations, upheld primarily by the army and the tax-gatherer; its industry was driven by slavery rather than by mechanical techniques; its trade, apart from pottery and cloth, was not for large-scale needs; its culture did not extend beyond its own ruling class. The greater part of the Roman Empire, therefore, remained untouched by its achievements, and was not deprived when it collapsed. The changes that ensued were mainly due to the loss of equilibrium which the Empire had provided. This had two aspects: the continual ebb and flow of invasion and settlement that lasted until the end of the tenth century; and the lack of any stable central authority by which order could be maintained. The history of the West during these centuries is dominated by invasions; more than anything else, these prevented any settled order from succeeding the collapse of the Roman Empire.

Of the Barbarian kingdoms formed out of the Roman Empire only that of the Franks endured. The others were swept away by succeeding incursions. In the earlier part of the sixth century, Justinian, ruler of the Empire in the East, attempted to regain North Africa and Italy; despite his initial success, the main effect was the devastation of Italy which rendered her powerless to resist invasion from the Lombards at the end of the century. The Lombards' fierceness and hostility to Rome eliminated Justinian's conquests and they permanently settled the north of Italy. In the seventh and eighth centuries came the Islamic invasions which overran the greater part of the Mediterranean, including Spain and North Africa, and were only checked in the West at the battle of Poitiers in 732. Then in the later ninth and tenth centuries there were the Viking invasions from Denmark and Norway which engulfed north-western Europe, including Britain and Ireland, and threatened to wipe out all traces of civilization. With the ultimate loss of their impetus and the assimilation of the Northmen during the tenth century, the great era of invasions ended and the siege of Western Europe was lifted.

With this background of external attack, to say nothing of internal wars, it is hard to define the stages of development during this period. It is only with the empire of Charlemagne, King of the Franks (768–814), that we are able to gain a glimpse of the new order of society that was emerging. Until the Carolingian Empire we are aware of a series of expedients and transitory shifts of power. Names like Gregory the Great, St Benedict, and St Augustine tell us of the growing authority of the papacy as the leader of the West, of the spread of monasticism, of the establishment of a coherent body of doctrine; rulers like Clovis and Charles Martel speak of the power of the Frankish Kingdom; men like Bede and St Boniface of the pre-eminence of Anglo-Saxon culture. With Charlemagne, however, we see the different elements come together for a fleeting passage of time. His Empire is the first clear sign of the changes that had taken place during the four centuries since the collapse of Rome, and if we examine them more closely it is not to imply that before Charlemagne such features did not exist; but rather to bring out the contrast between the classical and the feudal orders.

The most striking feature of the Carolingian Empire is that it confirms the shift in the centre of gravity from the Mediterranean to north-western Europe. This was to be the main area of development during the middle ages, and, although the Mediterranean and Italy again became of the first importance, the regions approximating to France, the Low Countries, and Western Germany were to be paramount. It also indicates the predominantly agrarian nature of medieval society. Though towns continued to exist and become increasingly more important, they were not the *foci* of power that they had been in the Roman Empire. Secondly, through Charlemagne's administrative measures we can see the way in which wealth and authority were bound up with landholding. The unit of society was the estate, with the lord or seigneur at the head of a descending hierarchy of tenants. The slaves and free peasants of the Roman Empire had tended to become a cross between the two: the dependent unfree peasant, or serf, holding his land and implements from his lord in return for rents (in labour, kind, or money) and subject to the latter's jurisdiction. This status expressed the changed circumstances of an agrarian society where freedom could only go with enough wealth and strength to defend it against both nature and man, and where independent cultivation was preferable to slave-labour. The protection offered by a lord was often the small peasant's only chance of survival in a world of famine and war. The relations of those in the upper reaches of society were regulated by vassalage, whereby one man took another for his lord, doing him homage and swearing fealty to him.

This compact of service and protection, one of the most remarkable features of medieval society, is, in its strictest sense, often taken to denote feudalism. It extended through all reaches of aristocratic society, usually for military purposes, to the king himself. It derived largely from the Companions of Germanic society who attended their leader unto death. All authority was, therefore, exercised through lordship, and one of the great stumbling-blocks to effective royal power was the rival jurisdiction of the aristocracy over their own retainers.

The third aspect of Carolingian society was the supreme importance of the Church. As we have observed, the Church had survived when Rome had fallen, and with it survived Roman organization and Roman civilization. These, added to its spiritual authority, which in its ends and interests was not that of the Roman Empire, gave it a prominence without parallel. The Church alone remained a cohesive force amid the welter of tribes and kingdoms: its bishops became the most important men in the cities, bereft of imperial officers, and in the dioceses. At a time when local authority was the only authority, the Church maintained its unity. In these circumstances it was indispensable to law and order. Its spiritual power played an important part in governing a conquered people, and from the time of Gregory I (590–602) conversion was one of the Church's leading activities. It held the monopoly of learning and literacy; and without clerics to help, even the simplest tasks of government – writing commands or making charters – could not be carried out. The monasteries were the only centres of organized education from the sixth century onwards and dominated intellectual life, as the academies had dominated it in ancient Greece and Rome; they belonged to a society whose unit was the estate and whose preoccupation was with survival. The Benedictine order's emphasis upon work and poverty was in keeping with the work and poverty of the earlier middle ages.

Thus, in an age which had so few resources of its own, the Church offered comfort and protection and leadership. It was indispensable to any ordered state, while its own interests demanded a strong ruler. Its great wealth, constantly increasing through endowment, was the first to suffer in a period of unrest. Hence the most successful attempts at government were those in which king and Church cooperated. The Carolingian Empire was the outstanding example.

Fourthly, Charlemagne's own achievements reveal the position of the king. He no longer possessed either the military and administrative power of imperial Rome or the absolute authority of its Emperors. Roman law had regarded the will of the Emperor as law in itself. 'What the Emperor decrees has the force of law' could have no meaning in the network of local custom and personal obligations of the ninth century. The king was dependent upon the local aristocracy for law and order. He could only delegate power to the man-on-the-spot who was able to exercise it by virtue of his lordship. In these conditions an independent central bureaucracy was out of the question.

Moreover, the status of the medieval king was affected by other important considerations. There was the tribal aspect, deriving mainly from the barbarian peoples, which regarded the king as the personification of the tribe and the guardian of its law. He was not able to raise himself above it; and he owed his own authority to election. With the development of the Church the king, although spiritually enhanced, was in practice further circumscribed. Kingship came to be regarded as a sacred office with the king more a priest than the magical being of tribal concepts. He was God's representative; and his supernatural character was symbolized in the ceremony of anointing, marking him off from other men. Medieval kingship therefore was subject to restrictions and obligations which were unknown to Roman Emperors. When we recall its lack of material resources we can realize how much depended upon the personality of the king. If it was a strong one, and he was able to wield an effective sword, when occasion required, he could create a strong authority; a weak king invariably meant lack of governance.

With Charlemagne, himself an outstanding personality, the relationship of king to Church was given a new turn; in addition to being king of the Franks, he became, at the hands of the Pope, Holy Roman Emperor in 800. This revival of the imperial idea shows not only the medieval belief that Christendom was the heir to Rome, but the central place that the Papacy occupied in Western Europe. The creation of an Emperor was an attempt to give the Pope a protector and a partner in directing Christendom; it put imperial power under papal auspices. Once revived, the imperial idea was to bulk large for the next five hundred years. That it was never, in practice, much more than a figment is hardly surprising. Only an international body like the Church could effectively transcend local boundaries, and the pope alone was able to make his voice heard throughout Christendom.

It was within this framework that culture and learning developed. They became inseparable from ecclesiastical and monastic life. They were directed towards a better comprehension of the scriptures and subordinated to the training of clerks and monks. Thus learning lost any independent rôle; it was the handmaid of theology. Yet, as the image of the Roman Empire became more distant and its aura grew, things Roman became evermore an object of veneration. The Carolingian renaissance in learning and culture is striking testimony to this attitude, which was to prevail during the middle ages. It marked a new phase in medieval culture. From the sixth century onwards learning had been in decline; there was a real danger that the heritage of the past would be lost. Thus the first need was to stop the rot, and to put learning once more upon an organized footing. This was the great achievement of the Carolingian reformers. Despite the blows by the Northmen against the main monastic centres, enough of their work survived to help the cultural revival of the eleventh century.

These centuries, then, often called the 'Dark Ages', had their moments of brightness. Even though its kingdoms were ephemeral, and Charlemagne's own empire collapsed under the stress of weak successors and the Viking attacks, the elements of medieval society were gradually forming. With the end of the last series of invasions in the tenth century, they began to come into the open.

CHAPTER 2

St Augustine and his Successors

THE centuries of the so-called 'Dark Ages' do not form any single outlook. They rather reflect a welter of different tendencies in which, for the most part, established ideas jostle one another and originality is virtually non-existent. Yet we may discern two marked phases in the thought of this period: the fifth and sixth centuries and the period beyond it.

The fifth and sixth centuries differ strikingly from the rest of the period in two ways. In the first place, they were, in character, still close to classical thinking and still maintained a high level of expression and culture. In the second place they contained two of the most prominent thinkers who were to influence the whole middle ages: St Augustine and Boethius. Both of these thinkers represent an earlier tradition besides helping to give rise to a new one. St Augustine is essentially the last in the line of the great African Fathers of the Latin Church: Boethius is the last Roman philosopher.

After these thinkers the West enters a period of decline, decline in the double sense of a lowering of tone and of a paling image of an original model. There was no really important thinker between Boethius and the eleventh century except for John Scotus Erigena. For the rest, we are confronted with a series of imitations and attempts to preserve the heritage of the past, both in philosophy and in learning, through encyclopedias and collections. Moreover, the whole organization of learning changed. At the time of St Augustine it still takes place in academies and schools and in the cities where the bishops have the headquarters of their dioceses. The classical stream of thought still flows, and a man like Cassiodorus in the next century was a senator as well as thinker. By the end of the sixth century this had all changed: henceforth, with society predominantly rural, and learning, of sheer necessity, the preserve of the clergy, the centre of culture changes to the monasteries. Here, alone, something of the social cohesion necessary for an organized life remained; here alone there was a chance of retreat from the turmoil of the erstwhile centres of civilization. Thus from the seventh century onwards most learning is monastic and most of the learned are monks.

This not only meant a break with the classical content of thought; it also meant that knowledge was primarily concerned with providing the sheer rudiments needed to train up a literate priesthood. The emphasis is upon preservation; only John the Scot attempts a new speculative system; for the rest, men like Alcuin, Bede, Isidore of Seville are content to compile what is already known in order that it may help to preserve learning and culture. In greater or lesser degree, this derivative attitude lasts down to the eleventh century; the prospect which the Carolingian renaissance gave to the revival of learning was shattered in renewed invasions, this time by the Northmen, of the ninth century. John the Scot had barely had time to elaborate his system at the court of Charles the Bald before the ending of the Empire which had made his work possible. Stable conditions had to wait for a century more until, with the assimilation of the Northmen, Western Europe was able to breathe more freely.

(i) St Augustine, 354-430

St Augustine lived at a time when the whole foundations of society were in upheaval. Born at Tagaste, in North Africa, he was the greatest of the great African Fathers who had been so important for the Western Church. During his lifetime the barbarians, after inflicting their first overwhelming defeat on the Romans at Adrianople, in 378, were pouring into the Roman Empire. Augustine lived to witness Alaric's sack of Rome and spent the last years of his life in organizing resistance to the Vandals besieging his own city of Hippo, of which he was bishop. His own life was equally stormy. Although his mother was a Christian, he soon succumbed to Manicheism, which explained the world in purely rational terms; it regarded all existence as a dualism of good and evil, with matter the

B

source of evil. Gradually, however, Manicheism lost its hold, and St Augustine, unable to find certitude, took up a moderate form of scepticism. It was in this state that he came upon the philosophy of Neoplatonism through reading a translation of Plotinus's work. It led him on to Christianity, whose spiritual interpretation had already deeply impressed itself upon him through St Ambrose, Bishop of Milan. Henceforth, St Augustine lived and wrote as a Christian, renouncing the ways and views of his previous life.

The whole of St Augustine's life and writings are therefore a progress towards certitude and faith. It is as an intensely personal journey, with its attendant phases, that we must regard his outlook. He does not simply start from a place of rest from which he surveys the world around. He moves on from position to position, so that some of his most formative doctrines come only at the end of his life. His writings reveal this unceasing quest, far more vividly than those of most thinkers. Consequently, no single work comprehends his entire outlook, which is itself of mixed descent and the product of his previous positions.

Strictly speaking St Augustine is not a philosopher at all, nor did he create a system. Like all the early Fathers, both Greek and Latin, his end was to defend and strengthen the faith. It therefore took in all those problems which needed solution. But in St Augustine's case, these were put on a lasting foundation and extended to all the fundamental questions which were germane to a Christian outlook. This was in part due to the width of his own experience: and the Manicheism, scepticism, and Neoplatonism of his early years remained influential throughout his subsequent life. From the Manicheans he had had confirmation of his own inclination to follow evil ways; and sin remained ever one of his deepest preoccupations. As a Christian he subsequently devoted much attention to its nature and cause, for which he was able to reach a solution. Scepticism, whereby he lacked any certitude, remains apparent in his distrust of all sensory and material knowledge and the realization that true faith comes only through inner conviction, independently of all external phenomena. Such a position ultimately buttressed his Christian belief that all truth was spiritual. Neoplatonism, the third stream in St Augustine's thought, was by far the most influential: it provided him with a cosmology, a pattern of the universe by which he was able to judge the relationship of the spiritual and the eternal to the material and the temporal. It was from Neoplatonism that St Augustine held that the truth was immaterial, residing in forms or Ideas (*rationes*) which derived from God; that God contained in Himself these immaterial archetypes of all things; that to know the truth is to know God, even though not directly; that only the soul, as a spiritual being, can attain to truth which is itself immaterial; that there is a distinction between such intelligible knowledge, alone the path to truth, and sensible knowledge which is dependent upon mutable things; that the soul can only reach the truth by dissociating itself from the sensible; that all being, as coming from God, is in itself good; that evil is negative, a privation of being; that everything material derives from seminal forms latent in matter, including those things yet to appear.

The affinities between Neoplatonism and Christianity were strong. As we have mentioned, the whole emphasis of Neoplatonism was upon the essentially spiritual, immaterial nature of reality. It therefore induced an attitude similar in many respects to Christianity: there was a common belief in a supreme author; a common orientation towards a contemplative, otherworldly attitude; a common desire to transcend the earthly realm of matter and to re-establish harmony with the supreme One. Lastly, many of their concepts were interchangeable: where the Neoplatonists spoke of the immaterial triad of the One, the Intelligence, and the Soul, Christianity saw the Trinity of the Father, the Son, and the Holy Spirit. But it was in those seeming degrees of harmony that the two outlooks differed so greatly.

In the first place Neoplatonism saw all existence as a procession of Intelligences from the One down to the material world. The whole process was involuntary, for each higher Intelligence, by virtue of its own goodness, transmitted its nature to a subsidiary Intelligence. There was, therefore, contrary to Christianity, no voluntary act of creation. In the second place, where Neoplatonism made existence an eternal process, for Christians it was *ex nihilo* and in time. There was no eternal hierarchical chain of beings as there was in Neoplatonism. In the third place, Christianity regarded creation as the immediate result of God's will acting directly upon all that He brought into being; with Neoplatonism it was essentially through intermediaries: each sphere was responsible for the sphere immediately inferior to it. In the fourth place, the Christian view was essentially based upon the world of actual existence, while Neoplatonism saw matter as an impediment to spiritual beings, and, in the case of man, regarded the body as the prison of the soul. Finally, since, with Christianity, God and His creatures existed at two completely different levels, the difficulty lay not in demarcating their provinces but in trying to find their meeting point. Neoplatonism, on the contrary, by identifying the One with goodness and making it above all being, was in danger of pantheism: the One as everywhere could be in all creatures.

Thus Christianity and Neoplatonism were concerned with different orders and with different problems. Christianity had to reconcile the actual existence of nature with God's will; everything in being had to be examined in the light of its creator. Its mysteries of the Trinity and the Incarnation were reflected in the experience of this world. Neoplatonism owed no such an obligation to explain the world; its main problem in an eternal, immutable system, was to return to the One, its source. In the soul's quest for the One, it could ignore the outside world entirely.

St Augustine, however much he might use Neoplatonic concepts, had to apply them differently: to provide a Christian explanation of the world. His starting-point was not the philosophical calm of contemplation, as with the Neoplatonists, but the Christian's desire to reach his maker. He was moved by the presuppositions of Christian faith; he sought not to prove them but to understand them, so that others might also understand them. This marks a difference in approach from a strictly philosophical enquiry, and St Augustine in this, as in so much else, provides a new groundwork for Christian thinking. Knowledge, he holds, can come only from belief. Before one seeks to know anything one must believe that it exists; there must be an idea in the mind. This was in keeping with his Neo-platonic view of knowledge. Yet it is only one element in his outlook, for the desire to know itself presupposes a state of mind – a love of truth; and this is a sign of grace, of the love of God within us. Only by God's grace can we want to know and believe. To know the truth requires intellectual clarity; but such clarity itself involves a whole way of life: the search for beatitude which only grace can bring. Before, then, there can be understanding there must be righteousness; without right-doing there cannot be right thinking. For St Augustine grace is the bridge between the created and the divine. It is the means by which man may enter into association with God, become His adopted son, and follow His ways.

As finally developed, St Augustine's doctrine of grace regarded it as a supernatural gift necessary for man's final salvation and preservation from evil. Whereas before the fall man had had need only of the grace which brought him to God (*elevans*), after the fall his nature was impaired. He therefore needed grace to heal his fallen nature (*sanans*) from concupiscence and ignorance. Without grace, man's free will, although still in existence, cannot overcome these impediments and so remain free from sin or achieve good. Grace, then, confers upon free will the added freedom of being able to give effect to its desires to do good. For St Augustine, God divided the damned from the saved according to whether He endowed them with a special grace (final perseverance) by which they might persevere in goodness and remain free from sin until the end. Such predestination to election or damnation rests with God's will alone; all that we can know is that sin destroys the love of God that grace alone can give: 'We cannot love God unless He already loves us' (*De gratia et libero arbitrio*, XVIII, 38).

The full rigours of this doctrine which, while asserting the independence of free will, seemed to ignore its powers to good, were not developed until the last years of St Augustine's life. From 412 he wrote a series of treatises against Pelagius and his followers who held that man was not tainted with Adam's sin, that his nature remained unimpaired, and that he could win grace by his own merits. The positions that St Augustine adopted in response to Pelagianism became the basis of the Catholic doctrine on grace, free will, and merit thenceforth. Yet even before these had been formulated in such works as his *De correptione et gratia*, *De gratia et libero arbitrio*, and *De praedestinatione sanctorum*, St Augustine had advanced far along the same path.

Now the importance of this attitude lay in the way it started with the real world and with man's actual state. Unlike the Neoplatonists, St Augustine's position took full cognizance of human history and the contingent nature of creation. Instead of dealing with contemplation and truth in the abstract it was centred on the limitations and capacities of man as a finite creature. In the second place, St Augustine's approach showed that the central problem of Christian thought sprang from the division between the divine and the created. He refused to acknowledge that the Neoplatonic view of spiritual contemplation sufficed for a return to the One, or God. The danger of pantheism, so manifest in Neoplatonism, prevented any direct contact between God and His creatures on the natural level. A supernatural aid was needed to transcend the finite, contingent, material world and to reach God's infinite nature. This awareness of the distinction between nature and grace sprang from the tenets of Christian belief: the personal concept of God who acted voluntarily, as opposed to the necessary hierarchy of intelligences, autonomous and eternal, which made up the Neoplatonic universe. The contrast between the two was the foundation of St Augustine's outlook; it made grace not just a question of theology but the expression of the Christian *Weltanschauung*: it put the relation between creator and creature as the central issue. All knowledge of the supernatural therefore was transformed from intellectual speculation into a state of awareness dependent on grace: only thus could true understanding emerge.

Within this framework St Augustine treated the problems

which confronted both the Christian and the unbeliever. His own previous experiences as Manichean and sceptic made him particularly aware of the need to explain the presence of evil and the evidence for belief.

As we have already suggested, St Augustine regarded knowledge as inseparable from belief; for him there was none of the later medieval distinction between the realms of reason and faith. As a result St Augustine does not try to establish proofs for God's existence on a purely rational basis. He is concerned to adduce support for the belief which he already has. Nor is he interested in the source by which we gain our knowledge. His task, as shown in his early *Contra Academicos*, is to ask where our knowledge can lead and whether it can satisfy our need for faith in a supreme being. This essentially theological approach turns from the world of the senses and material things to the immaterial world of our own ideas.

St Augustine's sceptical trait is seen in his dismissal of the fleeting world of things as unable to give us certain knowledge. Not that he denies the validity of the things we encounter there; in themselves they are true, but they do not allow us to pass from the individual facts to the general laws. In the case of refraction, for example, an oar in water appears bent. This is quite correct so far as its *appearance* is concerned, but *false* for the actual state of the oar. This failure to deduce the general from the particular means that we must look elsewhere for truth. For this, St Augustine turns to self-knowledge. Here, unlike the external world, our very doubts lead to certainty; for by doubting we become aware of ourselves: 'You, who wish to know, know you that you are? I know. Whence know you? I know not ... Know you that you think? I know. Therefore it is true that you think. It is true' (*Soliloquies*, II, 1). 'Everyone who is aware that he doubts, knows the truth and is certain of it ... and should not doubt that he has the truth within him' (*De Trinitate*, x, 10).

The starting-point, then, for knowledge lies in our own thoughts. This remains constant, even though we know nothing else. From this primary awareness of our own existence through thought, we can advance to awareness of certain ideas in our soul.* These, unlike the fleeting objects of the real world, remain constant and universal: number, colour, goodness, being, are all concepts that we possess and which are quite independent of external circumstances. They enable us to formulate certain laws such that, say, $2+2=4$, without needing to deal with actual numbers. Such truths are common to all men; they are eternal and immutable, transcending not only the material world but our own experience. They are signs of a higher Truth which we call God. He is the 'interior master', the light which illumines the truth in our soul.

This doctrine was the foundation of the Augustinian outlook which was to prevail throughout the middle ages. It took the Platonic emphasis upon the immaterial nature of knowledge as its starting-point; it identified the Platonic concept or Idea with truth and therefore equated mental images with intelligible reality. But St Augustine moved beyond Platonism and Neoplatonism in three important respects. The first was to harness these Ideas or concepts in the soul to their source in God. Unlike the Neoplatonists, they were not simply remote manifestations of the One; they were the direct result of God's own action. In this way, St Augustine is able to see God as first, immutable being – the He-who-is of the Old Testament. In God's own infinite immaterial nature reside the archetypes, or Ideas, of all that exists in the real world: they are indivisible from His own essence and are the signs of it. That which is distinct in this world is one in God. 'There are certain ideas, forms, or reasons, of things which are immutable and constant, which are immaterial and contained in the divine intellect . . .' (*De diversis quaestionibus*, 83, q. 46). It is from these that the soul is able to become aware of God. Now this is not the same as saying that the soul gains a direct knowledge of God. Such an interpretation was to be given to this view by St Anselm and later St Bonaventure, when they held that to have an idea of God was to know Him. St Augustine was content to adduce God's existence from the Ideas residing in the soul. He did not try to describe God beyond asserting the immutability of His

*See *De libero arbitrio* II, *De Magistro*, *Enarrationes in Psalmos*, 41.

nature which itself made Him unknowable to His creatures in this world.

The second consequence of St Augustine's view concerned the way in which the soul grasped these Ideas. This was by illumination, an inner light which enabled the soul to recognize them. In the *City of God* St Augustine referred to this incorporeal light as the means by which the soul reaches sure knowledge. Elsewhere he shows how all truth and understanding are part of the divine light, with God our master. The soul of itself is unable to see intelligible truth; it is therefore dependent upon an illumination from God. This is one more aspect of St Augustine's belief in the insufficiency of natural powers to transcend the natural; it is in keeping with his whole assumption that God can only be reached through the supernatural aid of His grace. But a difficulty arises when we enquire into the nature of this divine light. St Augustine himself, interested in its existence rather than in the mode of its operations, nowhere gave an unambiguous account of its working. Consequently, controversy has raged over whether it was an uncreated, divine light or part of reason's natural light, and over how reason actually grasped the divine Ideas. In the absence of any definite text in St Augustine's works, there will always be room for disagreement. Yet it would seem that, in keeping with his whole emphasis upon man's dependence upon God's influence and the inadequacy of the soul to know by its own resources, this added illumination was uncreated and divine. In any case, it remains true that the soul needed a special light, even if it came from itself, before it could comprehend the divine Ideas.

The third aspect of St Augustine's view of knowledge was the nature of the soul itself. Here, again, there are clear signs of Platonic and Neoplatonic influence. Unlike many Christian thinkers, including Tertullian, St Augustine affirmed that the soul was an immaterial substance.* In keeping also with the Platonists, he regarded the soul as indestructible and as the ruler of the body. He differed, however, in giving these concepts a Christian interpretation. The Neoplatonists had

*See *De quantitate animae.*

regarded the soul as imprisoned in the body. For St Augustine this was to fly in the face of the Christian belief in a divine providence whose creation was essentially good. The body, no less than the soul, was God's work; it was good in itself and only became bad when disfigured by sin. Similarly, where both the Platonists, and some Christian Fathers, believed that the soul, as an immaterial intelligence, had pre-existed from eternity, St Augustine upheld instantaneous creation. Although St Augustine does not specify at what stage the soul was created, he denies that it ever existed separately from the body.

In developing his own theory of the soul, St Augustine was concerned to stress two points: firstly that the soul, located throughout the body, not in any one place, is its active ruler. Not only does it guide the body in all questions of will and knowledge, but it also informs the body of its own state. Hence, St Augustine will not even allow that sensation is from the body; to do so would mean that the inferior could act upon the superior, an assertion that went against the whole Augustinian concept of hierarchy. On the contrary, sensation derives from the soul's own awareness of what the body is undergoing. St Augustine compares it with verse or music: although the physical sounds of the words are from the senses, their meaning and shape are provided by the soul's awareness. Thus through sensation the soul interprets the body's needs.

Secondly, the nature of the soul provides the strongest evidence of its contact with God. It is the mirror of the divine nature: it is immaterial (though not, of course, eternal), immortal, and its faculties correspond to the divine Trinity; its being (*essentia*) is the foundation for its understanding (*intelligentia*) and love (*amor*), just as the being of the Father is the foundation for the Word and the Holy Spirit. Moreover, it is by reminiscence that the soul gains contact with the higher truth; it does not so much learn the truth as recognize it in the light of eternal ideas. This is a further indication of its divine origin and is one more piece of evidence for the way in which Augustine turned a Platonic concept to Christian advantage. The Platonists regarded reminiscence as the soul's link with its spiritual source from which matter (its body) had separated it. It constituted a reminder of the free state of the soul before it had become imprisoned in the body; by turning away from the world of the senses and directing its attention to its inner being, the soul could catch faintly rays of truth and once more tread the path back towards the One. St Augustine had no need for this contradiction between the body and truth, but reminiscence enabled him to place the soul close to God.

In his view of God and the nature of the Trinity, St Augustine insists upon the utter simplicity of the divine nature; it allows of no categories or description: He is 'good without quality, great without quantity, the creator without need to create . . . everywhere without place, eternal without time . . . ' (*De Trinitate*, v, 1). He cannot be described save than by saying He is Being. We know with certainty only what He is not: this negative theology was to have great influence for the future. On the Trinity, too, St Augustine asserted the indivisible unity of the Godhead: his teaching in the *De Trinitate*, one of his most profound works, defined God as a unity subsisting in three persons. This was in marked contrast to the Greek view which by starting with the One saw the three persons as distinct, with the Word and the Holy Spirit subsequent to the Father. St Augustine's teaching on the Trinity formed the basis of subsequent Catholic faith.

In dealing with creation,* St Augustine distinguished between the immaterial models or Ideas which reside in God through the Word and the coming into being of individual things. The first, as we have seen, subsist in God eternally and are indivisible from His nature. Actual beings, however, were created simultaneously and so all that was ever to be is already in being. This naturally raised the problem of how new beings emerged if there was no further act of creation on God's part. St Augustine's answer was to adopt the Platonic idea of germs or seeds (*rationes seminales*) which were latent in matter and would germinate in the course of time. Thus, within the fixed eternity of a species, the individuals could evolve (but not develop) according to a pre-existing state. This condition

*See especially, *De Genesi ad litteram*.

applied to all material creatures, including man's body, though not to his soul.

Although this outlook did not allow for any individual variations or for evolution in the proper sense, it showed once again the essentially mobile character of the Christian world. It is in a constant state of movement. It makes the main contrast that between the immutable being of God, on the one hand, and the state of flux, of becoming, on the other. It puts the emphasis upon trying to find the connexion between the two.

This is particularly apparent in the problem of sin. For St Augustine, as for all Christians, the world, as the work of God, is essentially good. How, then, to account for the evil which prevails? The Neoplatonist Plotinus who had recognized all being as good saw the cause of evil in a lack of being; it was a privation which impaired the fullness of existence. By this view, sin could not have a positive cause, for it was a deficiency. St Augustine adopted this explanation and employed it both to absolve God from failure to create a good world and to counter the Manichean assertion that matter was the cause of evil. It enabled him to maintain the essential harmony and goodness of the world and to seek the cause for sin elsewhere. This he located in man's free will,* which, by Adam's transgression, had inculpated the whole human race and made man henceforth dependent upon the mediation of Christ. Sin, then, entered into the whole course of human history, and once more we can see how the real world of being of the Christians differs from the static cosmology of Neoplatonism.

In making the will the cause of sin, St Augustine introduced a trait that distinguishes the Augustinian outlook throughout the middle ages. While he insisted upon the indivisible unity of the soul's nature, he nevertheless, as in God, distinguished its various attributes, or faculties. He variously described these as memory, understanding, and will, or thought, knowledge, and love. Of these the will is the *leitmotif*: only by wanting to believe and by loving the truth can the soul turn towards the divine. Similarly, through the free activity which the will

*See *De libero arbitrio.*

possesses, man can be led along the path of transgression and sin.

We are thus back at our starting-point: the inseparable connexion between truth and faith; the necessity of grace to make the will receptive to God; the foundation of all knowledge in the love of goodness and the search for beatitude. This is the setting for St Augustine's outlook: it provides not a fully defined scheme of the universe but an enumeration of the milestones which can lead the soul to God. It was the founding of these milestones on firm philosophical positions that marked St Augustine's achievement. In doing so he gave the first sustained explanation of the tenets of faith.

This is nowhere more apparent than in his political philosophy. In his *City of God*, St Augustine shows the way in which all mankind is divided into the two cities, the terrestrial and the heavenly. These are not separate groupings but represent the saved and the damned. All men, good or bad, by their very natures have to live in the earthly city where they have earthly needs – sustenance, clothing, shelter, and so on. The division between the two cities comes when on the Day of Judgement they will be elected to eternal life or doomed to final reprobation. Only the Christians can, through grace, attain to the state which enables them to be saved. The whole of history therefore is a progressive movement towards the constitution of the heavenly city as it will finally emerge. So far as this world is concerned, it is the preparation for the next, and the state itself can only be justified in divine terms.

Now St Augustine lived at a time when the entire civilization of the ancient world was crumbling, and when the Roman Empire, itself Christian, was being overrun by barbarians and heretics. It could only seem that Rome was paying for her sins; that such suffering was a judgement from above. We meet in St Augustine's political theory the first full explanation of society in man's fallen state. Although men are naturally social beings, had there been no fall there would have been no need for the state, or government, as an authority imposed from above. Neither private property nor the division into masters and servants would have come about had men lived in their original state of righteousness. Peace and happiness, the desire of mankind, would have been preserved through man's own wholeness of nature. Original sin changed all this. It made necessary rulers and ruled to safeguard private property, to prevent war and disorder. Thus overlordship was a divine judgement, at once a chastisement and a remedy for sin. The State had a divine origin and rulers a divine authority. The Church was God's means of dispensing goodness; even bad rulers were the measure of society's sinfulness in calling them down upon itself.

Small wonder that St Augustine could not feel very enthusiastic for the State when he considered to what condition it had been brought. Yet he had, as in so much else, created medieval political theory. He gave a historical approach to its study, and, above all, he refused to see the evils of the world as eternal categories. Though slavery existed it was not in itself man's natural condition; there was no necessary relation between man's low estate in this world and his place in the next. Although St Augustine recognized the ills of this world to be necessary, they nevertheless remained ills, the result of sin.

St Augustine throughout refused to equate visible attainment with true happiness. In one sense his outlook was a critique of the static, regulated world of Platonists and Neoplatonists; where they stopped at concepts, he dealt with metaphysics, the actual state of being and its manifold aspects. Throughout he gave it a supernatural interpretation, but one which could have meaning for individuals and for societies. Although it was only one possible interpretation out of several, as we shall see in due course, it was the one most in keeping with the teachings of the early Church at that epoch. In a world where hope seemed to reside in personal salvation alone, St Augustine provided the grounds for such hope.

(ii) St Augustine's Successors

St Augustine was the last great thinker of the Patristic Age in the West. His was the dominant influence until the thirteenth century, when it was shared, but never overthrown, by systems inspired by Aristotle. During the fifth and the sixth centuries there remained a few final offerings of the classical outlook, before the stream dried up and the main intellectual efforts turned to preserving and transmitting its heritage. Of the thinkers who followed St Augustine the most outstanding was Boethius (*c.* 470–*c.* 525), a Roman who studied at Rome and Athens. He became consul to Theodoric the Ostrogothic king of Italy, by whom he was later accused of conspiracy and imprisoned. During his long captivity he composed *On the Consolation of Philosophy*, which became one of the most widely-read books of the middle ages.

Although it is open to dispute whether Boethius was actually a Christian or not, his great influence upon medieval thought is philosophical rather than theological. In a sense his work was complementary to St Augustine's: where the latter handed down an outlook which was largely a Christian synthesis of Platonism, Boethius transmitted Aristotle's logical work. Although far from complete, his translations and commentaries formed a major part of the Aristotelian logical corpus known to the West from the seventh to the later twelfth century. These translations and commentaries included Aristotle's *Categories*, *On Interpretation*, the *Prior* and *Posterior Analytics*, the *Sophistical Arguments*, and the *Topics*. He also translated and commented the Introduction to Aristotle's *Categories* (*Isagoge*) by Porphyry, the Neoplatonist, which was to be so influential in the twelfth century. These, together with a multitude of logical treatises, and his famous *On the Consolation of Philosophy*, gave him a place beside St Augustine as one of the main authorities of the middle ages, especially before the rediscovery of Aristotle's works at the end of the twelfth century. Boethius, more than anyone else, not only kept the philosophical tradition alive, but provided the means by which it could be renewed in the eleventh and twelfth centuries, over the problem of universals. Moreover, his application of Aristotelian categories to the structure of being was not without later influence.

Yet Boethius's subsequent fame was not of his own choosing. He had intended to transmit to the West all the writings of Plato and Aristotle, translated and commented by himself. His aim was to make a synthesis of their divergent outlooks. He only, however, reached the translations and commentaries of the logical works mentioned above, with the result that he preserved Aristotle for posterity. In his commentaries, and in his *Consolation of Philosophy*, he showed that his own position veered far more closely to Neoplatonism, even while expounding Aristotle.

Boethius's greatest contribution to medieval thought was over the question of Universals, that is, the relation of genera and species (animal, man) to individuals (Socrates, Plato). In his commentaries on Porphyry's *Isagoge*, Boethius answers the questions which Porphyry had raised, but not answered, on the nature of the genus and the species. Porphyry had asked three questions: first, whether universals were real substances or merely categories; second, if they were real, whether they were corporeal or incorporeal; third, if incorporeal, whether they existed separately from sensible things or were part of them.

While Plato had held universals to be real and incorporeal, Aristotle had regarded them as purely mental concepts. Boethius gives a solution which tries to reconcile them both; but since he is making a commentary on Aristotle he decides in favour of Aristotle. He shows that, since a universal is common to at least several individuals, it cannot itself be an individual and so cannot be a sensible substance. On the other hand, if it were simply a mental construction without reference to any object it would be meaningless; it would be a thought about nothing. Hence, a universal ought to correspond to some reality. To solve this predicament Boethius calls on the view which regards the genus or species as the result of the mind working upon the senses. From the confusion of objects encountered in the senses the mind is able to distinguish those qualities which are common to a group of individuals. In this way the universal subsists in material beings, though it is itself immaterial.

Boethius himself does not give unqualified support to this solution and refuses to commit himself for or against it.

Nevertheless, as taken up in the twelfth century, it provided the starting-point for the disputes between Nominalists and Realists which used to be regarded as the central feature of medieval thought. Boethius himself did not go beyond this position to apply the Aristotelian process by which the mind grasped the universal from the particular; and, in the absence of Aristotle's own work in the twelfth century, the problem likewise did not go beyond this point.

So far as nature was concerned, Boethius produced one distinction which was a fruitful source of future discussion. He regarded each individual thing as made up both of its matter and the form which determined it. Without both parts there would not be the individual substance: thus man is composed of his body (that which is) and the form (that by which it is) by which he is man. The form gives the substance being, and either without the other would not alone constitute man. These divisions were to become important in the thirteenth century in discussing the nature of being.

Boethius, in addition to his *Consolation of Philosophy*, which is on a religious theme but without reference to Christianity, is credited with theological works on the Trinity. The *Consolation of Philosophy* is concerned with finding true happiness in contemplation, despite the tribulations of this world. Among its many themes, including the different degrees of knowledge, the soul, and providence, Boethius deals with two which were to become prominent: the relation of free will to divine foreknowledge; and the different degrees of goodness in things, presupposing a sovereign good, which must be God. In the first, Boethius shows that for God to foresee the free acts of free will does not destroy their freedom and contingency; for God sees all things concurrently and eternally, even though they take place through the succession of time in the created world. The proof of God's existence from differing levels of goodness was to be taken up by St Anselm in the eleventh century.

With Boethius came the end of independent philosophical speculation until the eleventh century. There was no attempt by his contemporaries to utilize the works of Plato or Aristotle in the same way; and when with the Moslem invasions of the seventh and eighth centuries the links between the West and the Greek world were cut, renewed contact had to wait until the twelfth century.

With Boethius's pupil, Cassiodorus, the classical era was already at an end. After a highly successful career in the service of the same Theodoric who had had Boethius put to death, Cassiodorus founded a monastery, Vivarium, in Southern Italy. There he retired, building up one of the finest libraries in existence, which not only preserved the heritage of the past but introduced learning into the Benedictine Order as one of its pursuits. His own work consisted of a treatise on the soul and his *Institutes of Divine and Secular Literature*. Book 11 of the *Institutes* became used separately as a handbook for monastic schools. Entitled *On the Arts and Disciplines of the Liberal Letters*, it laid down the subjects which a monk needed to know, after the manner of an encyclopedia. These constituted what came to be known as the seven liberal arts, divided into the *trivium* and the *quadrivium*. The *trivium* dealt with the three subjects of grammar, rhetoric, and logic; the *quadrivium* with the four sciences of arithmetic, astronomy, geometry, and music.

Now Cassiodorus was not the first to formulate these groupings. As disciplines, they went back to Greek and Roman education; and in the second century B.C., Varro, 'the most learned of the Romans', had listed nine subjects, although throughout the Roman Empire only those of the *trivium* had been taught. In the early part of the fifth century A.D., Martianus Capella, though not a Christian, wrote a handbook on the liberal arts grouped into three and four. This was the tradition taken up by Boethius, who gave the name *quadrivium* to those sciences which studied physical bodies: in his own words 'they constituted a fourfold path to wisdom'. They were concerned with the acqusition of knowledge. From this he distinguished the three arts of grammar, rhetoric, and logic, which made up the *trivium*: as their generic title suggests, they did not aim at the acquirement of knowledge so much as at the ordering of experience; they provided the means for giving expression to what was known. This was the foundation of Cassiodorus's own educational principles, and through him and his predecessors they formed the basis of learning throughout much of the middle ages.

Boethius and Cassiodorus both bore witness to the relatively unimpaired state of culture in Italy under Theodoric; but by the time Justinian's conquest had ravaged the country and opened the way to the Lombard invasions, the continuity with the past had been broken. The foundation on which medieval learning had to be built was less exalted and lacked command of the resources which were still at men's disposal in the first part of the sixth century. Henceforth it was a question of consolidation rather than new advances.

This is already apparent in the renewed tendency towards encyclopedias in which the main elements of the different branches of knowledge were grouped together. In addition to Cassiodorus's, which we have already mentioned, Isidore of Seville (570–636), living in the comparative stability of Spain as yet unconquered by Islam, compiled his *Origines* or *Etymologiae*. It consisted of a mass of diverse knowledge, divided into twenty books, based upon the principle that all things could be traced to their etymology, thus deriving their meaning from their names. This naturally led to some fantastic conclusions, but the work remained one of the standard books of education until the thirteenth century. The first three books dealt with the seven liberal arts, and the rest were devoted to a combination of spiritual and practical knowledge, ranging from God to agriculture. Isidore also wrote separate books on theology (*De Fide Catholica* and *Sententiarum*) which bear witness to St Augustine's influence and authority: he upholds the absolute spirituality of the soul, and of angels; grace precedes all acts of merit and is an entirely gratuitous gift from God.

St Isidore was a product of the comparative peace which came to Spain in the sixth century. The schools which were opened by abbeys and cathedrals existed side by side with Jewish schools, thus retaining contact with oriental culture. His own interest, however, had been to place natural and scientific knowledge within a Christian framework and not to study it for its own sake. In this he was one of the fathers of medieval culture.

The extent of the break with the Roman world at the end of the sixth century can be seen in Gregory the Great (540–604). He is often regarded as the last of the Fathers, but as a Pope, and in his own writings, he is much more a harbinger of the middle ages. In the absence of any secular ruler to whom he could look for support, Gregory himself conducted the defence of Italy against the Lombards; as Pope he acted as the spiritual leader of the West and among his work must be included the conversion of the Anglo-Saxons. Gregory's main intellectual efforts were ecclesiastical: he reformed the liturgy and the chant, which have borne his name ever since; he wrote a pastoral rule on the duties of priests; his *Dialogues* were devoted to hagiography; and his *Moralia in Job*, among the most widely read books of the middle ages, was a commentary on moral aspects of the Bible. His own attitude to profane learning was hostile, as can be seen in his letter of rebuke to Archbishop Didier of Vienne for having included poetry in the education of his pupils. 'The same lips', he wrote, 'could not extol both Jupiter and Christ.' The liberal arts should only be taught to enable an understanding of scripture.

(iii) Pelagianism

The fifth and sixth centuries were a confused period in thought as in life. There was not, as yet, a clear stream to which the different outlets were tributary. Patristic mingled with classical, orthodox with heretical. Despite the dominance attained by St Augustine there were divergences which arose from the existence of other outlooks, as for example Boethius's, and from heresy.

St Augustine himself had been increasingly preoccupied with the heresy of Pelagianism. Unlike the other heresies which he had combated, such as Arianism and Donatism, that of Pelagius and his followers arose in his own lifetime, during the early fifth century. As we have already mentioned, the Pelagians denied the effects of original sin upon man. Adam's fall had been personal to himself; man was in any case mortal, and no man had been given immortal life through Christ's incarnation. Accordingly each man's destiny depended on himself; baptism was unnecessary, and grace, far from being the cause of merit, was its reward.

Pelagianism undermined the entire structure of ecclesiastical discipline and the *raison d'être* of the Church. It was founded upon man's independence of God and a belief in the self-sufficiency of human powers. Clearly it was incompatible with Christian authority, and St Augustine in combating it evolved the most far-reaching doctrine in reply: the seeming inexorability of predestination and the complete dependence of all goodness upon grace, so that even unbaptized children were condemned to everlasting death.

To many this seemed too extreme. Opposition developed, especially in the monasteries of Southern Gaul, where John Cassian had founded the abbey of Saint Victor at Marseilles. Cassian upheld what came to be known as semi-Pelagianism, whereby, following oriental tradition, although God conferred grace this was in response to an initial impulse by man. The human intellect had it in its power to follow the precepts of divine law, and if a man did so God rewarded him. What man initiated God crowned. God's will was not the only cause of predestination, for in addition to those whom He had eternally elected there were men who, by their own good deeds, could be chosen. This view spread to other monasteries; it was taken up by Vincent of Lerins (*fl.* 432), like Cassian one of the founders of monasticism in the West. He held that to make God the author of damnation, as St Augustine had, was to deny God His traditional attributes. Moreover, according to Vincent, the soul was corporeal, each one being created individually by God. The same outlook was to be found in Faustus, Bishop of Riez (*fl.* 452), and it continued into the sixth century, until Augustinianism triumphed at the Council of Orange in 529. Under the Bishop of Arles, the council approved a series of St Augustine's propositions on grace which formed the basis for Catholic teaching during the middle ages. Grace was the beginning of all merit, the means by which the will achieved good acts; it was an entirely gratuitous gift from God, not a reward. This doctrine became accepted throughout the Church and Pelagianism, with its variations, was overcome.

CHAPTER 3

The Carolingian Renaissance and its Effects

IT has become so much a habit to describe any sudden growth of culture as a renaissance that we are in danger of depriving the expression of any meaning. If carried too far, the whole of cultural development can be regarded as a series of renaissances: clearly a contradiction in terms, since all that is new would then be regarded as simply the resurrection of the old. Yet, if we take renaissance to mean rebirth, we have a certain justification in describing what happened in the Carolingian Empire as a renaissance. The reign of Charles the Great (Charlemagne), king of the Franks and first Holy Roman Emperor, witnessed to some degree a return of letters and learning. This movement was not in any way an all-embracing one, nor did it, in many respects, survive its authors. Yet it succeeded in two vital ways: it rescued culture from what appeared to be a slow but certain death; and it put it on an educational foundation firm enough to survive the collapse of the Carolingian Empire itself. In this sense, we can only understand the outlook and culture which the middle ages were to produce by a knowledge of its origins in the eighth and ninth centuries.

The Empire of Charlemagne was the first attempt at unified government since the collapse of the Roman Empire. It was, after Charlemagne's coronation as Holy Roman Emperor by the Pope on Christmas Day 800, regarded as the re-creation (*renovatio*) of the Roman Empire. Culturally, it took for its model the heritage of the ancient world. Its aim was to continue the classical tradition. As Alcuin, the main inspirer of Carolingian learning, put it, in one of his letters to Charlemagne, 'If your intentions are carried out it may be that a new Athens will arise in France, and an Athens fairer than of old, for our Athens, ennobled by the teachings of Christ, will surpass the wisdom of the Academy'. Herein lies the essence of the

Carolingian revival; it shows both its continuity with the past and its difference. While, on the one hand, the Carolingians regarded themselves as simply the modern representatives of the ancients, they were yet aware of their distinguishing mark. It was not merely the Athens of old to which they aspired; it was an Athens in a Christian setting. This distinction was in fact far more profound than the simple inclusion of Christ's name would suggest, and this more than anything marked off the Carolingian epoch from the days of Greece and Rome. Despite the superficial appearance of continuity between them, the Empire of Charlemagne was a theocracy steeped in an outlook far removed from the past. Though its power might rest largely upon the personality and sword of its ruler, Christian faith was both its justification and its support. In government and prestige alike Charlemagne relied upon the Church. It provided the surest means for strengthening and maintaining his Empire; its baptism and its bishoprics were the best guarantee of assimilating his enemies.

It is hardly surprising that education occupied a leading place in the Carolingian Empire. Only through a literate and trained clergy could the Empire endure and its objects succeed. Thus for the first time we see a conscious educational policy designed to stimulate learning. From the first, its end was a Christian one; and it was concerned not with reviving the philosophical speculation of classical times, but to train up ecclesiastics in an understanding of the scriptures. It is in this light that we must judge the Carolingian revival; it did not aim at original creation. An understanding of the established truths, found in the Bible and the writings of the Fathers, not the attainment of new truths, was its object. That it succeeded in this, and in stopping the rot of ignorance and illiteracy, cannot be gainsaid. It would have been as surprising as it would have been uncharacteristic had there been a great burst of creative works, and we must not condemn their absence.

If Charlemagne provided the authority for this revival, its resources came from elsewhere; and he was particularly fortunate in the conjunction of circumstances which made his aim possible. During the seventh century the thread of knowledge had been gradually unwinding. Throughout Western Europe there was a break in the pursuit of learning and the practice of letters, except in isolated places. Italy was suffering the effects of the continuous fighting and invasions of the sixth century; Spain was being attacked by the Moslems, so was North Africa, for long the home of Western Christian thought; Gaul, part of the Frankish kingdom, was lapsing from its former brilliant Gallo-Roman civilization. The schools of learning had come to an end during the fifth century and had not been replaced. Institutionally education had ceased to exist, and so, sooner or later, must educated men as well. Individuals like Boethius and Cassiodorus had been exceptions, the remnants of an extinct system. Only in a few private bishops' households, like that of Gregory of Tours (*fl.* 580), was learning kept in being. His *History of the Franks* gives a picture of the barbarization of the Church itself in a world of barbarism and violence: the towns have let culture perish; learned men are not to be found. 'Woe to our times.' Such is the message of Gregory. Clearly there could only be recovery if education were put on an organized footing. This is what Charlemagne and his helpers achieved.

(i) Anglo-Saxon Culture

Yet this would itself have probably proved impossible had there not been a source of learning on which to draw. While the continent was in the throes of decay, England, or more accurately Britain, was fashioning a living culture, and in the seventh century Northumbria became the centre of a brilliant civilization from which the lamps of Carolingian learning were to be lighted. This culture was itself the fusion of the two different streams of Benedictine monasticism and Irish monasticism. In this form it was transmitted to the continent of Europe.

When the barbarian tribes settled in the Roman Empire they had stopped at Britain, and Ireland had alone remained untouched. Its religious and cultural life was able to continue uninterrupted, with the result that it developed features of its own, distinct from the rest of the West. The most important of these were its monasticism and its learning. Irish monasticism was the dominant form of religious life. There was no civic tradition as there was in Roman territories and hence nothing resembling bishoprics. Moreover, Irish monasticism bore very strong affinities to the oriental type of extreme asceticism, and throughout it was noted for its fervour and missionary zeal. Traditionally the conversion of Ireland is associated with St Patrick (*c.* 389–461), a romanized Briton who had escaped to the monastery at Lerins in Gaul, the centre of oriental monasticism. Even if he was not solely responsible for bringing Christianity to Ireland, he helped to give it its individual stamp. The Irish Church became the main repository of culture, preserving its schools and its knowledge of Greek during the centuries when Europe was lapsing into ignorance.

By the missionary activities of the Irish monks, Christianity was carried to Scotland and Northern England, from Iona, bringing with it their monasticism and their culture. It was in the north of England, Northumbria, that the Roman stream met with the Irish. This was the result of Gregory the Great's dispatch of Augustine's mission to England in 596. Ultimately, after many vicissitudes, in which their different customs clashed, Northumbria was won for Roman Christianity. It was, however, in the seventh century that classical learning received its great stimulus in Britain. In 667 the Pope appointed as Archbishop of Canterbury, Theodore of Tarsus, a Greek. Under his influence the Church was reorganized and grew in effectiveness; and at the same time Benedictine monasticism, with its tradition of learning, was introduced by Benedict Biscop. His two foundations at Wearmouth (674) and Jarrow (681), richly endowed with books, became the sources of Northumbrian culture.

Their greatest product was the Venerable Bede (672–735), the first English historian and the most learned man of his day. His work and teaching gave the impetus to the learning which was to constitute the Carolingian renaissance. His own writings, apart from his history, were devoted to expounding the scripture and the compilation of treatises on different aspects of knowledge. His *De natura rerum* followed the model of Isidore of Seville's *Origines*. Like Isidore's work, it was an encyclopedia of all knowledge, and, similarly, it was in response to the same needs of educating the clergy. Bede also devoted treatises to combating the Pelagians – a suggestion that their doctrines might still have been current in the Britain of his time. Although outstanding as an historian, in his ability to sift evidence and to present an intelligible account of events, Bede was without originality as a thinker; this was not his aim. He set himself practical tasks of education, and in this he foreshadowed his less eminent successors.

In a sense Bede was the father of the Carolingian renaissance, for, through the activity of his pupil, Egbert, who became Archbishop of York, a school was established there. Egbert was succeeded as master of the school by his pupil Alcuin (735–804), and it was Alcuin whom Charlemagne invited to take charge of his Palace school at Aachen. Thus it was that the Carolingian renaissance was brought to birth.

(ii) The Reforms

In 782 Alcuin (735–804) began his association with Charlemagne, first as head of the Palace school at Aachen and then as Abbot of St Martin at Tours. Alcuin more than anyone else was the moving spirit of the Carolingian renaissance. His far-reaching reforms were to become a permanent part of medieval education. These can be said to have had three aspects. Firstly, measures for the preservation of literacy; secondly, the organization of schools and the establishment of learning on an institutional basis; thirdly, the content of education and the subjects taught.

In the first case, Alcuin was entrusted by Charlemagne with establishing a standard of correct spelling throughout the Empire. Moreover, as controller of the writing school, Alcuin succeeded in developing a clear script. The result was the beautiful Carolingian minuscule, which established a new standard of writing and was responsible for some of the finest manuscripts of the middle ages.

The re-establishment of schools was largely the result of Charlemagne's legislation and took place at different times throughout his reign. This provided for schools to be attached to monasteries and cathedrals, which should give education to those able to benefit from it. It was to include instruction in the psalms, the chant (music), computing the seasons, and grammar from standard texts. Later, after Alcuin's death, it was decreed that the parish priest should give similar instruction gratis. The monastic schools usually consisted of an internal school for the monks and children of the cloister, and an external school for secular priests who did not belong to the monastery. These were mainly centred around Benedictine foundations like St Martin of Tours, Fulda, Fleury, Reichenau. The cathedral schools belonged to the cathedrals of each bishopric under the bishop himself or a master; their pupils were children training for the priesthood. Outstanding examples were Paris, Chartres, Laon, and Rheims, all destined to become illustrious. It was mainly from the cathedral schools that the future universities of the North were to spring, though during the next two centuries the monasteries remained the dominant centres of learning. It is not hard to see how entirely dependent upon ecclesiastical institutions Charlemagne was. His policy was essentially an improvisation; it made use of existing facilities, endeavouring only to give them a more widespread application. Education as a separate pursuit, with a separate body of teachers, was unthought of.

The curricula of these schools was mainly the work of Alcuin. He took up the threads where they had been left by Boethius and Cassiodorus, and in doing so made a break with the Roman educational tradition. In Roman times, education had been almost entirely rhetorical and literary, a preparation for a public life, with Cicero and Quintilian for its models. By the eighth century, however, all this had changed: education was now for training up a priesthood; its need was not eloquence but an understanding of scripture. Alcuin's response was to constitute the curriculum from the seven liberal arts of the *trivium* and the *quadrivium*. Even though he gave most emphasis to grammar, rhetoric, and logic, as more in keeping with what was required, he was responsible for making them the permanent basis of medieval teaching.

In turning to the *trivium* and *quadrivium* Alcuin gave the final stamp to the work of Isidore and Bede; their encyclopedic method became the prevailing approach to knowledge. It emphasized the essentially conservative nature of Carolingian education. The close connexion between the seven arts and religious understanding gave them a new significance. As the means towards a theological end they themselves took on a sacrosanct character. 'The philosophers', he wrote, 'have not created but only discovered these arts; it is God who has created them in natural things; and the wisest men have found them there.' His own outlook was, therefore, in no way original; he was content to point the lesson from well-established texts. His works were mainly either contributions to the subjects of the *trivium* or in the case of his one philosophic work on the soul (*De animae ratione*) largely drawn from St Augustine. These were secondary to his greatest achievement as chief organizer of the Carolingian renaissance.

Yet it would be wrong to think of the revival of learning as entirely the work of one man. To Charlemagne himself must fall the credit for conceiving it and gathering about him an international company of scholars to help in its realization. These included Paul the Deacon (*c.* 725–797), who wrote a *History of the Lombards*, and revised a collection of *Homilies*; Peter of Pisa who taught Latin at the Palatine school and numbered Charlemagne among his pupils; the Spaniards, Agobard, Archbishop of Lyons, one of the luminaries of the Carolingian Church, and Theodulf, Bishop of Orleans, poet and man of letters. Nor did the flow of reformers dry up with Alcuin's death in 806. He was succeeded at his own monastery of Tours by his pupil and countryman Fredegisus whose *De nihilo et tenebris* displayed an unwonted taste for speculation in discussing the nature of nothingness, and called forth a counterblast from Agobard.

Meanwhile, another of Alcuin's pupils, Raban Maur (*d.* 836), carried forward the Carolingian reforms into Germany. Both as thinker and organizer he surpassed his master; and he was the founder of German education. In particular, his *De clericorum institutione*, a handbook for educating the clergy, became its model. Like Alcuin, he stressed the necessity of the seven liberal arts and justified the study of pagan writers, like the Platonists, as constituting an aid to Christian understanding – not for their own sake. True to the Carolingian tradition, he compiled an encyclopedia known as *De universo*, on the plan of Bede and Isidore of Seville.

Raban's work was carried on by Candidus of Fulda and Walafrid of Strabo, abbot of Reichenau, to whom, until recently, authorship of the standard Gloss on the Bible was mistakenly ascribed. The two monasteries of Fulda and Reichenau were the leading centres of learning in Germany, but Raban's influence also extended to France, where another of his pupils, Servatus Lupus, was abbot of Ferrières and one of the leading exponents of classical learning and textual criticism.

The increased importance of exegesis among the second generation of Carolingian thinkers showed that the programme of their forebears was bearing fruit. By the middle of the ninth century men like Paschasius Radbertus (*d.* 860) abbot of Corbie, in France, and Ratramnus (*d.* 868) and Gottschalk, both also of Corbie, were engaged in renewed controversy over such questions as predestination and the nature of the soul; while Remy of Auxerre (841–908) was an important grammarian. Clearly, intellectual life was quickening, though it still mainly comprised a series of individual islands which had not yet merged into a continuous ladmass. That it was not to do so for another two centuries was mainly due to the Viking invasions.

(iii) John the Scot (Erigena) c. 810–877

These developments formed the background to the work of John Scotus Erigena, who was born in Ireland,* and came to

*During the earlier middle ages Ireland was known as Scotia.

the court of Charles the Bald, where he taught at the Palace school. John stands out as the one original thinker during the period from Boethius to St Anselm. While all around him his contemporaries were content to try to understand their faith and to grasp the rudiments of knowledge, John ventured on new paths. Where his fellows hardly looked beyond the elementary questions of theology, contained in the writings of the Fathers, and kept within the bounds of the *trivium*, John constructed an entire system largely under the influence of Greek thought. At a time when the world around him limited itself to Latin culture, he took in that of Greece as well.

John's main distinction, apart from the genius of his thinking, lay in giving expression to a tradition quite foreign to the West. Both in space and in time his outlook belonged to another world. Its source lay in the near-mystical speculation of the Greek Neoplatonists, and in perpetuating it he largely stood outside the currents of his age. Yet, in emphasizing John's individuality, we should remember that he was a product, if an entirely random one, of the Carolingian reform: for it was in the Palace school of Charles the Bald, itself instituted by Charlemagne, that he was able to give expression to his ideas. Moreover, his doctrine of predestination issued directly from the controversies of his time.

No doubt the decisive factor in determining John's outlook was his knowledge of Greek. Thus he had direct access to the writings of the Greek Church, and it was there that he came to know not only the Greek Fathers but two writers who were to have a deep and lasting influence on the West, Denys the Areopagite and Maximus the Confessor. Denys the Areopagite, often called the Pseudo-Denys, was throughout the middle ages believed to be the pupil of St Paul and in the line of the first Apostles. In fact, however, his works first appeared in 532 and were probably written around the turn of the sixth century despite the author's pretence to be St Denys. His outlook was essentially the application of Christian concepts to a Neoplatonic system. Its importance for the middle ages lay in its mode of regarding creation as a manifestation of the divine nature; it pointed to ways of ascent to God which were to be adopted by the mystics of the fourteenth century, and it also provided a means of regarding God. The influence that Denys's writings were to have on John the Scot was only at the beginning of a line that stretched through St Anselm to St Bonaventure and St Thomas. Of Denys's works, which included the *Celestial Hierarchy*, the *Ecclesiastical Hierarchy*, the *Mystical Theology*, and the *Divine Names*, the latter was by far the most influential and was frequently commented.

The foundation of Denys's outlook lay in his conception of God as beyond all being and multiplicity. God's supremely simple essence allows of no definition or reference to anything outside it. Now this inherently Neoplatonic view of God as the One means that we have no knowledge of the divine nature. How, then, are we to regard the numerous names by which He is described in the Bible, itself the bearer of divine truth? Names such as being, love, omnipotence, cannot really apply to God, but are drawn from finite things in an attempt to make Him intelligible to us in our present state. To resolve the antinomy between what we can know about God and what is unknowable, Denys enunciated three stages in describing Him: the first is to give Him a name (affirmative theology); the second is to deny this name (negative theology); the third is to reconcile the contradiction by looking beyond the terms of human experience (superlative theology). Thus while, metaphorically, God is goodness, literally He is not, since our idea of goodness is drawn from the finite world. Any description of God must transcend these limits and so we must say that He is super-goodness. This enables us to reach a conception of God which is nameless, above all negative and positive predicates. It represents the highest truth that we can have of Him – mystical ignorance.

This conception of God, as above all being, is equally apparent in Denys's view of creation. God himself remains outside all that is, yet the super-goodness of His nature is manifest throughout existence. For this reason Denys regards Him as the supreme good, the fount of all being; every creature participates in His goodness as rays of light in the sun. God brings them into being through the divine Ideas, the prototypes and models of all things. Although the Ideas derive from God, they are not synonymous with Him, for while they are the manifestation of being, He is above being. This distinction was to have great influence upon John the Scot.

Thus we have a view of God as both transcending creation and immanent in it. He is unknowable to sense or reason because, as more than being, He is beyond description. On the other hand, we know Him through the different natures He has created: all nature is therefore evidence of God and all creatures are moved by love of Him. Such an outlook not only leads to a mystical desire for complete abnegation of the self in God (as St Bernard was later to portray); it also regards all creation as the unfolding of God's nature; it is part of a divine process by which God, through creation, reveals Himself to Himself.

Denys's doctrines became inseparable from the commentary on them by Maximus the Confessor (580–662), and for the middle ages the two went together. Unlike Denys, Maximus was concerned more with the dogmatic and mystical aspects of his outlook; while fully steeped in the Dionysian *schema* he tried to give it a more directly Christian content. He identified divine Ideas with the immaterial archetypes of all things, which God, the One (or the Monad), possessed in the Word. Thus they were an aspect of His own nature, a manifestation of His goodness. Similarly, man's relation to God was put within a christological framework: originally man's ability to reach God had lain within his own power, through contemplation; but he had turned away from God to things instead. Hence Christ's incarnation, in order to redeem man's contact with God. The return to Him is man's end; it brings him back to his source. Through ecstasy he can experience a foretaste of the final union in God, when the sensible world will be replaced by a spiritual world.

Maximus thus completed Denys's outline to give a rounded picture of the world as the manifestation of God, with His Word the source of its eternal essences. It makes the reunion of man and his creator dependent upon Christ's redemption of man from sin; it makes the ecstatic union of the soul with Christ the symbol of man's return to God. Such an outlook was at once a system and a mysticism. In both respects it was to reap a rich harvest in the West.

The influence of Denys and Maximus upon John the Scot is apparent above all in the metaphysical structure of his universe. Although there are equally clear and powerful traces of St Augustine as well, John's orientation derives from the former, and this is what so very largely distinguishes his system from that of any other medieval Latin thinker. In his aims he did not differ from his contemporaries: like them, he wanted to understand the scriptures, and in a very real sense his work was a commentary on the scriptures. Despite frequent accusations to the contrary, there was not a trace of the freethinker or the rationalist about him. He saw no distinction between faith and reason. Unlike St Thomas Aquinas, whose concern was to delimit one from the other, John took their indissoluble unity for his starting-point: 'If you will not believe you shall not understand.' Man, he held, in his present fallen state had lost his power of direct insight into truth; he was only able to know through the experience of his senses. To attain, therefore, to true understanding he was dependent upon the divine illumination brought by Christ. Hence, for man, certitude rested upon faith, and reason could only try to grasp the truths contained in faith. In fact, however, faith itself derived from reason and was the expression of the reason which came from God. This was essentially a theological outlook, quite in keeping with the mental climate of his time: 'Authority proceeds from true reason but never reason from authority'.

John's fundamental harmony with claims of theology can be seen in his own career. Initially, before he became interested in Greek writings, he studied the standard Latin authorities like St Augustine, Gregory the Great, and Isidore of Seville, and he engaged in the dispute over predestination with Gottschalk (c. 851). It was only in the 850s that he turned to the Dionysian corpus. Denys had already been translated into Latin by Hilduin, abbot of St Denis, whose patron he was. In 858 John made his own translation both of the Pseudo-Denys's works and Maximus the Confessor's *Ambigua*, together with the *De hominis opificio* of Gregory of Nyssa. Under the influence of these Greek thinkers, he composed his own master-work, the *De divisione naturae*, and a commentary on the Pseudo-Denys's *Celestial Hierarchy*. These both show the predominantly Neoplatonic character of his outlook, which he had developed and with which he is associated.

The supreme trait of John's outlook lay in regarding all nature as the mirror of God Himself. As with the Pseudo-Denys, God was both in nature and above it: in it by virtue of the essences through which He communicates being; above it because His own nature transcends all being. This can be seen in his work on the division of nature. Nature he regards as the general name for all things that are, and, in a certain sense, are not. In all that exists in nature, our thought can distinguish four aspects: first, nature which creates and is not created; second, nature which is created and creates; third, nature which is created and does not create; fourth, nature which is not created and does not create. These four divisions are really only two, between creator and created. The first and the fourth apply to God, while the second and third to creation. The first is God as the principle of all things; the fourth, neither created nor creating, is God as the end of all things, as immanent in nature, not as transcendent. The second division describes divine Ideas, the principles of all being, which derive from God; and the third are created things themselves.

Let us examine each of these in turn. John's view of God is, as we have mentioned, like that of Denys. He remains above all categories of being because to make Him being would be to delimit Him. We cannot know what He is but only *that* He is. Thus John applies the same Dionysian affirmative and negative theology: having given Him the names of goodness, being, and so on, we must deny them and acknowledge Him as super-goodness, super-essentiality – terms which place Him beyond all words.

Our ignorance of God is matched by His own ignorance of Himself. Here we see clearly the Neoplatonic germ of John's thought. Because he holds God to be beyond all fixed modes of being, for God to know Himself would be to define Himself; His knowledge would determine Him and He would become finite. Thus self-ignorance in God is supreme knowledge, an acknowledgement of His own immensity. In one sense it is parallel with our own ignorance, for each involves recognizing that His nature cannot be compassed. God only knows Himself in creating, for whatever He knows He creates, and what He creates derives from Himself. Accordingly, the whole of creation is a process of divine revelation, with each being an aspect, finite and limited, of God's own nature.

This is what John means when he calls nature a 'theophany': it is the revelation of God through creation. God Himself, however, is completely simple, with no division into parts, movement, action, or number. The distinctions that we make in Him are in our thought only. The Trinity itself surpasses any understanding of ours; it represents neither a division into different natures nor refers to different operations, but is simply a relation between its different persons. John's Neoplatonism is particularly apparent here, for he sees the Trinity more as the Neoplatonic triad with the Father as the unity, the Son as the source of all Ideas, and the Holy Spirit the cause of their division into actual beings. Although John in no way regards the One as prior to the other two, his very conception of God, as above being, tends to make creation more the hierarchical emanation of Ideas from the Son through the Holy Spirit than the direct act of His will. This can be seen most clearly in the second division of nature.

Traditionally the doctrine of divine Ideas, as expressed by St Augustine, was that they inhered in God eternally as an indivisible aspect of Himself. They constituted, therefore, God as creator, the expression of His own nature to what was outside Him. John, on the other hand, sees divine Ideas as posterior to God: they are created, in that they have their principle in God, not themselves: they are creators, in that they in turn provide the principles for everything else. Now, quite clearly, they cannot be synonymous with God and yet be finite and subsequent to Him, nor can they be the principles of all things unless they are their infinite archetypes. Such a position would present an insoluble problem to the traditional Latin view of God as the supreme being. But if God is more than being, being must itself come after God; it cannot be subsumed under the name God. Thus, for John, who puts God above being, divine Ideas, as the bearers of being, must in some way have been *endowed* with their power: they must be themselves created by God as creators of natural being.

The Word, as with the Neoplatonism of Denys and Maximus, is the intermediary from the One to the many. It contains all the immaterial archetypes of being, and these are transmitted through the Holy Spirit into actual things, divided into their genera, species, and individuals. Creation, strictly speaking, becomes a procession from God through these first causes or principles into incorporeal and corporeal beings. Moreover, it is an eternal process. Although Ideas are not eternal, in that they have a beginning, they are eternal in that they do not begin in time: they reside in the Word from which they are indivisible. 'We believe absolutely that the Son is entirely coeternal with the Father; as for the things that the Father creates in the Son, we say they are coeternal with the Son but not absolutely coeternal.' In this sense all things have existed eternally in their immaterial archetypes: there is no separate act of creation, for in the generation of the Son was the creation of the world. This, too, is more in keeping with the eternal manifestation of God through Platonic Ideas than the Christian view of God's direct creation of the world in time.

When we regard the created world, therefore, we are regarding God's manifestations. From what we have observed above, we can see that all that exists – as opposed to sin which is (following Augustine and Denys) a deprivation of being – is both good and from God. Everything is a participation in God's nature as expressed in creation; it is like the rays of light which reflect the sun. Because all creatures both derive from God as principle, and move towards Him as end, the whole of nature is a movement powered by love of God. This view of all being as originating in and returning to God was one of the most markedly Dionysian influences in John's outlook, and was to be of the utmost importance in succeeding centuries. In John's case, it led not simply to a personal attempt by the soul to grasp its connexions with God, but also to an objective analysis of the created world.

In the first place, the created world is a world of essences derived from the Ideas or archetypes in the Word. Thus knowledge of anything is through the forms which inform it: in looking at anything we are aware of its colour, its size, its shape, its quality; these are all essences by which we judge it: only matter cannot be recognized separately. Ideas, then, are the cause of all being and of all our knowledge of being. 'There is, I hold, nothing visible or corporeal which does not signify the invisible and the incorporeal.' Matter itself, far from being the means by which we can know the essence in things, is quasi-being, the cause of nothing. For John the problem of the relation of the universal to the particular did not arise. Each individual portrayed the natures of which it was composed and in turn belonged to genera and species with their source in divine Ideas.

In the second place, there is a hierarchy of perfection which is graded by proximity to God. There is a threefold division between immaterial natures (the angels), immaterial and material natures (man), and purely material natures. God participates in all of them, since they are all His gift. Their natures are the working out of the increasing multiplicity which accompanies the journey from the One to the many. The farther away from God, the less they participate in His light, and the lower they are in the scale of being. This is not through a divine dispensation over the relative merits of different creatures; rather, their different merits are the result of their position in the hierarchy. It is one more example of the almost inexorable working of the Neoplatonic universe which regards all being as progression of essences, steadily diminishing in value the farther they get from their source. Their point of return comes at the moment where they cease to maintain their own individuality and they are once more able to merge with their first principle.

Here John parts company from Neoplatonism and reverts to the more personal approach of Latin Christianity together with its tenets. Thus, in the case of man, John regarded him as in origin a compound of the intelligible nature of the angels and the sensible nature of the brutes. Through the fall, however, this nature had become impaired, with the result that man was now closer to the condition of animals, sharing the same subjection to instincts, sorrows, and death. Yet the soul, created in the triune image of God, has been provided with other means of rising above the world of senses. Through the Incarnation the soul was brought back into contact with the Word. Christ, then, became God's way of redeeming man and leading him back to Him. Consequently, contemplation by the soul does not suffice for a knowledge of truth; it has to come from a supernatural illumination specially added to man's ordinary faculties. John distinguishes between a natural gift (*datio*) and grace (*donatio*): the latter enables beings to return to their origin; it is the re-establishment of their primitive state of wholeness. This conception of grace shows that, though he professes a Neoplatonic universe, its end is Christian: he uses the philosophical base of the former to construct man's relation with God. This is utterly dependent upon Christ's grace and would have been impossible without the Resurrection.

John regards the return of all creatures to God as starting with death; for the point of greatest individual disintegration is the beginning of universal reintegration. He sees five stages in this return, finally bringing the divine Ideas back into God. This transmutation of being went beyond traditional theology. So did his view of the Day of Judgement when all evil would disappear and the difference between the saved and the damned would lie only in the latter's ignorance of the truth: for truth is beatitude and lack of truth damnation.

John's outlook remained an isolated landmark in medieval thought: it neither stemmed from the West nor did it carry Western thought into new channels. It was a stray sample from another world. Although John did not confine himself to the Greek Fathers, and although St Augustine is one of his leading authorities, he yet remained fundamentally a Neoplatonist. Just as St Augustine gave Neoplatonism a Christian foundation,

so John endeavoured to set Christianity upon a Neoplatonic base. While the first was both in keeping with the prevailing outlook and was a viable project, the second was not.
John did violence both to the modes of belief that had grown
up and to belief itself. Although it would be quite unfounded
to regard his outlook as pantheism it led to a blurring of the
line between uncreated and created, as evidenced in his view of
divine Ideas. God's hyper-nature tended to substitute a vague
grouping of attributes for the supreme being, with the result
that He was in danger of being the indirect cause of creation.
Lastly, the world itself tended to become confused with a
hierarchy of emanations, which had no sharply demarcated
beginning in time.

The Neoplatonic elements stand out in his system; even the
notions he took over from St Augustine were mostly in support of his Neoplatonism: the eternal Ideas in the Word; the
inability to apply categories to God; the soul as the image of
God and ruler of the body, including its sensations; the
nature of matter as semi-being; knowledge through Ideas –
none of these provides a specifically Christian content, but all
can be used to reinforce a Neoplatonic view. When joined to
the Dionysian concept of God as above being, the rôle of the
Logos as the source of all being, divine Ideas as the origin of
all things, creation as theophany, the ultimate return of all
things to God, the sempiternity of the world, we can see how
fully John echoed the leading ideas of the Neoplatonic progress from the One to the many. Such an outlook involved
too great a break with the past and the present of the West.
John's doctrine remained a monument to the power of speculation: like a gigantic structure it remained unoccupied, only
in due course to be condemned for its errors. But although
without effect in its own right, it helped to give a lasting
impulse to the dissemination of the Dionysian corpus.

Already during John's lifetime the threat of renewed attacks
and invasions was apparent and by the end of the ninth
century Western Europe, from Ireland to the Mediterranean,
was again under siege. The Vikings from the North, the
Saracens from Spain, and the Magyars from the East combined

to make the greater part of the tenth century a period of dis-
organization and decay. The imposing structure of Charlemagne's empire fell apart and its reforms in learning were
reduced to the individual monasteries in which it could survive. Yet it did survive, and the credit for this belongs to that
line of teachers and compilers from Bede to Raban Maur who
revived learning and laid the foundation of medieval education.

(iv) Political theories

Two main innovations distinguished medieval political
thought from that of the Greeks and the Romans. The first
was the notion of a providence from which the state directly
sprang; that is, its divine origin. As such, it was universal,
embracing all mankind. The second was to explain its coercive
authority and its evil aspects such as war, slavery, inequality of
economic and social status, unjust rulers, as God's remedy and
punishment for original sin. Both of these were given their
first full expression by St Augustine, who had been influenced
by the Stoics' conception of a law of nature to explain the
difference between the ideal order of things and their actual
condition as the result of the fall.

As we have mentioned, St Augustine, faced with the inunda-
tions of barbarians and heretics, had sought to show in his
City of God that the secular state could have no *raison d'être* in
itself; it was merely a transitory halt at which all men, the elect
as well as the damned, had to stop on their way to their final
reckoning. Although he had not identified the Church visible
with the City of God (which comprised the whole of the elect),
it had an important spiritual function in furthering God's will
on earth. In addition, men also had need in this world of the
lordship and protection provided by secular rulers. Thus there
had to be a secular authority no less than a spiritual one.

Strictly speaking, St Augustine's political ideas did not
concern the State as such; they were far more part of his wider
concern with man's place in nature and the effects of sin. Nor
did he look for justice on earth; for justice was essentially
supernatural – to give God His due – and therefore beyond

human reach. Consequently, although he put in motion a Christian view of history, he had not attempted to solve the forms of political organization. Above all, he bequeathed no precise idea of the relationship between the Church and the secular power. This was the task of his successors, and most of the theories of this earlier period were devoted to solving it.

The salient feature of medieval theory until the fourteenth century was the belief in a universal society. There was no such thing as a Church or a State as distinct bodies; but rather one Christian commonwealth in which there were both secular and spiritual powers. Moreover, these powers were regarded as deriving from God: neither was absolute in its own right. The problem to be solved therefore was how to establish an order of priority between them: what part was each to play in the hierarchy from God to the people? Despite the claims for papal primacy, by men such as St Ambrose and Gregory the Great, the doctrine of Pope Gelasius (A.D. 494) came to be the accepted one: this held that 'the two powers by which this world is chiefly ruled – viz. the sacred authority of the priests and the imperial power' together formed the government of a single society, each with its own law and functions. Their relationship should be one of 'mutual helpfulness', with each complementing the other. The doctrine of the 'Two Swords', as it has often been called, met with general acceptance in an age when neither kings nor popes were in a position to assert an independent and all-embracing authority; it fitted well with the interdependence of spiritual and secular authority which has already been noted in the Carolingian Empire.

PART II

THE TRIUMPH
OF SCHOLASTICISM

(*c.* 1000–1300)

CHAPTER 4

Introduction to the Period

WITH the eleventh century medieval society began to come
into its own. The following centuries present an almost new
world in comparison with the past. For the first time we can
see a society that is at once stable and expanding, a society that
is coherent politically, socially, and economically, a society
with its own forms of law, its own culture, its own ethos, a
society, in short, no longer governed by a series of fleeting
makeshifts but firmly based. To look at the richness and the
quickening of life in these later centuries, away from the
afflictions of the previous epoch, is like turning to health after
sickness. It is this difference in condition which very largely
accounts for the great changes. More than anything else they
represent the lifting of the state of siege under which Europe
had existed since the fifth century. This enabled life to take on
a new direction, away from the continuous threat of attack and
the periodic devastations. It marked the change from war to a
condition of relative peace with all its attendant developments.
Thus what we see in the flowering of medieval civilization is
not a new social order, but the same one when at last able to
emerge from the constrictions of war.

It would be false to make the distinction between the
Dark Ages and the latter middle ages too sharp. There was
no millennium at the year 1000, ushering in a new life.
Not only was the change gradual and often halting, but, in
terms of modern society, the middle ages never enjoyed real
stability or prosperity. There was always the threat of civil
war, robbery, murder, and lawlessness, in addition to the
havoc that armies and armed bands could wreak; life for the
majority of mankind, if not 'nasty, brutish, and short', knew
little or no guarantee against injustice, oppression, sudden
death from plague or famine, and ceaseless, back-breaking
toil. In government, a state was as strong as its ruler and

liable to sudden collapse when he died. State authority in our sense was unknown, and even the power of the strongest kings left the majority of the population untouched. The Church, the repository of spiritual authority and culture, ministered to illiterate peasants who remained quite outside the confines of learning and knowledge. Despite the imposing cohesion with which the Church universal ordered its affairs, at the lower reaches many of its parish priests were hardly more enlightened than the peasants from whom they were mainly sprung. The same caution applies to every walk of life: when we talk of towns we mean insalubrious clusters of what would largely appear to us as hovels, separated by narrow, evil-smelling alleys; when we talk of production for the market we must think mainly of small proprietors with a few larger concerns. Travel and communication were slow, dangerous, and difficult; roads, in the modern meaning, non-existent and easily rendered impassable. Food was restricted in quantity and narrow in variety. In matters of health men were at the mercy of nature and their own constitutions. Altogether, then, the changes that we hail must not be thought of as the sudden leap to a new life; it was rather a laborious climb taking men from the bottom of the pit to the edges: but the bottom was never far away.

The ending of the invasions before the year 1000 marked the ending of the first phase of the middle ages. Henceforth we are confronted with an array of new features making up what is often called the second feudal age. It is distinguished from the first in a variety of ways. The first age was essentially a regrouping after the breakdown of the Roman Empire. While it would be untrue to describe it simply in negative terms, it had little chance to provide a constructive alternative to Rome. It was forced to concentrate upon survival and confined to improvisations in the face of almost continuous emergency. Only for a time under Charlemagne was it able to advance beyond this state; even though the Carolingian Empire did not long survive, it pointed to the distinctive medieval society which had developed over the preceding centuries. We can see there the feudal nature of social relations, the local estate as the unit both of life and of authority, the primacy of the Church as a spiritual and a political force, and the changed conception of culture which ensued. Yet throughout the earlier period, the West was hemmed into its own corner of the map; it had little opportunity for wider contact, and the final measure of authority was the sword. What is so striking about the second feudal age is the rounded society which emerges once these barriers have been broken. It not only gives full expression to existing ways but compasses new areas previously outside its range.

The return to something like conditions of peace brought with it a revival in the standards of life. The invasions of the preceding century had come near to obliterating the last remnants of organized life, particularly in the towns: population and trade had shrunk. Now, however, there was a sustained increase in population and trade until the fourteenth century. The eleventh and twelfth centuries were the great periods of colonization, when areas of woodland, marsh, and waste were brought under the plough and settled. Estates, particularly those of many of the large ecclesiastical foundations, produced not only for their own needs but for the market as well. The self-contained life of the estate, the result of circumstances during the first feudal age (and not a universal law of feudalism), expanded into trading activities; areas of specialization grew up, as for example wool production in England and cloth manufacture in Flanders; trade, which had always existed locally, took on a renewed international character as well, extending to the East through the Mediterranean and through the Baltic Sea to Russia; special international fairs grew up by the side of local markets and fairs, the most famous being in Champagne on the route between the great commercial centres of Flanders and Lombardy. By the thirteenth century a credit system had been established and utilized both by secular States and the Papacy.

It was against this background of expanding wealth and population, increasing amelioration in the conditions of life, ever more elaborate divisions of labour, the revival of trade and the growing importance of towns, renewal of contacts with the far richer and older civilizations of the East, that medieval society developed during these centuries. They helped to make for the growing complexity which is so marked a feature of this period. Although Charlemagne's attempt at an Empire unifying what are now the Low Countries, France, Germany, Switzerland, and Italy was never repeated, he provided a model constantly to be emulated: a universal Christian Empire presided over by an Emperor and drawing its spiritual authority from the Pope. From the tenth century the emperorship passed to Germany, and throughout the ensuing three centuries that land was regarded as the seat of the Empire.

The difficulty in harmonizing the temporal claims of the kings of Germany with the far more intangible, but universal, spiritual authority of the Pope remained the most vexing of all political problems. It gave rise to repeated wars between the two sides, beginning with the conflict over Investitures in the eleventh century and continuing into the fourteenth century until the virtual annexation of the papacy to France at Avignon. Although the Emperor was in fact little more than the holder of an honorific title which in itself bestowed no real power, and although his universality was confined in theory to Western Europe and in practice to his own estates, his position *vis-à-vis* the Pope was a very real expression of the complex relation between spiritual and secular authority. It was assumed that, following St Augustine, both were agents of divine authority; the problem arose over their respective extent and limits. It led to a whole literature of the rival claims of king and priest, Emperor and Pope, in an essentially theocratic society.

Yet, in reality, the Pope alone had a universal authority, and one of the most striking aspects of society after 1000 is the growth in papal power. In the earlier stages it is primarily spiritual, yet none the less effective for that. The ban of excommunication was a far deadlier weapon than even the strongest of strong-arm methods employed by a secular ruler: it cut off the offender from the society of his fellows and rendered him helpless and unprotected. Its effect upon Henry IV,

German Emperor, in 1075 was seen when in the following year he stood for three days as a penitent, bare-headed and bare-footed at Canossa awaiting the Pope's forgiveness. With repeated use, excommunication lost its edge and the history of the Papacy from the end of the twelfth century is largely the record of a spiritual power becoming secularized, adopting both the machinery and the methods of government used by ordinary rulers. What distinguished papal government was its universal efficacy, extending to the whole Church, and its international composition, drawing upon ecclesiastics in all lands. Even the most Italian of the popes could not reduce the Papacy to purely Italian limits.

There was a parallel growth in secular authority during these centuries, and the originally amorphous welter of tribes and localities gradually gave place to a group of comparatively distinct states or regions – England, France, Germany, Spain, Flanders, Burgundy, Sicily, the Lombard cities. By modern standards they were hardly nations or states, if these are taken to mean firm national groupings sharing a common tradition and consciousness, and submitting to a uniform political and legal authority. Nationalism as applied to the middle ages is an anachronism; group sentiments remained nearer to tribalism. Government, likewise, is far more descriptive of our own experience than of medieval life. Yet, at its broadest, these different groups showed enough identity to warrant their description as states.

This cohesion became more marked as time went on: the initial basis of authority had rested with the man best fitted to exercise it. This involved more than mere military ability – though authority would not long endure without it; it also required some wider, non-personal sanction indicating a particular fittedness to rule and invariably associated with royal descent. Concurrently with a widening conception of kingship went the widening of royal authority. In time the personal element, which was throughout an incalculable asset, gave place to something more like a regular machinery of government with departments like the chancery and the exchequer, staffed by royal servants, and concerned with the routine of administration. Increased governance gave a stimulus to the revival and development of both canon and civil law, one of the foremost intellectual influences of the age.

Apart from the general increase in the level of civilization, a diversity of new forms appeared. Foremost among these was the renewal of religious fervour giving rise to a series of reforming movements from the tenth to the thirteenth centuries. They began with the founding of a monastery at Cluny, in French Burgundy, by William the Pious of Aquitaine, in 910. It was to be a model for observing St Benedict's rule, in reaction against the steep decline in monastic and ecclesiastical standards through the disorders of the time. Under a series of remarkable abbots it became the generator of religious reform throughout Christendom. By the eleventh century it had led to the foundation of over 200 abbeys affiliated to Cluny and virtually constituting a new monastic order.

Cluny was only the most outstanding example of the general movement towards religious reform extending to the papacy itself, which, until the synod of Sutri in 1046, had been largely at the mercy of the rival aristocratic factions dominating Rome. Gradually, however, it lost the momentum of its first zeal, and gave place to a new movement which sprang from Cîteaux, also in France.

In 1198, a community was established there by the Benedictine Abbot of Molesme and six followers. In protest against the growing laxity of Cluny, their aim was to observe the Benedictine rule in its full rigour. The Cistercian emphasis upon austerity was in keeping with the general trend of the age towards asceticism. Like Cluny before it, Cîteaux was only the most striking manifestation of a whole movement. It was characterized by the desire to settle in the wildernesses away from the goods and temptations of the world. Yet, paradoxically, this very withdrawal to the uninhabited regions led to the spread of settlement, for by their colonization of new lands they helped to foster the growing prosperity, and by the end of the twelfth century the Cistercian estates were leading Christendom in methods of estate management and production. During the twelfth century, the Cistercians became the driving force in religious reforms, mainly through the magnetic power of St Bernard, Abbot of Clairvaux, one of Cîteaux's daughter foundations; and at the time of his death in 1153 they numbered over 340 monasteries.

Yet, in their turn, the 'white monks' also lost their impetus; nor was withdrawal and monastic reform enough in a world of growing wealth and privilege. The Church had been one of the greatest gainers from the return to stability: its monasteries had suffered cruelly from the devastation and pillages of the Northmen, its lands were as vulnerable as the laity's in times of unrest, and more than the laity it was dependent for its well-being upon a strong ruler. It had, from the first, played a leading part in helping to govern, while at the same time asserting its rights and its independence from secular interference. Consequently both the papacy and individual churches had attained to a privileged position, its princes and its wealth too often making it appear as just one more ruler: it collected its dues in the form of tithes, enforced tariffs for marriage, baptism, and burial; it often occupied the finest lands with which it had been endowed; in the cities of Northern Europe especially, the bishops were usually the most obdurate opponents of communal liberties. Thus there were very real signs that the Church as an institution was losing contact with its flock and had forgotten its first principles.

At the other end of the scale, the growth of towns was giving rise to an under-privileged employee class, which differed from the ordinary artisan in not being its own master. This was particularly so in the cloth manufacturing industry in Lombardy, but such people were also prevalent in many of the towns of Europe, such as Lyons. The renewed contact with the East, which came through trade and especially the Crusades, brought with it also such Eastern heresies as Catharism and Manicheism. It led to the formation of communities pledged to the observance of Christ's laws, but inevitably, in seeking communion outside the Church, they constituted a challenge to the Church.

By the end of the twelfth century heresy had taken hold in many parts of Italy and France. Its centre became Languedoc (Provence) in Southern France, where, taking its name from the town of Albi, it became known as the Albigensian heresy. It assumed such dimensions that finally in 1209 Pope Innocent III, having previously failed by persuasion, agreed to a Crusade against the Albigensians. That it was, in fact, used by the nobles of Northern France as a pretext for their own greed and that its main result was to destroy the unique Provençal culture is a matter of history. Its significance here lies in the changed nature of the third religious movement for reform, which arose from these protests against Church privilege – that of the mendicant Friars.

The Friars differed from previous movements in not being monastic. Their emphasis was upon going into the world, not withdrawing from it; their aim was the salvation of others, not directly that of their own souls; theirs was a social mission rather than a personal régime. Foremost were the two orders of the Franciscans and the Dominicans, both pledged to poverty and preaching. Though they differed in certain respects (especially at first), together they came to constitute the main intellectual force of the thirteenth century; the majority of the leading thinkers were drawn from their ranks; and they dominated the universities.

The universities themselves were another creation of the second medieval age. In northern Europe they were the direct heirs of the cathedral schools which had been established during the Carolingian renaissance, and which largely formed the intellectual centres in the first phase of the return of learning in the eleventh and twelfth centuries. From assemblies of clerks they gradually tended to group round a famous master, such as Abelard, and lived in hostels and lodgings. They never lost their ecclesiastical character and ultimately a university came to be defined as having received a licence from the Pope to be a place of studies. South of the Alps, especially in Italy, the universities, although including clerks, were mostly lay, and arose not from ecclesiastical foundations, but directly from the study of law and medicine. It was at such universities as Oxford and Paris in the north, Bologna and Salerno in the south, that the main intellectual life of Europe was centred. As we shall have to discuss in more detail, they not only fostered the study of arts, science, and theology, but individual universities evolved their own distinctive outlook.

Directly connected with universities was the development of urban life with its own institutions, law, and ethos. Far from being the solvent to the rigid structure of feudal society, towns played an integral part in it. There was never a time during the middle ages when towns did not exist; but they took on an entirely new importance during the eleventh, twelfth, and thirteenth centuries. They not only fulfilled a vital economic function but became a force in their own right. The communes which they established, and the privileges which they wrung from bishops and lay lords, led to their independence. They evolved customs and laws best suited to their needs, and inevitably differing from those of the countryside. Yet, except in Flanders and Lombardy, they were never able to assume anything approaching complete autonomy. To an overlord they represented an important asset both as a source of tolls and revenue and as allies against recalcitrant nobles. Moreover, they became the centres of administration, wealth, and culture. A university or a capital or a cathedral would have been inconceivable away from the resources, situation, and protection of a town. In a very real sense, then, medieval government and culture, to say nothing of economic considerations, were largely based upon towns, even while we recognize that they were not the predominant form of social life.

Throughout this period Europe was itself expanding geographically. This was in marked contrast to the constriction of the previous era and is perhaps one of the best gauges of how great the changes in Europe's fortunes were. This expansion has at least three aspects: there was, firstly, the gradual eastward movement of the Germans into Slav lands: a movement both of conquest and of colonization. Secondly, there was the reconquest of the Moslem possessions in Spain and Sicily and the Mediterranean. Thirdly, there were the periodic crusades against the Turks for the regaining of Jerusalem and the Holy Land. While the first two movements were largely the result of localized efforts, the crusades were part of a European movement under papal direction. Whatever genuine zeal there might have been was overshadowed from the first by motives of adventure and plunder, and the Fourth Crusade in 1204 ended as an assault upon Constantinople itself, from which the Eastern Empire never really recovered. Yet this contact with the Moslem world, by crusade, pilgrimage, and trade, had a fruitful influence upon the West; it introduced it to a higher civilization and helped it to regain the full heritage of Greek culture as well as the riches of the Moslem world. Without these sources, scholasticism would have had a very different history and probably an incomparably poorer one. Just as the West was dependent on the East for so much of its trade and luxuries, it owed it a debt also for its civilization.

Such, then, is the backcloth to the development of medieval thought and the rise of scholasticism. It takes place in a general upsurge which left nothing unaffected. The ideas that we are to discuss are only one aspect of this general state. It is equally evident in the evolution of Gothic architecture, the appearance of vernacular literature, the revival of letters and classical Latin, and the writing of poetry. They helped to make up the climate of thought from which the greatest intellectual achievements of the middle ages were to spring.

CHAPTER 5

The Renewal of Letters and Speculative Thought in the Eleventh and Twelfth Centuries

DESPITE the failure of the Carolingian Empire to endure, its educational achievements were far from lost; indeed, they formed the starting-point for the renewal of learning in the eleventh century. In the first place, they provided the seven liberal arts as the basic curriculum and with them the main books for study. Throughout the following centuries these subjects were the foundation of all university courses, even though their content changed with the discovery of Aristotle. In the second place, the organization of all teaching into monastic and cathedral schools maintained continuity in learning until the universities became the main centres: during the ninth and tenth centuries, the monastic schools had remained the main seats of education at such centres as Tours, Fulda, Reichenau, under such men as Raban Maur and Walafrid Strabo, whom we have mentioned before. With the eleventh century, however, the cathedral schools took over the leadership, in turn giving place to the universities. In the third place, one of Alcuin's special achievements had been his emphasis upon correct writing and the proper copying of manuals. This had led to the copying of most of the classical authors during the next two centuries, an achievement that very largely facilitated the great developments of the eleventh and twelfth centuries.

In these ways the Carolingian achievements laid the groundwork of a coherent body of knowledge and a method of study. Yet, while the Carolingian reforms had provided these essential prerequisites for the renaissance which began in the eleventh century, the latter was of a quite different order. In the first place, it extended to the greater part of Christendom. Starting in North Italy and France, it subsequently spread to England, Germany (mainly in the West and the South),

Southern Italy and Sicily, and to the northern areas of Spain. Unlike previous renaissances, it was not confined to individual pockets, but became a broad front embracing every centre of learning. This universal aspect was more than one of geography; it was also one of outlook. From the eleventh century to the end of the fourteenth, a single culture informed all education and a common language, Latin, transmitted it. The centres of learning were themselves composed of diverse nationalities, and in the case of the universities students were usually grouped according to 'nations'. To read most of the treatises of the time is to be outside place; it needs a forcible effort of will to think of St Thomas as Italian, or Duns Scotus as Scottish; and, having made the connexion, one is aware of how irrelevant, even distracting, such distinctions were.

The second important trait of the new renaissance was the very diversity within this overall framework. The Carolingian reforms were essentially the result of a deliberate act of policy and legislation: they were limited in scope and character, and their products bore a common stamp. It is quite the opposite from the eleventh century onwards. To begin with, there was a marked difference between north and south of the Alps. In the North, as we have already mentioned, the culture was entirely ecclesiastical, centred either in the monasteries or the cathedral schools. In Italy, it was mainly through schools established in the cities. The two regions, therefore, developed in different directions and at different rates.

North of the Alps, the cathedral school became the most important and widespread form of education: where previously many cathedrals were without schools, between c. 1050 and c. 1200 every cathedral had one, under the chancellor of the diocese. As the Church moved from strength to strength, so did the schools attached to it. They became the most illustrious centres of culture, and much of the thought and learning during these one and a half centuries derived from Chartres, Laon, Paris, Orleans. Meanwhile the monastic schools tended increasingly towards internal education. The externe schools were gradually discontinued, during the eleventh century, as education passed to the cathedral schools.

Despite this withdrawal, the monasteries still continued to be one of the main cultural influences. In an age of monastic fervour, the monks made up the majority of educated men; the monasteries remained the chief repositories of books; and in men like Lanfranc, St Anselm, and St Bernard they possessed some of the giants of the time. From an intellectual point of view they represented the older tradition: their approach to theology was still by meditation rather than by dialectic; the writing of history was one of their main pursuits at a time when, in the schools, dialectic was ousting the more literary activities. Nevertheless two outstanding examples of monastic culture had an important influence: Monte Cassino in Italy and Bec in Normandy. Monte Cassino was at its height in the second half of the eleventh century and gave a great stimulus to learning, especially medicine. At about the same time, Bec was one of the most influential centres of theology under Lanfranc and his pupil Anselm: their writings, particularly Anselm's, were powerful forces in changing the intellectual climate.

While in northern Italy the urban schools played a similar part to the cathedral schools north of the Alps, there were marked differences between them. The urban schools were not only independent of ecclesiastical control but they were largely secular in interests: theology and philosophy were throughout the hallmark of the cathedral schools; but the urban schools were primarily devoted to the study of law and medicine. Already by the end of the eleventh century, Bologna had become the centre of legal studies, a foundation for which there was no parallel north of the Alps. The universities which sprang up north and south of the Alps were, therefore, very largely the products of these initial differences.

In thought, the eleventh and twelfth centuries were the centuries of reawakening everywhere. Whatever the subject, and whatever the region, there was a universal sense of discovery. The eleventh century, in particular, witnessed a genuine renaissance in the humane studies, and at first letters and style were the main preoccupations. Only in the second half of the twelfth century did the more specialized techniques of dialectic come to dominate the scene, until, in the thirteenth century, philosophical and theological speculation had ousted other pursuits.

(i) The eleventh century

There was no sudden beginning to this new movement. Perhaps the first straw in the fresh wind was the Cluniac foundation at Fleury on the Loire where, under Abbo (d. 1004), a flourishing culture grew up. Whether he was himself responsible for a treatise on Aristotle's *Categories* or not, the earliest manuscript containing Aristotle's *Analytics* dates from Fleury during this period. But the only outstanding name during the tenth century, the *saeculum obscurum* of invasions and disorder, is that of Gerbert of Aurillac; he, too, was the product of the Cluniac reform, and after studying in Spain, where he gained a knowledge of Arabian science, he became head of the cathedral school at Rheims in 972; in 999 he was made Pope Sylvester II; and he died in 1003.

Gerbert's interest lies largely in his breadth of outlook, which extended to the *quadrivium* as well as to the *trivium*; he not only accepted the full classical tradition of the Carolingian reforms, but he also displayed an awareness of the world of science and mathematics with which he had come into contact in Spain. Gerbert was a portent, both in his interest in science and in his approach to dialectic. Like Abbo, he included in the latter Boethius's commentaries on Aristotle's *Analytics*. These were to become an essential part of the Aristotelian corpus of logic until the translation of Aristotle's own texts in the thirteenth century. They marked a new advance in dialectic, for where previously Aristotle's logical works had been confined to the *Categories* and the *Interpretation* (*logica vetus*) Boethius's treatises on the first and second *Analytics* were now added and helped to constitute the new logic (*logica nova*). Thus, in a century singularly barren of cultural developments, Boethius was introduced to Western thought: an event which was to have direct bearing on the future of dialectic and the controversy over universals. That Gerbert himself regarded dialectic as an important means to the understanding of Scripture can be seen from the attention he devoted to it. Altogether he presents the classic picture of the renaissance man, which is usually reserved for the fifteenth and sixteenth centuries; he was one who had a taste for many kinds of activity and knowledge.

The intellectual history of the eleventh century is dominated by the growing importance of dialectic. In one sense the conflicting claims of faith and reason were the motive force in medieval thought from this time forward. Yet it is particularly marked at this period when their different spheres had not been clearly delimited. On each side there was a pronounced tendency towards extremism. The exponents of dialectic showed little or no awareness of reason's limits, in applying it to nearly all the truths of dogma; as a reaction, its opponents virtually denied reason any place in faith at all.

This struggle between the dialecticians, upholding the claims of reason, and the anti-dialecticians, who rejected them, was to be the first of many. It was sharpened by the wider issues which arose from the struggle between the Church and secular rulers then being waged. Although it reached its first climax in the contest between Pope Gregory VII and the German Emperor Henry IV, loosely known as the Investiture contest, it extended to most of society. It was part of the general movement for religious reform and the ending of such abuses as simony and lay investiture, which came from secular control. There was a general desire among Church reformers, like Humbert, Damian, and Hildebrand, to shake the Church free to enable it to pursue its own spiritual mission. This assertion of the independence, and indeed the superiority, of the Church was no less apparent in the attitude of many of the same reformers to dialectic and reason. Peter Damian, for example, rejected the claims of reason to interpret revelation as he denied the dependence of the Church upon the Emperor.

While it would be untrue to regard every thinker during the eleventh century as a dialectician or anti-dialectician, few were uninfluenced by the currents their opposition produced. For the first time there was something like a universal awareness of logic and a growing recognition that it had an importance in all thinking, including matters of faith. Even men who, like Lanfranc and Anselm, opposed the extreme claims made for dialectic, acknowledged its efficacy, while its foremost opponent, Peter Damian, himself employed dialectic to rebut it.

(ii) Scholasticism

One of the outstanding consequences of this atmosphere of ferment lay in the development of what is loosely called scholasticism. Scholasticism has long been a subject for controversy. By some it has been seen as an attitude or state of belief which takes Christian revelation for its subject; to others it is a method of disputation, and this has been its distinguishing trait; while others have regarded it as the rational aspect of belief, a philosophy in its own right.

While none of these is necessarily self-exclusive, in my view scholasticism was essentially the application of reason to revelation. It was an outlook in which rational enquiry was governed by the assumptions of faith, and faith was supported by the powers of reason. Both were indispensable, and to separate them, or to neglect this inherent unity, is, I believe, to do violence to scholasticism. It belonged to reason to elucidate, explain, and support the fundamental Christian tenets as found in Scripture; it was the province of faith to direct reason and to provide it with the terms of reference for its explanations. Scholasticism, therefore, went beyond either mere dogma or natural philosophy. It was knowledge within a dogmatic framework, and, ultimately, faith and reason had to harmonize. When they no longer did so, scholasticism disintegrated.

At its broadest, this outlook characterized all medieval thinking from the Fathers onwards. The Christian truths were no less fundamental for Duns Scotus in the fourteenth century than they were for St Augustine in the fourth century. Their differences were due to a new relationship between faith and reason as well as to new methods of discussion. The main changes in both came with the eleventh century. For the first time reason, as expressed in dialectic, was asserting itself and making claims to discuss all that belonged to faith. It was later reinforced by the steadily growing corpus of logic, metaphysics, and science which gradually became available with the transmission of the works of Aristotle and the Arabian thinkers, towards the end of the twelfth century. By the thirteenth century reason was therefore able to stand, independent of faith. This made for an entirely new situation as compared with the period before the eleventh century.

As we shall see, the impact upon faith of the growing power and self-reliance of reason provides the main thread in the intellectual history of these centuries. With this great emphasis upon rational processes came a change in method. Formerly, reading, and meditation on, texts, as appropriate to monastic life, had provided the main means of expression. Now, in the eleventh century, it was increasingly taking the form of disputation and discussion, whereby a problem was framed in the form of a question (*quaestio*). By this method a question would be posed (for example whether God is the highest good), the arguments for and against stated, and a balance struck.

The *quaestio* became universal in medieval thought from the twelfth until the fifteenth century. Yet in itself it neither originated then nor was it peculiar to philosophy. It was already in evidence as early as the tenth century, among the codifiers of canon law. Both the canonists and the scholastics were governed by the same need to sift the conflicting arguments, drawn from authority, in order to arrive at the truth. It led largely to the method of *pro* and *contra*, and, concurrently with its use in philosophy, it can be seen among such lawyers as Burchard of Worms, Ivo of Chartres, and Gratian. The use of dialectic was also greatly stimulated in the eleventh century by the controversies between Emperor and Papacy. By Abelard's time, therefore, it was already widely used and he, more than anyone else, codified it as a method of theological discussion. Moreover, in addition to its non-theological antecedents, the *quaestio* did not constitute such a radical break with the past as has sometimes been suggested: its task was to weigh conflicting evidence often from the same authority and always from accepted authorities. This attempt to arrive at the most probable interpretation, through the resolution of discordant opinions, had lain at the basis of all exegesis from the earliest days of Christianity. All the Fathers, St Augustine, St Jerome, St Ambrose, had been preoccupied with interpreting Scripture, and, in that sense, the guiding aim of the *quaestio* was firmly rooted in tradition. The difference lay in introducing logic to help in reaching a solution; and although this transformed the mode of expression, and of thinking, the same authorities continued to figure in its arguments, as well as many of the same problems. At the height of the so-called scholastic age, in the thirteenth century, we can still trace the lineage of its thought to earlier times: the main authorities remained the Scriptures, the Fathers, especially St Augustine, and Boethius's logical commentaries. Even when the vast weight of the Aristotelian and Arabian corpus had been added, it could not diminish the power that these authorities wielded throughout the middle ages.

We may, then, regard scholasticism as an outlook extending over a thousand years and undergoing a variety of developments. Yet, in essence, it was directed to Christian ends and guided by scriptural and ecclesiastical authority. Throughout, it was dependent upon the use of profane knowledge and logic, mainly from Greece in general, and Aristotle in particular. The changes in the relative proportions of the sacred to the profane were largely responsible for the change in scholasticism itself. But even when reason was at its height, faith still had the last word. When it was no longer heeded, scholasticism died.

(iii) Dialectic and Anti-Dialectic

The eleventh century gave a powerful impetus to the growth of scholastic method. All the leading thinkers were preoccupied with the claims of dialectic: was it to be the universal arbiter in everything, including dogma? Or did it have any place at all? The different standpoints taken towards it marked the main discussions of the times. Dialectic itself meant more than the rules of discussion; it constituted the logical works of Aristotle then known (the *Categories*, *Interpretation*, and the *Analytics*), together with Porphyry's *Isagoge* and Boethius's *Commentaries*. These involved not only the classification of concepts, but also, in the case of the *Categories*, extended to things themselves. Accordingly dialectic approximated far more to a method of discussion and verification; it used logical and metaphysical criteria to judge concepts, those of faith included.

Gerbert had already acknowledged its importance, and it fell to his pupil, Fulbert, Bishop of Chartres from 1006 to 1028, to further Gerbert's teaching. In 990 Fulbert opened the school of Chartres, which was to be the most illustrious centre of learning in the twelfth century. Its foundation may be said to mark the beginning of the new era. Together with the traditional subjects taught, a very high place was given to dialectic. Fulbert himself was aware of its limitations and its dangers; God, he held, was beyond the reach of all logical concepts. But his pupil Berengarius, head of the school of Tours (*d.* 1088), recognized no such restriction. He represented the new outlook which regarded all truth as amenable to dialectic. Berengarius himself is best known for his attempt to apply dialectic to the Sacrament of the Eucharist. He opposed the view that the bread and wine were really changed into Christ's body, on the grounds that, as long as the accidents remained the same, so did the substance. The bread and wine were only symbols of Christ. Thus by applying arguments taken from dialectic, Berengarius was led to denying Transubstantiation. His doctrines, together with John the Scot's, were condemned at the Synod of Vercelli in 1050.

Berengarius was only the most extreme example of the dialectical outlook. Anselm of Besate (*c.* 1050), often called the Peripatetic, was another who stressed the need to emancipate dialectic from theology. He was one of the first examples of the new type of professional scholar, wandering from place to place and gathering around him a following of students. The peripatetics were among the foremost influences on the intellectual life of the eleventh and twelfth centuries, with Abelard as their outstanding representative. Anselm himself went from Italy to Germany, teaching the principles of dialectic with especial emphasis upon contradictory statements. Where Berengarius had applied dialectic to faith, Anselm remained content to treat it for its own sake.

These views, whether directed against faith or confined to grammatical statements, were regarded as a challenge to theology. They threatened the supremacy of faith by their attempt to be independent of its dictates. Reaction was bound to come; and it took the form of an attack upon dialectic. It was led by the representatives of the older monastic culture, where from the first all learning had been subordinated to theology, and dialectic had no greater claim to prominence than any of the other seven liberal arts. Gerard of Czanad (*d.* 1046) had been one of the earliest upholders of the sovereignty of faith, but it was Peter Damian (1007–1072) who became its most outspoken protagonist. He had himself opened a school at Ravenna before his conversion, and he was well equipped to attack dialectic with its own weapons. Damian was not only concerned with dialectic, he was also one of the leaders in the movement for Church reform.

Yet it was in combating the dialecticians that he displayed his greatest extremism. In his treatise *On Divine Omnipotence* Damian threw doubt upon all knowledge, by invoking God's absolute power, by which He had absolute freedom to act as He willed. God could do anything; accordingly, there could be no certainty. His will was above all laws, unrestricted even by impossibility. Dialectic and reason therefore can have no place in discussing God or matters of faith: 'That which is from the argument of the dialecticians cannot easily be adapted to the mysteries of divine power; that which has been invented for the benefit of the syllogisms ... let it not be obstinately introduced into divine law ... let it [dialectic] be like a servant ready to obey her mistress' (P.L. 145, 603c*). Damian did more than refute the claims of dialectic; he questioned its

*Migne: *Patrologia Latina.*

96

validity at all. There was not only no means of arriving at the truth, but there were no logical principles to distinguish it at all. This was essentially the response of one who distrusted all reason. It was too extreme to have any immediate influence, for it restricted all intellectual activity to the study of the Bible and its commentaries, which Damian recommended in his *De ordine eremitarum*. Although Damian's outlook, as it stood, could lead to scepticism, in his hands it was the most extreme form of fideism.

Manegold of Lautenbach (*d.* 1103) and Otloh of St Emmeram (*d.* 1073) were others who shared Damian's contempt for secular knowledge. Manegold followed Damian in regarding philosophy as the handmaid of theology and the temptation of the devil. He is, however, especially important for his political philosophy, where, besides making the Pope supreme over all rulers, he regards the king as elected by his people and so, ultimately, liable to deposition if he fails them (P.L. 155).

Between these extremes of dialectic and anti-dialectic there lay a middle way, which, if less spectacular at first, was to prove the most enduring. It emanated originally from the monastic school at Bec, in the second half of the eleventh century, under Lanfranc and St Anselm. Lanfranc (*c.* 1010–1089) was born at Pavia and studied law at Bologna, before becoming Prior of Bec; he was Archbishop of Canterbury from 1070 until his death. He was not against dialectic in itself but against its misuse. He countered Berengarius's eucharistic views not, like Damian, by an all-out attack upon philosophy, but by showing its misapplication: not only had Berengarius abandoned the voice of authority, but he had broken the rules of dialectic in taking a particular proposition to be universal (P.L. 150, 427a). Lanfranc therefore tried to establish the meeting-place of dialectic and theology, at a time when one was being upheld to the exclusion of the other. Although there was little that was original in his own thinking, the fruit of his efforts must be seen in the achievements of his pupils, especially Anselm and Ivo of Chartres; the former was the first thinker to try to apply dialectic as an aid to belief, the latter furthered the growth of canon law.

(iv) St Anselm

With St Anselm (1033–1109) we reach the first great original thinker in the West, since John the Scot, and the first creator of a system in the tradition of St Augustine. Born at Aosta, in Italy, he followed Lanfranc as Prior of Bec and Archbishop of Canterbury. Like Lanfranc, though in a very different way, his importance belonged to the future rather than to his own day. All around him men continued to direct their enquiries to the more limited questions raised by the struggle between the dialecticians and the anti-dialecticians; an accommodation between faith and reason had still to be reached; the scope of reason had still to be tested. For St Anselm, on the other hand, this was not the main issue; far more than his master Lanfranc, he was a monk first and foremost, and in the interests of faith he was prepared to use reason. Not for him the dichotomy between dialectic and belief; on the contrary, to use his own words, Anselm 'believed in order that he might understand' (*Credo ut intelligam*). In a sense, this was the programme of scholastic thinking: it had been St Augustine's starting-point that belief was the condition of knowing. Similarly, the faith had, as its aim, love of truth, or, put in St Anselm's words, faith sought understanding (*fides quaerens intellectum*).

Three important traits mark St Anselm's system. The first was the application of dialectic to every aspect of dogma. In this respect St Anselm was a child of his age; there were not as yet any recognized limits to the scope of rational enquiry; the boundaries between natural and supernatural knowledge had not yet been drawn. It was still the first age of reason's new-found voice. Anselm's second trait is that he took purely theological themes. He did not set out either to create a system or to explain the world, but to understand the faith he held. His outlook, although a coherent body of thought, is marked by the theological nature of its subjects. They are concerned with God, the Trinity, the Incarnation, the Virgin, original sin, and the way of arriving at these truths.

In his lack of concern to explain nature and being, Anselm

was, again, not out of harmony with his age. There was not yet a comprehensive knowledge of metaphysics; this had to await the arrival of Aristotle's works in the later twelfth century. Dialectic, when not dealing with faith, was still primarily concerned with classifying concepts and ordering knowledge, rather than examining being itself. Moreover, the exploratory nature of Anselm's investigations can be seen in the way he wrote. He did not attempt any overall examination of faith, but confined himself to separate studies on his chosen topics. This monographic treatment is a feature of the eleventh and twelfth centuries. It contrasts with the broad themes and vast *summae* of the thirteenth century. By this means we are, as with St Augustine's works, able to follow up the development of St Anselm's thought through each of its stages.

In the third place, St Anselm was in the direct line of descent from St Augustine: even if we cannot accept his claim that he had been 'unable to find anything which I have said that does not belong to the writings of the Catholic fathers and especially blessed Augustine' (*Monologium*: Prologue), it remains true that they shared a common approach. They both made faith the starting-point for knowledge; they both regarded the Idea of truth (or beauty or goodness) as evidence for its existence; they both sought for knowledge of God through these eternal Ideas; they both regarded the human soul as an image of the Trinity. Anselm differed from St Augustine in going farther along the same path and in drawing conclusions for which St Augustine had not looked. His striking novelty came from applying dialectic to Augustinian premises.

St Anselm's entire position rests upon the primacy of faith. We must recognize that, like St Augustine, he allowed reason no independent validity. For both, reason was an instrument in demonstrating what was already believed; of itself it could not add to certitude, although it could give additional evidences of its truth. Like St Augustine, Anselm held to the maxim 'If you do not believe you will not understand'. Reason, therefore, could never be more than a meditation upon faith, and it always presupposed it.

St Anselm's thought is dominated by what we may call the Augustinian or Platonic view of truth. He regarded everything as an aspect of some ultimate source. Thus beautiful things all held beauty in common and were participations in the beautiful – a complete essence in itself. His treatise *On Truth*, devoted to showing that anything true was dependent upon the Truth, clearly expressed this view, that all reality transcended individual things; the latter were simply the signs of a higher truth. This was the foundation of St Anselm's theory of knowledge and he employed it to prove God's existence.

His proof followed a similar progression to St Augustine's proof: from the existence of independent, immaterial concepts, or truths, he concluded that they must have an author who was God. This was worked out in his two treatises, the *Monologium* and the *Proslogion*. The *Monologium*, meditations and reflections on God, started from the principle, which we have already discussed, that unequal degrees of goodness presuppose some absolute good. This is developed in three proofs. The first begins with goodness in things. Through our senses we experience many types of good. These must all have a cause, participation in which leads to their specific goodness. This ultimate good is God. The second proof shows that there is a common goodness which ultimately must have a single cause – God. The third proof assumes a hierarchy of goodness (e.g. that animals are superior to vegetative beings and that man is superior to animals) which must culminate in a single perfection.

It need hardly be stressed how much all these proofs derive their inspiration from St Augustine. They all express the same view of reality as lying outside things. Yet they also show the way in which St Anselm was prepared to look to things themselves for evidence of God's existence. He did not, however, stop there. In his *Proslogion* he desired to find a single proof for God which was more immediate and belonged to inner experience. It was in this work, originally called *Fides quaerens intellectum* (faith in search of understanding) that he developed the famous ontological proof: so called by later generations to denote its reliance upon mental concepts rather than the experience derived from facts.

This proof differed from the three of the *Monologium* in starting from faith; and it must be understood as deriving from Christian experience. Its validity, from Anselm's point of view, did not rest upon its verification by objective tests, but solely upon the knowledge which came through God's illumination. 'That which I first believed thanks to your gift, I now understand through your illumination' (*Proslogion*, ch. iv). Such knowledge of God, therefore, presupposes grace.

The actual proof was the simple assertion that when we say God we conceive a being than whom no greater can exist. Even the fool in the Psalm (13: 1) who says that there is no God has an idea of God. This idea of God must exist in reality, for otherwise it could not exist in our minds, and we could then think of a being greater than God. This would be a contradiction; therefore God must exist. 'O Lord, who givest understanding to faith, give me to understand, as far as you know it to be good for me, that you exist as we believe and that you are what we believe you to be. We believe that you are that than which nothing greater can be thought. Or is there no such being, since "the fool hath said in his heart 'There is no God' "'? But when the fool himself hears what I say, a being than which no greater can be thought, he understands what he hears and what he understands is in his understanding, even if he does not understand that it exists. It is one thing for an object to be in the understanding, and another to understand that it exists' (*ibid*. ch. ii.). As the painter has an idea of a picture without supposing he has painted it, so the fool can believe that God exists in the mind without existing in reality. But, in fact, the cases are not the same: 'Clearly the being than which none greater can be conceived cannot exist in the understanding alone. If it is in the understanding alone it can be thought of as existing also in reality, which is greater. If therefore that than which nothing greater can be conceived is only in the understanding, this same being than which a greater cannot be thought is that than which a greater can be thought. But this is not possible. Without doubt, therefore, that than which no greater can be thought exists both in the understanding and in reality' (*ibid.*).

This argument was something quite new, and has ever been the subject of controversy. Before passing judgement we should note its assumptions and its intentions. In the first place, its descent can be traced back to Anselm's underlying belief that ideas represent a higher truth and so can ultimately be identified with reality. St Augustine, too, had discovered God through the truth which we recognize in our soul. But where Anselm differed was in making our idea of God synonymous with God's existence. St Augustine had stopped at the evidence that God existed; he did not identify that evidence with God Himself. St Anselm, on the other hand, included God in his definition of Him. This meant that so far as God was concerned, Anselm made no distinction between that which exists in thought and that which exists in reality. But only so far as God was concerned. This is the second aspect of Anselm's ontological proof; despite many assertions to the contrary, it was for those who started with faith. Not only was the whole argument directed towards believers, the fool included, but Anselm's reply to the criticism of Gaunilo the monk makes this clear. Gaunilo had objected that this was to make real all that we think. But, he went on, because he thought of the Fortunate Isles lost in the Atlantic this did not mean that they existed, any more than to think of God was to infer His existence. To this St Anselm countered by saying that knowledge of God could not be compared to knowing the Fortunate Isles. It was this special knowledge that came from faith that lay at the base of Anselm's ontological proof.

What, then, the ontological proof shows is the inference that dialectic can draw from faith. It takes the belief in God as established: it offers rational evidence to support that belief. Once taken out of the *milieu* of revelation it loses the special protection that saves it from Gaunilo's criticism. Because God is God he cannot be regarded in the same way as other knowledge. This approach, although not immediately influential,

was to be taken up again in the thirteenth century by St Bonaventure, and in the fourteenth century by many thinkers who
saw no way of proving God's existence from reality. It marked
the extreme limit of the Augustinian outlook, in transferring
full sovereignty to the Idea derived from faith. This extremity
made for its selective use in an age where more and more care
was to be bestowed upon demarcating faith from reason.

In his view of man, Anselm also followed Augustine closely:
the human soul, composed of memory, intelligence, and love,
was in the image of the divine Trinity. Its knowledge came
through recognizing the Ideas within it. In one sense,
St Anselm's whole outlook derives from this Augustinian
foundation. He upholds illumination of the soul by God as the
means to knowledge of the truth: his *Monologium* is really an
aspect of this special belief.

Theologically, St Anselm made important contributions to
the doctrine of the Incarnation. In the case of original sin, his
modification of St Augustine's view was particularly influential. Where St Augustine had seen the main consequence of
sin as concupiscence, St Anselm saw it as a loss of righteousness. Man's original free choice had led to the loss of his
freedom against sin. He had lost the inclination to justice,
rather than become the slave to sin.

Anselm's importance lay in the future; his new methods of
reasoning mark him out as the first thinker of the 'scholastic'
age. Yet he also retained his links with the past. This was not
so much in his devotion to St Augustine; indeed one of the
most important streams of thought throughout the middle
ages was the Augustinian school. It was far more in his
unawareness of any boundary between faith and reason. He
did not attempt to restrict the use of reason to the support it
could derive from experience. He did not make the distinction
between natural and supernatural knowledge which the later
scholastics were to make. For him all aspects of faith invited
meditation, and it was reason's purpose to further meditation.
If for the first time both the ingredients, faith and reason,
were employed, their exact proportions had still to be
measured.

(v) Universals, Abelard

Anselm had written against a background of growing dialectical activity. The first phase, with its dispute between the dialecticians and the anti-dialecticians over the very existence of dialectic, was giving way to problems confronting dialectic. Already during Anselm's life-time the question of universals had appeared. Put simply, this concerned the relation of genera and species to individuals. What were the nature and the status of general terms like 'animal' and 'man', in the actual world of individual animals and men? Were they simply mental concepts (words) or did they really exist (things)? The answers given to these questions marked off the Nominalists from the Realists. The nominalists held that universals were merely words, that only individuals existed, and that the genus or the species corresponded to nothing in the real world. The realists, on the other hand, recognized, in some degree, the existence of genera and species and their correspondence to reality. Those who saw them as coming before all individuals, with the individual a mere variant on a common essence, were extreme realists. Those who acknowledged their presence in individuals, while preserving the separate identity of the latter, were moderate realists. Yet, even so, there is a borderland which often seems to veer between nominalism and realism. In such cases we can most usefully concentrate upon the position itself rather than its pigeonhole.

It used to be held that nominalism and realism were synonymous with medieval thought. But in reality their dominant phase covered the fifty years or so from the last two decades of the eleventh century, spanning the careers of Roscelin at the beginning, and Abelard at the end. This is not to say that universals suddenly disappeared as an intellectual issue, but rather that they began to take their place as one among many problems. The problem itself was not peculiar to the middle ages; it is one that has vexed all epochs: the source of the discrepancy between our understanding and the physical world. In itself it did not imply theological criteria. The issue during the eleventh and twelfth centuries was not over the existence or non-existence of divine Ideas, but over the grouping of things into genera and species; it did not therefore go beyond being and its relation to knowledge. Moreover, it arose before the systematic application of reason to faith which St Anselm had foreshadowed; the equipment for a full-fledged natural philosophy was still wanting, and hence the battle was waged primarily in terms of logic and epistemology. Only with Abelard's solution, and the new impetus to metaphysics given by the translations of Aristotelian and Arabian works, did this restricted approach give way, and universals become part of the wider problems of theology and metaphysics.

The subject of universals did not arise by accident: it was one of the few legacies of ancient philosophy handed down to the West and preserved into the eleventh and twelfth centuries. The agents in this transmission were Porphyry and Boethius: each had, in dealing with the Introduction to Aristotle's *Categories*, broached the nature of logic and of universals. They took Aristotle's ten categories, classifying the particular attributes of a substance, to mean terms, not things, with the result that logic was regarded by some as the science of words. This seems to have influenced Roscelin (*c.* 1050–1125) who is usually regarded as the first nominalist. Born at Compiègne, he studied at Soissons and Paris and was Abelard's master at Loches. None of Roscelin's writings survived, except for a letter to Abelard on the Trinity, and his ideas are only known through references to them by Abelard and Anselm. Roscelin's chief fame attaches to his view of the Trinity for which he was condemned by the Council of Soissons in 1092. According to Anselm, who combated them, Roscelin's errors arose from refusing to recognize universals. This meant that where he should have seen the unity of the divine Persons, Roscelin tended to see three separate Gods, a heresy. 'He who does not understand that several men are specifically one man,' wrote Anselm, 'how would he understand that, in the most mysterious of all natures, several persons, each of whom is a perfect God, are one God?' (P.L. 148, 265b). Although Anselm did not take any direct part in the dispute over universals as such, he joined issue when theology was involved. Anselm's own attitude was at the opposite pole – what we could call extreme realism: he saw all reality as inhering in universals, and this had governed his view of truth and his arguments for God's existence in the *Monologium*.

Roscelin himself is said to have described universals as sounds (*flatus vocis*), signifying merely words. The individual was the sum of all reality, neither divisible in itself nor part of a whole. Clearly such a doctrine made any approach to theology bound to end in heresy.

Apart from Roscelin, the issues were not directly nominalism as such, or theology. They revolved round the different aspects of realism, and were concerned mainly with Abelard's attack on the extreme realism of William of Champeaux, together with his own solution. William of Champeaux (1070– 1121) was himself Abelard's teacher for a time at Paris. His career, like that of Abelard and Roscelin, testifies to the growing influence of individual masters, as opposed to any fixed places of learning: he had studied under Manegold, Anselm of Laon, and Roscelin, whom he opposed, before becoming a teacher. His importance is not confined to his teaching on universals, though it is its most prominent aspect. Like Roscelin, his views are mainly known at second-hand – through Abelard's *History of Calamities*. According to Abelard, William held that the species existed fully in every individual; the latter was differentiated only by local modifications. 'The same reality remains entire in each of the individuals of a species; they contain no diversity of essence but receive variety only from the multitude of accidents.' Thus Plato and Socrates, for example, both shared the same essence of human being; they differed only in individual particulars which were extraneous to their common nature (accidents). This meant that, in effect, Plato and Socrates were the same and that in seeking to preserve the unity of the species William had sacrificed the individual. Later, under the weight of Abelard's attack, he modified this community of essence to one of non-difference. Plato and Aristotle belonged to the same species because they did not differ; they were united by absence of difference. Although this, too, was attacked by Abelard it was to have some bearing on his own views.

It was Peter Abelard (1079–1142) who brought the controversy to an issue; and if it gained its great prominence from him it also received a solution which largely settled the matter in that form. Without doubt, Abelard was the dominant intellectual figure of his day. He gave a new impetus to dialectic, developed its method, and extended its use; the strength of his personality set the seal upon the pre-eminence of the individual master; and it was largely through him that Paris University became the foremost centre of dialectic and theology. He was primarily a dialectician, concerned neither with evolving a philosophy of nature nor with creating a theological system in St Anselm's manner. His was an essentially critical approach to the meaning of words and concepts. This rather than ideas or speculation was his *forte*, and he applied himself to examining matters of theology and logic with equal keenness.

We cannot class Abelard among the great original thinkers, for this was not his intent; nor can we regard him as a rationalist or the founder of scholasticism. His greatest contribution lay in furthering rational and dialectical argument, and in helping to develop it as an aid to faith. If his immediate impact was far greater than Anselm's, his ultimate achievements must be seen more in the general development of scholasticism than in any specific personal influence.

The first stage in Abelard's stormy career, and the most spectacular, was with universals. Although much of his fire was directed against William of Champeaux, Abelard was mainly concerned with the questions which Porphyry had raised, but had not answered, in his *Isagoge*: firstly, was the universal real, or a mere verbal expression? Secondly, if real, was the universal corporeal or incorporeal? Thirdly, did the universal exist separately or was it to be found in sensible things? To these three questions Abelard added a fourth: whether, if the individual ceased to exist, the universal would remain; that is, was the species 'rose' dependent upon the existence of individual roses?

Boethius, who, as we have seen, had been the first to attempt a solution to these questions, had regarded the individual as the embodiment of the universal; it represented the universal as particularized by matter and individual accidents (such as shape, colour, quantity, and so on). Thus Plato and Aristotle were the material expressions of the species 'man' which in itself was immaterial and could only be recognized in thought. This position was (to use the terminology of the twelfth century) realist; it recognized the existence of the universal as a thing (res). On the other side was Roscelin's viewpoint which regarded only the individual as real and the universal as a mere word (vox).

Abelard, therefore, was presented with these two alternatives, and he rejected both.* He criticized the realist position taken up by Boethius and, initially, by William of Champeaux, for denying the individual its own essence, thereby going against the evidence of nature: 'although many authorities appear to agree, it contradicts nature in every respect'. In the first place, since according to the realists the form or essence came before the individual, there would be no difference between one individual and another. They would share the same genus and they would share the same categories (substance, quantity, quality, and so on) of which each individual was comprised. Moreover, to say that Socrates differed from Plato, not in species (which was the same) but in individual accidents (height, colour, eyes, and so on), would be to give the accidents priority over the species; this would then make the species itself contain accidents and so accidents, not species, become the foundation of individual being. Each of these contradicts the realist position. In the second place, Abelard showed that if the genus 'animal' really meant the same essence for all its members, men would share a single nature with irrational creatures, like dogs and horses, thus making the genus rational and irrational at the same time. Abelard also criticized William of Champeaux's principle of non-difference: positively it was

*For what follows see B. Geyer's edition of Abelard's Philosophical Works: *Die Philosophischen Schriften Peter Abaelards*; and V. Cousin, *Ouvrages inédits*.

only another way of saying that if Socrates and Plato were united by absence of difference, they shared a common existence; negatively it had no more meaning than to say that they did not differ from a stone.

Against the nominalists' repudiation of universals, Abelard also invoked the evidence of reality. If logic were simply a matter of grammar there would be no other standard than the correct use of words; but in fact statements can be meaningless though grammatically correct, as, for example, to say that man is a horse. The answer to these difficulties, as Abelard saw it, lay not in denying universals but in ceasing to regard them as things. In this it is possible to say that Abelard came nearer to a nominalist than a realist point of view. The mistake of the realists, he asserted, lay in thinking of genera and species as things. It was this that led to the impossible task of reconciling them with individuals: 'It is monstrous to predicate the thing of a thing.' Accordingly, Abelard reverted to Aristotle's definition of the universal as 'that which can be predicated of several things, like man'. In contrast, 'the individual is that which cannot be predicated of more than one thing, as with Callias'. Thus the universal was not a word *qua* word, but a word which could be predicated of things. This was the great difference between Abelard and Roscelin.

The problem Abelard had to solve was why the same word could be used to describe a group of individuals. His reply took him beyond the categories of logic into the realm of knowledge. A universal, he said, corresponded to what existed in things. This was not the same as making the universal a thing: instead of taking the universal to be the essence of the individual, it must be seen as referring to its status. Thus it does not signify man, which is nothing, but to be a man, a condition common to all men. Now this state is inseparable from the individual; therefore the universal can only be derived from the individual. This was the novelty of Abelard's position, for he made knowledge of the universal come through intellectual activity. Through our minds working upon the things encountered in the senses we are able to distinguish their common status. In the final analysis, the universal is a concept which the mind abstracts from the individual: 'because all clear understanding seems to derive from individuals, when we have grasped them through the senses we recall them through the intellect'. Consequently, Abelard has to examine the processes of thought leading up to recognition of the *status*.

The great difference between the individual and the universal was that, while the individual gave a clear and exact picture, that of the universal was vague and blurred: 'that which is a universal word presents a common and confused image of many things; that which an individual word produces keeps to one and the same form, restricting itself to one person only'. The *status*, then, in dealing only with the general characteristics abstracted from a number of individuals, presents an overall impression. This impression, once in our minds, no longer represents any particular object and can survive any changes to the original object. Thus our impression of a tower does not have to correspond to any single, real tower, and it therefore lacks the precision of a real tower.

Since, then, the universal was inseparable from the individuals in which it inhered, Abelard's reply to the original questions could not go unqualified. Firstly, over the existence of universals: on the one hand, a universal, as a word, did not exist in itself, but, on the other hand, it designated something real, which Abelard had described as a state. Secondly, universals were not corporeal, except in so far as a word was a physical sound; thirdly, universals existed in sensible things and yet they represented concepts which could only be understood when abstracted from sensible things. Finally, although the universal could only derive from individuals once abstracted they were independent of real things.

Abelard's solution, for all its novelty, never fully passed beyond the logical plane. While he was the first medieval thinker to recognize the psychological aspect of the problem, in his view of abstraction, genera and species remained primarily logical concepts. He did not attempt to analyse the nature of universals in themselves or ask how they came to be common to a group of individuals; he in no way sought the meaning of essence, or its relation to accidents. In short, Abelard did not examine the sources of knowledge; he never translated the concepts derived from abstraction into real terms. Above all, his starting-point was that a universal was a term (*sermo*) which could be predicated of other things. Hence it had no reality in itself; it was an attribute of things or of words.

For this reason we run the risk of confusion in describing Abelard as a moderate realist; that is, one who recognizes the existence of the universal in individuals (*in re*): Abelard's universals lack any independent existence; they are not grounded on being. The moderate realism of St Thomas, on the contrary, is founded upon the independent existence of the universal, even though it subsists in individuals. For Abelard, it was only a logical category; for St Thomas it was a metaphysical entity. Abelard refused reality to anything but the individual; St Thomas saw individual reality as the embodiment of universal reality. The universal for Abelard was never more than a concept of the mind and it could only be located in the mind; for St Thomas it corresponded with ultimate reality. Thus, if we take, as the criterion of realism, the reality of the universal, Abelard's position seems to belong to nominalism. More important than the category, however, was the powerful impetus which his solution gave to the autonomy of logic as the study of concepts independent of real things. This grammatical aspect was to become ever more prominent in the thirteenth and fourteenth centuries.

Abelard did not confine himself to purely logical topics, and indeed the greater part of his later life was dominated by the condemnation, and the threat of condemnation, of his theological views. From the point of view of the history of thought, perhaps his most important work was the *Sic et Non*. This brought to theology the method of reconciling contradictory authorities already practised by the canonists. The aim, he said, was to arrive at the truth through a rational investigation of the different opinions given: 'By doubting we come to enquiry, by enquiring we perceive the truth.' This approach has been justly called 'methodical doubt', and it was equally apparent in Abelard's other theological works. For example, in his *Dialogue between a Christian and a Jew*, he made the philosopher reject both their arguments on the grounds that they were unsupported by proof. Dialectic, therefore, was a necessary means of explaining faith to the infidel and of elucidating it for the believer. 'If philosophers attack us they must be convinced through their own philosophy.' The *Sic et Non* contains 150 theological questions each supported and opposed by conflicting statements, which were resolved by the rules of logic. Although, as we shall mention again later, this was not in itself a new and revolutionary step, it helped to establish the dialectical method in theology. It was the first comprehensive exposition of theology as a science rather than as a meditation; it prised theology away from authority and exposed it to the scrutiny of reason. In this sense, the *Sic et Non* crystallized scholastic method; it was a milestone on the road to the systems of the thirteenth century.

On the wider questions of theology, we have already remarked that Abelard did not share Anselm's desire to provide a speculative foundation to dogma; indeed what is striking in Abelard's work is the absence of any attempt to relate his logical discussions to a general outlook. This is particularly apparent in the way in which he distinguishes between genera and species on the one hand, and divine Ideas on the other: the latter, he says, are in no way to be regarded as the former. Divine Ideas are the archetypes that God has, as creator, while man's ideas are quite different. Unlike John the Scot, for example, he did not try to find their meeting-point. In his approach to questions of dogma, Abelard, far from following Anselm's enumeration of necessary reasons in support of faith, was chary of the indiscriminate use of dialectic: 'Insofar as reason is hidden', he wrote, 'let us be content with authority.' Many of the heresies that he combated in his introduction to theology he regarded as coming from wrongly-applied dialectic: 'What greater affront can believers receive than to have God Himself examined and for small intellects to be able to understand Him and language to discuss Him?' Yet Abelard was condemned for those very offences by

St Bernard, who wrote of him: 'When he discusses the Trinity he sounds like Arius, when grace he sounds like Pelagius, when the person of Christ, like Nestorius.'

Abelard's main theological offences were over the Trinity, original sin, and grace. So far as the Trinity was concerned, he did not try to emulate Roscelin, thus risking tritheism. He pointed out that the same distinction between things and words must apply when discussing the Godhead. The main outcome of his different discussions was to see, contrary to Roscelin, the unity of the Divine Persons, whom he tended to regard as expressions of power, understanding, and goodness. His view was condemned at the Council of Sens in 1142.

More striking were his ethical opinions, which are contained in his *Scito teipsum*. These were very largely due to his novel views on original sin. Unlike St Augustine and Catholic tradition he saw sin far more as a punishment than a fault. He distinguished between vice, which was an inclination to sin, and sin as an action which affronts God. Moreover, in following the accepted definition of sin as a negation of being, he concluded that it did not of itself constitute anything. Abelard held that an action was the result of individual intention and could only be judged according to whether the intention was for good or evil. 'All acts are in themselves indifferent and only become good or evil according to the intention of their author' (P.L. 178, 644a). This led to his ignoring the need for a supernatural aid in achieving a good act; it in effect denied the need, specified by dogma, of a prevenient grace in every good action. Its novelty lay in transforming morality from a supernatural into a personal matter; in an age of objective criteria, Abelard turned to subjective values. This was in keeping with his whole bent; it made reality rest with individual certainty, rather than with general concepts of good and evil; but it also violated the tenets of faith. As with his epistemology, there is more than a hint of the attitude which Ockham, also, was to adopt in the fourteenth century.

When all is said, however, Abelard was an adventurous spirit, not a rationalist. A great part of his writings was devoted to refuting heresy; his innovations were from trying to make faith intelligible to reason. His passionate advocacy and his highly individual approach created complications which in a lesser man would have not have arisen. As he himself wrote: 'I do not want to be a philosopher if it means resisting St Paul; I do not wish to be Aristotle if it must separate me from Christ.' This is the testimony of a man of faith whose temper led him beyond his inclinations.

(vi) The twelfth century

In many respects it is artificial to make a division between the eleventh and twelfth centuries. Many of their topics were the same, as were their controversies: the struggle over universals spanned both centuries; Anselm, the first great thinker of the eleventh century, lived into the first decade of the twelfth. Yet there was a difference, and it lay in the increasing diversity of expression as time went on. At the time of St Anselm the main intellectual positions were principally either theological, in the Patristic sense of glossing Scripture, or dialectical, with emphasis upon classification rather than enquiry.

Already, as we enter the twelfth century, we are aware of the change. In the first place, there was the marked turn which had been given to dialectic by Anselm and which was furthered by Abelard. Different as they were in age and outlook, and although Anselm's system remained a solitary testimony to intellectual greatness, they shared a constructive approach to dialectic; it was not to be used for its own sake (as, for example, Anselm of Besate had implied), but for elucidating problems of faith – God's existence, the Trinity, the Incarnation – and matters of philosophy – universals. This extension in the application of reasoning was furthered by the rediscovery of more of Aristotle's logical works, mainly the *Organon*, which came to constitute the 'new logic'.

Secondly, there was the growing interest in Platonism, and with it, nature. This, too, was a marked development on the purely Patristic outlook which had so far prevailed. There was now a curiosity in natural phenomena, where previously creation and the physical world had been largely taken for granted. This, too, was stimulated by new sources of knowledge: in this case, the translations of scientific works from the Arabic, mainly by Constantinus Africanus and Adelard of Bath, and including works by such authors as Galen, Hippocrates, and Euclid. These, aided by an incomplete version of Plato's one known work, the *Timaeus* in Chalcidius's translation, with commentary, and Boethius's writings on music and arithmetic, combined to produce a strongly Neoplatonic outlook. Thus the first stage to an independent philosophical approach was provided by Platonism. It was, in a sense, a halfway house between the exegetical studies of the old thought and the full-fledged natural theology of the thirteenth century. The Platonism of the twelfth century still lacked what Aristotle and the Arabian philosophers were to provide – a thoroughgoing analysis of the structure and the constituents of being, in its different aspects of form, matter, movement, substance. It led, rather, to a desire to trace back the things found in nature to a divine source. Nevertheless, the Platonists of the twelfth century were the first to examine the connexion between the existence of the world and the existence of God.

With this greater interest in nature and speculation, there tended to be a change in the humanism which accompanied it at Chartres, its centre. While there was still a great emphasis upon the classics, so ardently fostered by the Carolingians, the purely stylistic and rhetorical aspects of grammar became less important as the century progressed. Gradually, though not immediately, the effect of Abelard's logic made itself felt; grammar was drawn increasingly into the orbit of dialectic; its concern was with the meaning of words and their combination rather than with style as such. From this point of view, it would be true to say that the eleventh century was more the age of literary humanism, with men like Peter Damian, Hildebert of Tours, and St Anselm, than the twelfth century. The element of rediscovery was being displaced in the twelfth century by exploration of new forms, and exemplified in the type of theological writing known as the *Sentences*. Foreshadowed in Abelard's *Sic et Non*, these were logical discussions of theological truths; they bore witness to the triumph of dialectic over both literary eloquence and the traditional theology.

Finally, in contrast to the ever-widening domain of dialectic, we see the equally new form of mysticism. This was more than the sheer rejection of reason in faith, of, say, Damian. It constituted an inner experience of God, transcending all ordinary understanding. St Bernard of Clairvaux and Hugh and Richard of St Victor were its leading, though very different, exponents. It, too, was to become stronger with the years.

(vii) The School of Chartres

The centre of humane studies and Platonism was the school of Chartres. Founded by Fulbert in 990, it was early associated with an interest in grammar and the subjects of the *quadrivium*, furthered by the translations of Constantinus and Adelard of Bath. Constantinus Africanus, born at Carthage, spent thirty-nine years in the Orient and in Egypt before settling at Monte Cassino, sometime after 1060. There, he translated medical works from the Arabic, helping to make Monte Cassino one of the foremost centres in the study of medicine. His translations, besides those of Arabic works, included writings by Galen and Hippocrates. These translations spread first to Salerno, pre-eminent in the study of medicine, and then to Chartres.

Adelard of Bath was born in England and studied at Laon and Tours. He was both translator and author. Among his translations were the *Elements* of Euclid and Arabian astronomical works. His own writings consisted of the *Natural Questions*, embodying his scientific studies, and his *De eodem et de diverso*, written between 1106 and 1115, based upon the *Timaeus*, St Augustine, and Boethius, whose *Consolation* he followed in alternating prose with verse. His outlook, far more strongly influenced by the natural elements of the *quadrivium* than that of most of his generation, was Platonic. Truth lay in Ideas; the senses were a source of deception:

'. . . there is no knowledge from the senses, but opinion only. Hence what . . . Plato called the irrational senses' (*De eodem et de diverso*, 13, 2). On the question of universals Adelard takes a point of view which shows his own strong Platonism, while doing justice to Aristotle. He accepts Aristotle's definition of genera and species as describing what exists in things. But they are just as real as the individual; in fact everything is at once individual, genus, and species. The greater a man's degree of percipience, the greater his ability to look beyond the individual. He follows Plato in holding that universals can only be seen in their true purity freed from imagination, 'outside things, that is to say, in the divine intellect'.

Adelard's view amounts to making the individual the same as the universal; it is the senses which impede our minds with the individual. This explains the viewpoint of Aristotle, who saw only the individual. Adelard himself did not try to reconcile Plato and Aristotle, but to explain the source of their divergence. He was the first thinker of this period to trace the immediate connexion between divine Ideas and actual being. This was largely the result of his knowledge of Greek and Arabian science.

The first great name at Chartres, after Fulbert, was Bernard, master of the school from 1114 to 1119 and Chancellor from 1119 to 1124. His own writings have not survived, and he is known only through John of Salisbury's *Metalogicon*, the source for so much of our intellectual knowledge of the period. Bernard was deeply influenced by the ancients, to whom he likened his own age 'as ants sitting on the shoulders of giants'; they were able to see further not through their own stature but through the elevation to which the ancients had brought them.

John of Salisbury describes Bernard as a grammarian and 'the most perfect Platonist of our age'. This gives us the clue to Bernard's main influences. They were twofold: on the one hand, following the tradition established by Quintilian, the grammarian's task was the cultivation of style and taste and feeling through a study of classical literature. Bernard made this traditional literary outlook the main pursuit of the school.

Yet he also turned to the more logical aspects of grammar, which were ultimately to displace its moral and rhetorical side. Here he gave a Platonic answer to the problem of species and genera and their relation to God. Universals, he held, did not exist apart from Ideas: similar words were really expressions of a single idea, as 'white' and 'to whiten' really derived from 'whiteness'. The Idea in itself comprehended both form and matter; these were two aspects of the same being instead of two different things. Thus, as with Adelard, the Platonic view prevails that a thing directly represents its Idea. Bernard, however, distinguished between the eternal Ideas in God and the Ideas inhering in things themselves and immanent in them. Divine Ideas, exemplars in the divine intellect, were not coeternal with God since they came after Him.

Bernard set the tone for his successors, both in his humanism and his Christian interpretation of Plato by which he identified divine Ideas with the divine nature. Moreover, unlike Abelard, he shows the close connexion between all that he is discussing and God. This combining of the natural with the supernatural is one of the most marked characteristics of the Augustinian-Platonic outlook.

Bernard's younger brother, Thierry of Chartres, succeeded Gilbert de la Porrée as Chancellor of the school in 1142, having previously spent eight years as a teacher in Paris. Described by John of Salisbury as the 'most zealous inquirer into the arts' he displays a similar range of interests to Bernard in his humanism and Platonism. So far as the first is concerned, his *Heptateuchon*, a manual of the seven liberal arts, gives an invaluable picture of the state of knowledge in the first half of the twelfth century. From it we are able to learn what works were available for the study of the different subjects. In logic, Aristotle's *Organon*, comprising the *First Analytics*, the *Topics*, and the *Sophistical Questions*, were mentioned for the first time, and went together with Boethius's works. In grammar Priscian and Donatus were the main authorities; in rhetoric Cicero and Martianus Capella. Equally important were the translations of Arabian astronomical works by Hermann of Dalmatia and Robert of Rétines, which included Ptolemy's *Planisphaerum* as well as numerous treatises on medicine and works on arithmetic, geometry, and music.

This strong leaning towards scientific knowledge is apparent in Thierry's speculative pursuits. He was less concerned with strictly logical questions than Bernard and Gilbert de la Porrée. His *Concerning the Works of the Six Days*, a commentary on the story of creation in Genesis, is a cosmogony strongly influenced by Plato's *Timaeus*. It is an attempt to bring the support of science, as found in the *quadrivium*, to the word of the Bible; to show, by an examination of causes and of the six days of creation, how all being shares its common source in God, who is Himself above being. 'The sovereign Trinity operates in matter which is the totality of the four elements.'* There is a fourfold causality. 'God the Father is the efficient cause, the Son is the formal cause, the Holy Spirit is the final cause, and matter the material cause.' Thierry discusses the different ways in which the philosophers (i.e. pagan philosophers like Plato) have regarded the final cause by which creation is disposed. He himself holds to the Platonic view of the final cause as the demiurge or world soul, with which he identifies the Holy Spirit. Thierry utilized each of the four sciences of the *quadrivium* to describe God; but in the surviving fragment of his work we see only arithmetic employed to this end. By it, we are shown, following the tradition of Boethius and the Pythagorean theory of numbers, that unity is common to all numbers; that unity alone is stable and immutable, as opposed to all other numbers; and that the difference between unity, as stable, and other numbers, as mutable, is the difference between God, who is eternal, and creation, which is not. 'The eternal is none other than God; unity, therefore, is divinity itself' – God is the form of being, the source of all that is, though He remains above being. In this, also, Thierry says, the philosophers have recognized God's uniqueness, whatever the name which they have ascribed to Him. This is further evidence of their affinities with Christian doctrine.

With Thierry we have approached the Neoplatonism of John the Scot (Erigena). Despite their different starting-points we

*See B. Haréau: *Notices et extraits*, p. 173 ff.

can recognize the almost mathematical delineation of the One and the many. The Hellenistic world was coming into view once more.

This attempt to find a correspondence with Christian dogma in a Platonic view of nature is clearly to be seen in the *De mundi universitate sive megacosmus et microcosmus* of Bernard of Silvestris (or Tours). This is so much the product of Plato's *Timaeus* that it is hard to see its immediate bearing upon Christianity. That it was closely in keeping with the spirit of Chartres is apparent in its being addressed to Thierry of Chartres. Moreover, like Thierry's *De sex dierum operibus*, it was designed to show the presence of God in creation. It was written as a dialogue, in prose and verse, after the model of Boethius and Martianus Capella, between Nature and Providence. 'Nature addresses a plea to *Nous*, that is, the Providence of God, over the confusion in the first matter (*hyle*), and asks that the world be more beautifully fashioned. *Nous*, moved by her prayers, willingly agrees to the request, and he separates the four elements from one another. In the first book the order of elements is described. In the second book, entitled the *Microcosmus*, *Nous* speaks to Nature and glorifies the beauty of the world, and promises that in the completion of her work she will fashion man. *Physis* [Nature] therefore forms man from the rest of the four elements.' Bernard's view of creation follows the Neoplatonic triad of the Good, the Logos, and the World Soul, corresponding to the Trinity of the Divine Persons. From the Good emanates the Logos: 'He is the understanding of God which surpasses everything', and contains the eternal Ideas of all things, together with the different genera, species, and individuals of all that come from the elements (*hyle*). The world soul (*Entelechia*) in turn emanates from the Logos, translating the Ideas into the concrete being of nature.

Another prominent member of the school of Chartres was William of Conches (1080–1145), a pupil of Bernard of Chartres. William, like Bernard Sylvestris, tended to follow natural knowledge to the point of excluding faith, and his more unorthodox assertions were collected and presented to

St Bernard for condemnation, by William of St Thierry. William of Conche's main concern was with providing natural evidence to support the Christian belief in creation. In this, like all his confrères, he was largely influenced by the *Timaeus*. His works included a commentary on the *Timaeus*, glosses on Boethius's *Consolation*, a work on morality inspired by Cicero and Seneca, and two treatises, the *Philosophia mundi* and *Dogmaticon philosophiae*, on nature and science. As with many of the Chartrains, William identified the Holy Spirit with the World Soul which 'extended the divine will from power and wisdom to the creation and government of the world'. But William went beyond this Platonic position by regarding it as immanent in all things, 'a natural force infused into things by God by which some live, others live and feel, others live, feel, and discern' (*Philos. mundi*, Bk. i, ch. v). This extension of the Holy Spirit into nature, which became its expression, was pantheism.

A similar unorthodoxy is apparent in William's scientific outlook. He transformed the prevailing tendency of emphasizing the importance of the *quadrivium* into making it alone the fount of wisdom; the *trivium* was only a means to the *quadrivium*. In examining nature he took up the atomic theory of Democritus, which had been reintroduced into the West by Constantine Africanus and Adelard of Bath. Atoms, he held, were the first principles. This was to make the elements of being material, an extension of his view that nature was a manifestation of the World Soul. William faced opposition not only from William of St Thierry but also from Platonists, like Gilbert de la Porrée, who regarded immaterial Ideas, not unstable matter, as the source of ultimate reality.

Perhaps the most important thinker to come from the school of Chartres was Gilbert de la Porrée (1076–1154), pupil of Bernard, chancellor of Chartres (until in 1141 he left to teach at Paris) and bishop of Poitiers from 1142 until his death in 1154. One of the greatest teachers of his time, Gilbert was regarded by his contemporaries as, and was, one of the foremost thinkers of the twelfth century. His works included a series of biblical commentaries, a commentary on Boethius's theological works and his treatise on the *Categories* of Aristotle, *De sex principiis*, which became one of the standard texts on logic in the thirteenth century, taking its place beside Aristotle, Porphyry, and Boethius. Gilbert's work may be said to have had two aspects: the more strictly logical where he dealt with Aristotle's *Categories* and the wider metaphysical aspect where Platonism, mainly that of Boethius, was the guiding element. Unlike Abelard, with whom he shared the intellectual pre-eminence of the epoch, Gilbert was far more a metaphysician: being and its modes were his main preoccupation. Moreover, individual though he was, he bore the common stamp of Chartres in relating existence to God. Hence his view on universals cannot be directly contrasted with Constantine Africanus and Adelard of Bath. Atoms, he held, Abelard's, for each was interested in different problems.

Gilbert's metaphysical approach is apparent in his discussion of Aristotle's ten Categories in his *De sex principiis* (P.L. 188). These, it will be recalled, constituted the different attributes of any one individual: substance, quantity, quality, relation, place, time, action, passion, situation, and having. Although as logical distinctions they did not differ, translated into real (metaphysical) terms they did: for example, substance is not equivalent to place or time. Accordingly, Gilbert distinguished between the inherent qualities in anything and its accessory qualities. The first four of the ten categories (substance, quantity, quality, and relation) made up its substance; the other six were simply additional. The inclusion of relation as an absolute substance was to become a matter for great discussion, as it involved the Divine Persons of the Trinity. It was especially prominent during the fourteenth century.

On the wider issues of being, Gilbert's main importance lay in taking up Boethius's distinction between being, which is (substance), and the form by which it is (subsistence). In his commentary on Boethius's *De Trinitate*, Gilbert shows that a substance is an actually existing individual with qualities peculiar to itself (accidents); a subsistence is simply the property or essence in itself, devoid of accidents. Thus the substance Socrates contains the subsistence, humanity, without which Socrates would not be a man, together with the accidents without which he would not be Socrates. All being, then, derives from subsistences, and each individual comprises a collection of subsistences – corporeity, animality, humanity. As Gilbert says, 'subsisting things are the being of their subsistences' (P.L. 64, 1265c). This view represents the fullest Platonism, where each individual is the embodiment of the forms which inhere in it. These forms Gilbert traces back to the divine Ideas in God, though they are not identical with them.

According to John of Salisbury, Gilbert 'attributed universality to innate forms . . . the innate form, however, is not the image of the original and does not reside in God's intellect, but inheres in created things'. Thus the principles of all being are in simple forms, themselves deriving from divine Ideas. Matter itself is made up of the four elements (fire, air, water, earth), a view which Gilbert opposes to William of Conches's atomic theory. By this means Gilbert was able to regard genera and species as the inherent forms in individuals – the subsistences themselves devoid of individual determinations. 'Sensible in sensible things, it [the universal] is conceived as a non-sensible [i.e. as immaterial] by the intellect; it is singular in singular things, and universal in everything' (*ibid*). It is for the mind to group these different forms, which it perceives through individuals; from these arise genera and species as general and special subsistants which make up individual substances. Thus the individual is the compound of form and matter, and this marks it off from the form.

We have here the opposite of Abelard's view of universals. Whereas Abelard never enquired into the constitution of being, and regarded abstraction from the psychological aspect of how the *mind* arrived at general concepts, Gilbert's is concerned with being itself. The very constituents of form and matter explain the relation of individuals to universals. Abstraction, therefore, is only a recognition of inner reality, and not the *explanation* of reality, as it was with Abelard. Similarly, where Abelard stopped at abstraction, Gilbert went on to distinguish God's being from that of things. God alone, as the source of all being, is pure being. While His different creatures have only different aspects of being (hence genera and species) God is without determinations. In Him there can be no distinction between His substance and His sub-sistants. Nevertheless, this way of thinking so permeated Gilbert's outlook that on several occasions he applied it to God, whereby God's being derived from His divinity. 'God, one in three persons, is a diety or divinity, a single form in God by which He is God.' For this Gilbert was attacked by St Bernard at the Council of Rheims in 1148, though not condemned.

Gilbert's importance lies in his making the first systematic attempt to explain God by principles drawn from metaphysics. Hitherto, and for some time afterwards, the emphasis in discussing God was to show Him as the author of creation. Gilbert went further than this; and, in acclaiming the new modes of thought which came with knowledge of the Arabic thinkers, there is a tendency to neglect his own very similar achievement. His weakness lay in his reliance upon solely Platonic concepts. He lacked the Aristotelian divisions of being which could alone have made possible the attempt to subsume God under metaphysical terms. Nonetheless, his overall outlook, the presence of a series of essences in all that exists, was to become one of the main supports of later Augustinian thinking.

Gilbert's own immediate influence was great and gave rise to such a strong following that they were called the *Porretani*. Among them we may mention Nicholas of Amiens, Raoul Ardoul, and Otto of Freising (influenced also by Abelard and Hugh of St Victor) whose *Deeds of the Emperor Frederick* [Barbarossa] provides much valuable knowledge of men like Roscelin, William of Champeaux, Abelard, and St Bernard.

From John of Salisbury (1110–1180) above all others we are enabled to gain a living picture of Chartres and of the age. He was himself the clearest example of the humanist and the international man of letters. He knew nearly all the leading men of his time, both kings and scholars. He was in turn the pupil of Abelard, Robert of Melun, William of Conches,

Gilbert de la Porrée, secretary to Theobald and Becket, Archbishops of Canterbury, and knew well Pope Adrian IV and Henry II of England. He spent the last four years of his life as bishop of Chartres.

It is through John's *Metalogicon* that we have a picture of the first generation of Chartrains and of the humanism for which Chartres stood. He was not an original thinker in his own right, and out of the eight different standpoints which he enumerated on universals, his own is not clear. In the *Metalogicon* his main fire is directed against *Cornificius*, the imaginary figure of the dialectician, the logic-chopper who is obsessed by the insoluble and the futile, especially the problems of universals. 'Disdaining everything except logic, they spend their entire lives on it; having become old they are puerile doubters; they discuss every syllable and even every letter of words and books; they hesitate over nothing, they search everywhere and they never come to knowledge' (*Metalogicon*, Bk. i, ch. 7 and 8). He recognized the importance of logic in all knowledge: the scientist and the moral philosopher reach their conclusions only by logic, and without it they could not proceed. His own work included the new logic of Aristotle, as it was coming to be known – the *Analytics* and the *Topics*. The latter he regarded as providing the rules not only for dialectic but for all knowledge. Only a limited number of things were certain, and, in the tradition of the Academy, he upheld an attitude of doubt to matters which defied proof.

John was in no way a thoroughgoing sceptic, but one who was prepared to keep an open mind on what was not certain. He accepted the testimony of the senses which, he said, 'were the first power or the first activity of the soul' and the foundation of all knowledge. Following the *Posterior Analytics*, he upheld the Aristotelian theory of knowledge through the mind's abstracting truth from the senses. The senses and reason, together with faith, formed the source of all our knowledge. Thus John, in contrast to the growing belief in intellectual certitude, preferred the elegant modesty which he associated with Cicero. He reflected the essentially humanistic aspect of Chartres, which regarded eloquence and cultivation of the mind as the most desirable qualities. Unlike, say, William of Conches, he represented the *trivium* rather than the *quadrivium*.

John also wrote an important work on political theory, the *Policraticus*, where he regarded the king as the intermediary between the Church and the people. 'The prince is the minister of the priests; he is less than they', and his task is to uphold God's law. He can, if necessary, be overthrown. This theocratic outlook was from one who had supported, even if he had not always agreed with, Becket in his struggle against Henry II.

The attitude of Chartres, then, was not a single homogeneous one, but it had certain fundamental tenets which were shared in greater or lesser degree by all its members. Firstly, the surpassing interest in tracing creation to God; secondly, the common influence of Platonism, especially the *Timaeus* in Chalcidius's translation and his commentary on it, Boethius's works, and those of Cicero and Apuleius; thirdly, the strong interest in the subjects of the *quadrivium*, as well as in grammar and rhetoric; fourthly the tradition of classical culture, the belief that cultivation and elegant expression were a matter of moral tone. Within this overall outlook there were many variations, but one thing that all its thinkers shared in common was a strong realism: the belief that all being ultimately derived from the Ideas in God, and that all nature was ultimately informed by Him. The same traits are in evidence in another member of the school, Clarenbaldus of Arras (*d.* 1170), a pupil of Thierry of Chartres and Hugh of St Victor. He wrote a commentary on Boethius's *Trinity*; his natural theories were strongly influenced by Thierry; he regarded God as the 'form of being', and he took up a position of extreme realism over universals which, in contrast to Gilbert de la Porrée's view that each man had his own form, held that all men shared 'one and the same humanity'. What was novel in Clarenbaldus's outlook was his view of God as pure actuality and matter as pure 'possibility', needing a form to make it actual. We are here on the brink of Aristotle's physics, destined for such importance in the next century.

(viii) Pantheism and heresy

By the end of the twelfth century the school of Chartres had given of its best, and its varying traditions had become diffused. It had been the main forcing-house of philosophy as opposed to pure logic, and much of the outlook of men like Gilbert de la Porrée was re-echoed in the different *milieu* of the thirteenth century. Its influence was also apparent in other directions. The end of the century witnessed the growth of pantheism, which had been at least implicit among thinkers like Thierry of Chartres and William of Conches. Two of its main exponents were Amaury of Bène and David of Dinant, both condemned at the synod of Paris in 1210 and again at the Fourth Lateran Council by Innocent III in 1215, together with many of Aristotle's works. Amaury of Bène (*d.* 1206 or 1207) had taught at Paris and is known only by citation. He apparently held that God was not only in all things, but was all things. This was an easy, but momentous, step from the Neoplatonic view of Erigena and the Chartrains who saw God in all things; it meant that God lost His separate identity.

Amaury's condemnation in 1210 came at a time when heresies were once more becoming a powerful threat to ecclesiastical authority. His own teachings, which had given rise to a group of 'Amaurians', tended to the same result. He is said to have said that 'as light is not seen in itself but in air, so God is not seen by angels or by man in Himself, but in creatures'. This immediately negated all the main tenets of Christian teaching: good and evil, sin and merit, the beatific vision or eternal reprobation lost all meaning in a world which was the same as God. There could be no need of salvation, of the sacraments, or ultimately, of the priesthood itself when everything participated equally in God's nature. It is not difficult to see the dangerous implications of Amaury's doctrine.

David of Dinant's pantheism was of a very different kind, and is also known primarily through citations – by Albert the Great, St Thomas Aquinas, and Nicholas of Cusa – so that we cannot be certain whether he actually held the conclusions which they drew. Like Erigena, David regarded nature as falling into divisions; in his case these were three: matter, thought, and God. Unlike Erigena, however, David made these divisions identical, thus including God within them instead of maintaining Him above all being. By a series of deductions David reached the conclusion that, as neither prime matter nor God has forms by which we can identify them, and yet we know them, they must be included in things. David's reasons were taken largely from Aristotle. Although it has been argued that this was not pantheism so much as monism, it seems apparent that, as with Amaury, David had identified God with matter, since his whole emphasis was upon making God the substance of all bodies and souls.

Another tendency to heresy was in the views of Joachim of Flora (1145–1202), Abbot of St John, Calabria. In common with Amaury of Bène and David of Dinant, though from a directly social and ecclesiastical standpoint, Joachim saw this world as the theatre of all God's operations. He translated the persons of the Trinity into different epochs in the history of the world. The age of the Father began with creation and extended over the period of the Old Testament; that of the Son began with the Incarnation and was due to end with the ending of the twelfth century. From then onwards there would be the eternal reign of the Holy Spirit in which, with the coming of the Eternal Evangel, the true Spirit of Christ's teaching would prevail, and the Church would be spiritualized and reformed. This desire for Church reform coupled with an apocalyptic vision was to have a very powerful influence over the next century, particularly among the Franciscans, including John of Parma, general of the order from 1247 to 1257. It became associated with heretical movements, especially in Southern France, where Joachim's works were burned in 1263 by a synod at Arles. His works were also condemned by the Fourth Lateran Council in 1215, for tritheistic leanings.

(ix) The new theology: the Sentences

These outbreaks of unorthodoxy were closely connected with both the growing wealth and power of the Church and also with the influx of heretical ideas from the East. Already, however, much earlier in the century, works had been composed to combat heretics and to explain the faith, in particular by Abelard. This was part of a widespread attempt to systematize faith and to put it on an intellectual foundation. Abelard in his *Sic et Non* had been one of the first to broach the problem, and although he had not originated the method, he gave a great impulse to it. As a result, there grew up what is known as the new genre of the *Sentences*. These, as expressed in Peter Lombard's *Four Books of Sentences*, became the main vehicle of scholastic thought in the succeeding centuries. They constituted a systematically ordered collection of questions drawn primarily from the Bible and the Fathers. Each question dealt with the conflicting answers given by authority, and resolved them by dialectic. Hence they crystallized the method and outlook of mature scholasticism, with the *quaestio* as its centre, and with all discussion guided by the interplay of *pro* and *contra*.

Peter Lombard was born in Italy and taught in the cathedral school at Paris from about 1140, before becoming bishop of the city in 1159. He died in 1160. His four books became the standard theological textbook of the middle ages, and in the next century a commentary on them was one of the requirements for all those studying to become a master of theology. Among the most formative works of the thirteenth and fourteenth centuries were the commentaries on the Lombard's *Sentences* by such men as Alexander of Hales, St Bonaventure, Duns Scotus, and William of Ockham.

The four books of the *Sentences*, following an accepted division, dealt with God, creation, the Incarnation and Redemption, and the sacraments of the Church. The work itself was original neither in content nor in form. Its content was largely taken from St Augustine's thought (it has been estimated that 90 per cent of the Lombard's citations were from St Augustine); but it included references to the Fathers and to one or two moderns, like Abelard and Hugh of St Victor. It also contained the first references to John of Damascene's *De fide orthodoxa*, translated from the Greek in 1157, and doubtless an important influence upon the Lombard.

More interesting, from an historical point of view, is the form of the *Sentences* themselves. They marked the emergence of the works of systematization which were to dominate the thirteenth century; they constituted a break with the monographic treatment of, say, Anselm, although they did not yet constitute a system. In this sense, they brought to fruition a new phase in medieval thought. This did not originate with the Lombard; and in tracing the antecedents of the *Sentences* it is necessary to go back to the end of the Patristic age, to the compilations of Cassiodorus and later of St Isidore, Julian of Toledo, Bede, Alcuin, Walafrid of Strabo, and others. From the stem of their compilations sprang a series of branches. Firstly, there was the work of the jurists, concerned to return to the true texts of the law. This was a general movement both in civil and canon law and involved purging the false from the genuine by something like a dialectical process. It was particularly prevalent in canon law, where, to the revival of interest in law and order generally, came the added stimulus of the Investiture Contest between Papacy and Emperor in the eleventh and twelfth centuries. A series of spurious collections, directed towards asserting the independence of the Church, which had started with the *False Decretals* in the ninth century, made the task of clarification particularly urgent and difficult.

Among the search for the genuine, two collections were particularly important – those of Ivo of Chartres and Gratian. Ivo (1040–1117), who was one of the outstanding members of the school of Chartres, laid great emphasis upon the grouping of texts, and his effect was very great upon his contemporaries and successors. But it fell to Gratian in his *Decretum*, which harmonized the conflicting canons, to make the complete synthesis. The activities of the canonists both influenced and were influenced by the similar efforts of the theologians. Thus it is very likely that while Abelard himself derived much of the method of the *Sic et Non* from the canonists he in turn stimulated Gratian in his work.

The second stream, of theological systematization, had its source at Laon during the twelfth century. It was, under

Anselm of Laon, the 'Master of Masters', and William of Champeaux, the principal school of theological studies in the early twelfth century, though Paris, under Manegold of Lautenbach, was also important. A great number of its members engaged in systematizing dogma and in expounding theological questions. It was at Laon that the first sentence collections originated, as well as the standard Gloss on the Bible. The extent of the debt of all subsequent theological system to Laon is only now coming to be recognized. From Laon it spread throughout the schools of France, helped on its way by Abelard's *Sic et Non* and the biblical commentaries of Gilbert de la Porrée. One of the most important centres became the Abbey of St Victor, in Paris, where Hugh of St Victor wrote his *Summa of the Sentences* and the *De sacramentis*. These two works together with Abelard's *Sic et Non* and the *Sentences* of Robert of Melun, Abelard's opponent, were of the greatest influence upon the Lombard's *Sentences*.

Finally, there was the growth of dialectic itself as the arbiter of all intellectual activity. From the days of Roscelin, Lanfranc and Anselm, when it had been first applied to faith, its influence had grown steadily. Its laws of discussion had by the second half of the twelfth century largely ousted the older method of reading and meditation. John of Salisbury's harsh words (already quoted) on the dialecticians were directed against the new school of logic at Paris, on the left bank of the Seine, under Adam of Petit-Pont, where discussion was alone sovereign.

Peter Lombard's *Sentences* crystallized this long process of applying the principles of dialectic to dogma. Although lacking the depth or the originality of Gratian's *Decretum*, they have been aptly compared as doing for theology what Gratian did for canon law. Already by the second half of the twelfth century, the Lombard's *Sentences* were being glossed and commented by such thinkers as Peter of Poitiers and Peter Comestor, and had given rise to similar works by Prevostin of Cremona and Simon of Tournai, all of the cathedral school at Paris. By 1300, therefore, Paris was securely established as the home of the new theology, just as Bologna was the home of law.

Another aspect of the regulation of faith by dialectic can be seen in the works of Alan of Lille (1125–1203), one of the foremost intellectual figures of the century, who taught at Paris and at Montpelier before retiring to Cîteaux. He gave fullest expression to the tendencies mentioned above: that is, the attempt to formulate rules for the exposition of theology, in order to refute and convince heretics and unbelievers. Alan's work does not answer to any one school, though there are two main elements in his outlook: its content is largely Neoplatonic, influenced particularly by Boethius and Proclus; and its method is an accentuated dialectic.

Much of both these elements can be attributed to the so-called *Book of Causes*, which became known to the West at about this time. In reality, this work constituted the *Elements of Theology* of Proclus, the third-century Neoplatonist, in which he had transmitted the teachings of Plotinus. Alan was one of the first to use it, knowing it by the name of *Aphorisms on the Essence of the Supreme Good*. Its influence upon Alan is all too apparent in his *Rules of Faith*, an exposition of the rules of theology which had been inspired by Boethius. Alan's aim was to expose the laws which were peculiar to faith in the same way that the other sciences had their own laws. The *Rules* began with the most universal law from which, following Euclid's method, the others could be deduced. The first is that 'the Monad is that by which everything is one'. From this Alan went on to deduce the relationship of the One, who is God, to the many. With the help of the *Book of the Twenty-four Philosophers*, wrongly ascribed to Hermes Trismegistos, he reached a formula on the Trinity that was to become famous: 'The monad only engenders the monad and only reflects its own love in itself.' This was taken up by succeeding thinkers to show the essential unity of the three persons in one nature: each was an aspect of the same nature.

The attempt to give rational support to the tenets of faith was carried to its farthest extent in his *On the art of Catholic faith*, the authorship of which has been attributed in turn to Alan of Lille and Nicholas of Amiens; recently it has swung back in Alan's favour. This treatise was directed to providing arguments in favour of Christianity against those who did not believe in it. As with his *On Catholic Faith against the heretics*, Alan had in mind those within Christendom (like the Cathars and Waldenses) as well as the Jews and the Moslems. He followed Euclid's method of theorems, governed by a series of definitions and postulates. It did not pretend to be conclusive; its starting-point, in contrast to, say, St Anselm's, was not faith but disbelief. In structure, the work followed the *Sentences*: it was divided into five short books on God, the world, creation, the Incarnation, and the sacraments; similarly dialectic, not authority, was the means of resolving the problems. There could be no rational knowledge of God; only that which came from faith: accordingly demonstration of His existence depended upon the Aristotelian view of the necessity of a first cause. Alan realized that reason was, at best, only probable, but nevertheless his work showed the degree to which faith now rested upon it. 'I have carefully put in order the probable reasons in favour of our faith . . . so that those who refuse to believe in the prophets and the Evangelist may find themselves led there at least by human reasons.'

Alan's view of nature was largely Neoplatonic; he regarded it as the symbol of God in which there was a correspondence between everything and the World Soul. He took up a position of extreme realism over universals, which, together with his use of Aristotelian categories – form and matter, substance and accidents, the four causes – showed the influence of Gilbert de la Porrée as well as of Boethius.

(x) *Mysticism in the twelfth century*

The most striking change effected by the growth of reason was the attempt to support faith by objective criteria. These ranged from the laws of dialectic to the evidence drawn from natural phenomena; they also varied in the degree to which they were applied. Yet they shared in common the desire to convince by demonstration. This was in marked contrast to the older tradition, of faith as its own justification; and although there was no inherent contradiction between belief and demonstration, the latter tended to be regarded with suspicion, especially by the monastic orders. In its most emphatic form, the belief in the supreme validity of inner experience meant what is commonly described as mysticism: that is, a state in which, by contemplation and self-abnegation, a direct contact with God is established, transcending all external mediation. Whatever the differing degrees of such experience, they share a common belief in the sovereignty of personal experience as opposed to knowledge by intellectual processes. Life, will, and love, rather than learning, intellect, and proof, are its agents, though these do not necessarily exclude the latter.

In the twelfth century there were two main centres of mysticism, themselves quite distinct from one another – among the Cistercian abbeys, particularly of Clairvaux and Signy, and the Abbey School of St Victor in Paris. The leader of the Cistercian mystics was St Bernard (1091–1153), who became Abbot of Clairvaux at the age of 24, a position which he occupied until his death. To talk of the twelfth century without mentioning St Bernard would be like talking of the sixteenth century without mentioning Luther. He was one of its guiding spirits in everything that concerned religious life and Church discipline; if anyone personified the new reforming ardour of the time it was he. His thought is only one aspect of his manifold personality, which was equally prominent in preparing the Second Crusade and in securing Abelard's condemnation, at Soissons and Sens, for theological error. Although he did not, in any way, share Peter Damian's hatred of knowledge, he distrusted it when divorced from belief. Like St Augustine, he held that it should be harnessed to faith, not pursued for its own sake. 'Thus', he wrote of Abelard, 'the human intellect usurps everything to itself, leaving nothing to faith; it wants to go too high in enquiries which go beyond its power.' It was when reason tried to rule faith that St Bernard was moved to oppose it.

St Bernard's outlook was above all drawn from his own inner experience and, although he was the founder of medieval mysticism, the very nature of his experience made it impossible to transmit. His philosophy, he said, was 'to know Jesus and Jesus crucified' (P.L. 183, 995b). It was not concerned with ratiocination: 'What do the apostles teach us? Not to read Plato, nor to turn and return to the subtleties of Aristotle, not always to learn in order never to reach knowledge of truth; they have taught me to live. Do you believe it is a little thing to know how to live? It is a great thing and indeed the greatest' (P.L. 183, 647). Thus it was not to logic that he turned, but to his own soul. The first stage to true knowledge is humility. This enables us to recognize our own wretchedness; in doing so, we have compassion for the misery of others (charity), and this in turn moves us to detest our own sins and to look upon the truth (contemplation). The culmination of contemplation is ecstasy an immediate contact between the soul and God, involving the separation of the soul from its body in the union with God. 'For in a certain way you lose yourself, as if you were not' (P.L. 182, 990). It is a communion of wills, though man still maintains his own substance.

It is here that St Bernard differs sharply from the mystical theology associated with Denys the Areopagite, and maintains the tradition of St Augustine: for this return to God is not simply the work of contemplation, the retracing of the path to the One; it is the work of grace. It is therefore the result of a supernatural aid, and man cannot know the truth without it. This foretaste of the beatific vision is ultimately dependent, then, on the inclinations of man's will, which through original sin has turned away from love of God to man's love of himself. Only through Christ's grace was his power of loving God restored. Here lies the great difference between St Bernard's outlook and that of the majority of his contemporaries: the knowledge that they derived from reason could not deal with divine truths; the latter could be reached only through grace. A supernatural end required supernatural means; it involved not proof but a condition of life in which the will to love God was the *sine qua non* of knowing Him. In this we have returned to St Augustine's path. Not without reason has St Bernard been called *Augustinus redivivus*.

St Bernard's friend and disciple was William of St Thierry

(*d.* 1148) who spent his later life at the Cistercian abbey at Signy. He was one of the leading opponents of dialectic, and especially of Abelard, whose mistakes he recounted in a letter to St Bernard. He showed strong Platonic and Augustinian influences in the importance he attached to memory as helping the soul to recognize its divine origin. This in turn influenced reason and will, and these three faculties corresponded to the Trinity – memory to the Father, reason to the Word, and will to the Holy Spirit. Like St Bernard, William stressed the primary rôle of grace in restoring man's love of God which had been distorted by sin. Thus the path to God lay in the soul illumined by grace.

Another Cistercian, Isaac of Stella, abbot of Stella (1147–1169) was more deductive in his approach. As with St Bernard, much of his thought was expressed in sermons and letters. He regarded the body, the soul, and God as the three realities: little that was certain could be known about any of these, but most about God. Like St Augustine, he held that, in a certain way, the soul is the image of God, and that as the intermediary between Him and the body it has a base, a middle, and a summit. While its base can be seen in imagination, which is the summit of the body, its summit is intelligence, which is connected with God. Between them is a hierarchy of faculties, where, following the Aristotelian theory of abstraction from the experience and images supplied by the senses and the imagination, reason is able to abstract the forms from material things. These are themselves incorporeal, even though they only subsist in corporeal forms, and the intelligence perceives incorporeal being itself – God. The distinction between intellect and intelligence derived from Boethius, to which must be added St Augustine's theory of illumination by which the intelligence is enabled to see God. Isaac showed the full extent to which the Augustinian position of self-knowledge had become elaborated by arguments based upon reasoning.

This influence of reason upon mysticism is even more in evidence with the Victorines. The abbey of St Victor had been founded in 1108 by William of Champeaux, Abelard's opponent; but it did not attain renown until the time of Hugh of

St Victor (1096–1141). His chief works were his *Didascalion*, his *De sacramentis*, and his *Summa sententiarum*, which were so influential upon the Lombard's *Sentences*. His outlook was, in one sense, much more consonant with the Carolingian epoch; for his aim was to make knowledge serve theology rather than to partner it. Yet the effect of his compilations, especially *De sacramentis*, was to give an impetus to systematization, from which the *summae* of the thirteenth century sprang. The difference was that, for Hugh, knowledge should be the object of contemplation, a means of 'tasting in this life that there will be a day of reward for good works'.

His *Didascalion* was a guide to knowledge, designed to provide the essentials for a liberal education. Its first three books dealt with the seven liberal arts, the next three with theology. In the first three books, Hugh divided knowledge into the following categories, of theoretical (mathematics and theology), concerned with truth; practical (ethics, economy, and politics); mechanical (including agriculture, navigation, and medicine); and logic (grammar, rhetoric, and dialectic). Of these he regarded logic and mathematics as the instruments and foundation of knowledge, and the prerequisites of all demonstration and practice. 'Because logic and mathematics are naturally first in order of learning, and act, in a certain manner, as instruments, everything else should be shaped by them' (P.L. 176, 758d). These two subjects in effect were the seven liberal arts, for in addition to logic's subdivision into grammar and rhetoric (the *trivium*), mathematics covered arithmetic, music, geometry, and astronomy (the *quadrivium*). The latter dealt with the material forms of things which could only be reached through the Aristotelian method of abstraction. Thus, in the case of mathematics, such concepts as quantity, number, line, were the result of the mind separating these intelligible realities from the confusion of material things.

Nature, then, provided the starting-point for understanding. It was the first stage in the threefold ascent to truth in God, where the eye of the flesh knows the world of things. The second stage is where the eye of reason knows itself; while in the third the eye of contemplation comes upon God.

Through sin, only the eye of the material world has remained unimpaired; whilst the eye of contemplation has become closed. Hence the need of revelation to know God: 'Faith, therefore, is necessary in order that the unseen may be believed' (P.L. 176, 330a). Faith is a form of certitude above opinion but below the highest form of knowledge, which is a true experience of things as they are. Like Augustine, Hugh puts personal experience as the highest form of knowledge. He follows St Augustine's concept that the experience of one's own soul is the guarantee of existence. 'No one has proper wisdom who does not see that he exists' (P.L. 176, 825a). Thus Hugh used the knowledge of the world and the arguments of the philosophers to fashion a *rationale* of mysticism. He made all that is open to experience germane to the knowledge of God – which only contemplation could bring.

Richard of St Victor (*d.* 1173) followed Hugh in giving his mystical speculation an empirical foundation. His main work was the *De Trinitate*, which had an important place with the scholastics of the thirteenth century; so also did his two mystical treatises known as *Benjamin major* and *Benjamin minor*. Richard bears a strong resemblance to St Anselm in his attempt to found all truth on necessary reasons. 'I am firmly convinced that as for the explanation of realities whose being is necessary (and the Trinity and the existence of God are such) there must be not only probable reasons but necessary reasons, although they sometimes happen to escape our inquiries' (P.L. 196, 892c). Like Anselm, also, he started from the world of the senses in reaching necessary truths; and he showed the same lack of constraint towards the scope of dialectic.

This can be seen in his proofs for God's existence. The world of the senses presents a picture of constant change, of things coming into existence and vanishing, and which are therefore not eternal and cannot be self-caused. 'Nothing can be entirely from itself which is not eternal' (P.L. 196, 894a). Thus there must be some eternal being from which these finite things derive, 'otherwise there was a time when nothing was, and then things which were to be in the future were not, because there would be nothing which would have given or had been able to give them the principle of their being' (*ibid.*). The impossibility of such a situation showed that there must be a first immutable being. Similarly Richard drew upon Anselm's use of differing degrees of perfection to show that God is the highest good. In the case of the Trinity, he used the argument of the difference between necessary being and possible being to show that the Divine Persons shared a single nature. It was to have an important effect upon such thinkers as Alexander of Hales, Bonaventure, and Duns Scotus.

So far as knowledge was concerned, Richard followed Hugh in enumerating its degrees, through imagination (which concerned the world of senses) and reason (which dealt with the intelligible world) to intelligence (with God as its object). As with Hugh, contemplation was the highest stage. The eye of intelligence in common with the eye of the sense, and in contrast to the eye of reason, can see its object. 'As we are wont to see corporeal things by corporeal senses, as visible, present, and corporeal, so also can this intellectual sense grasp the invisible, indeed as invisible, but immediately and essentially' (P.L. 196, 118d). Richard enumerates nine stages in the soul's ascent to clear knowledge of God – through the different stages of imagination aided by reason and reason helped by imagination until, above pure reason, the soul loses itself in contemplation of the pure truth. Such a position can only be attained with supernatural aid.

The Victorines, as with all the thinkers of the twelfth century, betrayed the omnipresence of reason. This was the great distinction between the eleventh and twelfth centuries. Neither St Bernard nor the humanists of Chartres, neither the Victorines nor the extreme realists, were prepared to reject the experience of natural phenomena or the laws of dialectic. Yet the very impact of reason as an external adjunct to faith left its different aspects still largely unexplored. Reason has not yet been broken down into distinctive categories. Aristotle and Plato – to the extent that they were known – mingled freely in the same outlook; men as different as John of Salisbury, Peter Abelard, Hugh of St Victor, could all share the Aristotelian view of knowledge by abstraction; Plato, Pythagoras, and the atomic theory jostle together in William of Conches's thought. It was essentially an age of eclecticism, of taking different parts from different sources. It was also an age where the parts were still more in evidence than the whole: there were no great systems as yet; only with the appearance of those from the Moslem world did they also emerge in the West.

CHAPTER 6

The Philosophy of Islam

INTELLECTUALLY, the difference between the twelfth and
the thirteenth centuries was, at its broadest, the difference between isolation from the Islamic world* and contact with it.
Islam provided the West with the twofold benefit of
Aristotle's works and of its own philosophical systems. Both
were of inestimable importance for the development of
western thought in the thirteenth century. It has often been
implied that it was by the agency of Aristotle that scholasticism developed as an outlook peculiar to the West and that
the Arabic thinkers added little that was new. It is true that in
terms of new philosophical or scientific ideas the Islamic
world was mainly dependent upon Greece; so, too, was the
West. The yardstick, however, is not novelty of invention so
much as novelty in applying known concepts; and here the
rôle of Islamic thought cannot be exaggerated.

Already in the ninth century, Islam was making the attempt
to supplement Moslem revelation by reason. In this, Aristotle
(or Aristotle neoplatonized) was the main instrument, and
during the tenth and eleventh centuries systems had arisen
which, in scope and speculation, if not in content, were to be
comparable with the greatest in Christendom. The more
closely we examine thinkers like St Bonaventure, St Thomas
Aquinas, and Duns Scotus, the more clearly we can see how
indebted they were to Jewish and Arabian thinkers like
Avicebrol and Maimonides, Averroes and Avicenna. The
latter did more than simply transmit Aristotle's ideas; they
provided an example of how to relate Aristotle's philosophy
to faith; they had established a method of treating a problem
which, in essence, was the same as that confronting Christian
thinkers. Many of the concepts and arguments of Islamic
thinkers, therefore, were frequently adapted to Christian

*The same also applies for Jewish philosophy.

needs, and a full understanding of the great scholastics is only possible with reference to the Arabian and Jewish thinkers.

This is not to minimize the direct influence of Aristotle; yet even here there has sometimes been a tendency to distinguish too sharply between his pure form and the Neoplatonic garb in which he was first introduced into the West from Islam. All the Christian thinkers of the thirteenth century (except the Latin Averroists) shared in the same mingling of Aristotle and Neoplatonism as the Arabian thinkers. Even Averroes had been compelled to add certain things to Aristotle in order to make his thought provide for God. St Thomas Aquinas, like-wise, although going to the true texts of Aristotle, was com-pelled to incorporate important Neoplatonic ideas in order to harmonize the doctrines of Aristotle with the tenets of faith. Thus, although he would be a rash man who said that scholas-ticism in the thirteenth century would have been impossible without Arabic and Jewish thought, it would be equally questionable to pretend that they did little but introduce Aristotle. Their great contribution was in pioneering full-fledged systems of thought with Aristotle as their main support.

(i) Arabian Philosophy

The term Islam can be misleading if it is taken to imply a homogeneous civilization with a dominant outlook. As much as, if not more than, the old Roman Empire it consisted in a vast assemblage of diverse states, stretching from Spain in the north-west to Syria, Arabia, and Persia in the east, through North Africa and Egypt – all under the dynasty of the Caliphs established in the eighth century. Its different sects and out-looks upon which Mohammedanism was imposed were equally divergent; they included the dualism of Persian Zoroastrian teaching, with its belief in the God of light, the different sects of animism and astral worship, as well as the influence of Indian philosophy. The Hellenistic tradition formed just one more element amidst this welter of outlooks. Syria had become its centre from the sixth century, after

Justinian had closed the schools of philosophy at Athens in 529. A series of schools grew up at Edessa, Kinnesrin, Risaina, where the philosophy of Aristotle was taught, in addition to the medical works of Galen and Hippocrates. Even when that at Edessa was closed by the Emperor Zeno the knowledge of Aristotle – mainly his logical works in the *Organon* – survived and much of it was translated into Syriac in the monasteries.

Although Greek thought had also spread into Persia, Syria was to be the source for its transmission to the Arab world, and ultimately to the West. With the coming of Islam, in the seventh and eighth centuries, came the demand for Greek science and thought. Under the caliphate of Haroun-al-Raschid (785–809) there began the translation of the works of Aristotle, Archimedes, Galen, Hippocrates, Euclid, Ptolemy. The effect of Greek thought upon the orthodoxy of Moslem belief was, in many respects, similar to that on the West in the thirteenth century. Different groups or sects arose, distinguished by their attitude to the place of reason and its relation to faith. The mutakallamin (those who discoursed), despite their diversity, held to the view that theology was the source of truth. The motazilites, on the other hand, upheld the use of reason in faith and the liberty of human free will in moral actions. In the doctrine of al-Askari (873–935), however, these attempts at flexibility in theology were opposed by an outlook which became the accepted orthodoxy. This enunciated the absolute sovereignty of God's will, which was unknowable and entirely free. It therefore closed the door to all speculation in theology and, in contrast to the West, it was the non-ecclesiastics, doctors and judges, like Avicenna and Averroes, who were largely responsible for the development of thought. In essence, however, the lines of conflict were not between pure rationalism and faith, but, as in the West, over the scope and the validity of reason in faith. The philosophers, though not clerics, were nevertheless believers, and their belief conditioned their outlook as much as it did that of the Christian theologians.

Now among the translations into Arabic of Aristotle's

works, there were two which belonged to the Neoplatonists, Plotinus and Proclus. These had been included in the Syrian catalogues as the *Theology of Aristotle* and the *Book of Causes* (*Liber de causis*), to which we have already seen Alan of Lille refer as the *Aphorisms on the Essence of the Supreme Good*. In reality the *Theology of Aristotle* constituted Books IV–VI of Plotinus's *Enneads*, treating of the spiritual nature of the soul, and its relation to intelligible reality, and the procession of the One, the first Intelligence, and the Soul. The introduction to the *Theology*, moreover, had little bearing upon the contents. According to the introduction this consisted in translating the four causes of Aristotle's theory into God as final cause, the Intelligence as formal cause, the Soul as efficient cause, and nature as material cause. 'It is the explanation of God's dominion . . . the light from God illumines the Intelligence, and, through the medium of the Intelligence, shines upon the Soul of all the heavens, and from the Soul, through nature, upon things which are born and die.' Although it was generally regarded as authentic Aristotle, this work was in fact pure Neoplatonism.

The same was true of Proclus's *Elements of Theology* which, as we have already seen, was a series of theorems, in the style of Euclid, dealing with the same triad of the One, Intelligence, and Soul. The One, as first cause of all being, was itself eternal and above being. It was indefinable, but could be called the Good, for through its agency everything existed. The first being was the first Intelligence, which, in Neoplatonic style, is separate from the One, though in itself simple. It contained the sum of all intelligible Ideas, which through the World Soul became souls, reaching down to the human soul. Thus man is able to grasp truth by intellection and so work back to the One. In its translation into Arabic it received certain alterations to make it more in harmony with Moslem theology, with the One tending more towards God the Creator.

The effect of these works was of the first importance both for Aristotle and Neoplatonism as well as for Arabian and Christian thought. Firstly, it had the effect of neoplatonizing Aristotle. Upon his essentially physical interpretation of the world, drawn from the observations of the senses, was imposed the intelligible universe of Neoplatonism. Where Aristotle, starting from experience, had arrived at the concept of a final cause, this was now joined to a theory of generation: a hierarchy of Intelligences provided the basis of existence. The human soul was now connected to the One by means of thought and meditation. The effect on Neoplatonism was no less profound; it gave a more directly astronomical interpretation to its spiritual world; the hierarchy of intelligible beings, stretching from the One to the human soul, became more like a chain of cause and effect; the Neoplatonic Intelligences more like the souls of the spheres. To this mingling of Plato and Aristotle must be added the widely diffused view of light as the fount of being, gradually fading the farther it gets from its source in God. This theory of light was an important element in Neoplatonism and the various oriental philosophies, like Zoroastrianism, and it had a powerful effect upon Arabian, and later Christian, thought.

The overriding consequence, then, of the inclusion of these Neoplatonic works was to introduce under the title of Aristotelianism a composite *Weltanschauung* which provided a thoroughgoing explanation of the universe at both the sensible and the intelligible level. It offered a series of propositions which, as they stood, flew in the face of Arabian, no less than Christian, teaching: it substituted the impersonal power of the One for the personal concept of God; it made God's actions indirect and his effects determined; it looked to contemplation, instead of revelation, for knowledge of God. As we shall see in the next chapter, the working out of the Arabian systems brought in their train many other problems which were specific to Christianity. For the present it suffices to say that they also exercised Islam.

One of the first among those thinkers most influential upon the development of Aristotelian and Greek thought in Islam was Alkindi (*d.* 872). His efforts were devoted to commenting Aristotle's works and to writing a series of scientific treatises on medicine, optics, meteorology, as well as geometry, arithmetic, music, and astronomy. His importance lies in his being the first to apply himself to problems raised by Aristotle over demonstration, and in using what was to become the characteristic combination of Aristotle and Plato to solve them. The question to be answered was how to arrive at a definition of things (as in Euclid's geometry) when our mode of knowing is discursive: that is, since we can only reach, say, the concept quantity by counting individual things, how can we start by saying what quantity is. To overcome this apparent contradiction between our way of knowing and what we know, Alkindi invoked Aristotle's distinction between the active intellect – an intelligence which contained eternally all intelligibles outside the soul – and the possible intellect, in the soul. The possible intellect, under the impact of the active intellect, is able to pass into act and can receive from it knowledge of intelligibles. This knowledge, derived from the workings of the active upon the passive intellect, produced the acquired intellect in which the knowledge of intelligibles, once achieved, resides; from this intellect, in turn, comes the demonstrative intellect, from which we are able to understand the quiddities, by which we can define things.

The importance of Alkindi is twofold: in the first place, he introduces the Aristotelian distinction between act and potentiality, which is central to Islamic and Christian Aristotelianism. Since to be potential, or in potency, is for an essence or nature to remain unrealized – to await being made actual – all possibility is inferior to, and dependent upon, a state of actuality. It can only be brought into being through the agency of something already in act. The second important aspect of Alkindi's outlook is the introduction of the active and the passive intellects and their distinction not simply in terms of activity but as different beings: the active intellect is a spiritual being existing outside and above the soul. This Platonic interpretation of Aristotle was to give rise to one of the most marked features of Islamic thought – the belief that there was only one active intellect for all humanity, and that every human soul was moved and informed by this separated active intellect.

Alfarabi (*d.* 950) is a much more complex, and indeed

confusing, example of the combination of Aristotle and Plato; in his case this is directed towards arriving at a theological account of existence. It involved two distinct problems, first, of reconciling Aristotle and Plato with Moslem teaching, and, second, Alfarabi's own strictly religious, almost mystical conception of God as the sovereign and direct cause of everything.

Although it is difficult to bring his various views into a unified whole, there is common to them the distinction between God as necessary being and everything else as merely possible. We can here see the distinction between essence and existence that was to prove so formative, from Avicenna to St Thomas and Duns Scotus, though Alfarabi himself did not endow it with the nuances of Aristotle's metaphysics. What he did was to take the Aristotelian dictum 'that the notion of what a thing is does not include the fact that it is' to show that only God is necessary; natural things are contingent, as liable not to exist as to exist. Their existence is only accidental to their essence, just as, say, Socrates's existence is not inherent in the essence man. In God, on the other hand, existence and essence are identical, since God is necessary and therefore must be: He cannot not exist. This view of essences as independent of actual existence shows the Platonic nature of Alfarabi's attitude, by which essence was made the condition of all individual existence.

Alfarabi's cosmology was dominated by this same juxtaposition of necessary and possible being and a Neoplatonic view of essences, and he used it to develop a hierarchy from God to sensible things. God as necessary being is at the summit of everything. Because He is necessary His nature must be simple, for it can only arise from Himself. Similarly, in accordance with the Moslem view of God as a single person, Alfarabi uses God's necessity to free His essence from the Neoplatonic triad: God gives rise to the first Intelligence by knowing Himself; but this Intelligence is, in its own nature, only possible since it derives from an external cause. The World Soul, which is in turn produced by the first Intelligence, is also possible being and so are all those which come after it. Alfarabi conceives these intelligences within a Neoplatonic framework whereby each engenders the next, until finally the sub-lunar world of generation is reached. The Intelligences themselves, however, are conceived according to the Aristotelian view of celestial spheres and are essentially material bodies. Thus it is here that we see the intermingling of Aristotle and Neoplatonism in its clearest light.

So far as man's knowledge is concerned, Alfarabi shows two different faces. In one, following his view of existence, he makes human understanding come through abstracting from things the intelligible forms which have been imprinted in them by the active intellect, the tenth and last of the celestial spheres, or Intelligences. The forms abstracted pass through three different intellects, each of which is the act of the other, and above them is the active intellect, the source of their illumination. On the other hand, Alfarabi strongly upheld the essentially contingent character of all possible being as subject only to God's unfettered will and devoid of intrinsic laws. Difficult though it may be to reconcile in detail however, Alfarabi's outlook remains throughout one in which God's omnipotence and necessity are alone sovereign.

In Avicenna (980–1037) we see the ideas of Alfarabi given a lasting and deepened form in which so much of what was specifically Arab was transmitted to the West. Avicenna himself was one of those great men whose greatness extends to almost all that they touch. Apart from his pre-eminence as one of the most important philosophers in the middle ages, he was equally illustrious in science and above all in medicine. He was born at Bokhara, in Persia, where he devoted himself to writing voluminously on logic, metaphysics, mathematics, physics, and medicine as well as leading an active public life and being a celebrated physician. His *Canon of Medicine*, in particular, long remained a fundamental work. His main work on philosophy and allied topics was his eighteen-volume *Book of Recovery* which was made available to the West in individual translations of its different sections. By the end of the twelfth century part of his physics (under such separate titles as *De sufficientia*, *De coelo et mundo*, the *Sixth book*) his psychology, his logic and his *Canon of Medicine* were known to the West.

Basically, Avicenna's thought is a refinement on Alfarabi's leading idea of the difference between necessary and possible being. It extends to all the ramifications of the modes of being, the relation of knowledge to existence and the hierarchy of being, from God to the world of matter. Within this wide area, Avicenna's prevailing tendency was to diminish the Neo-platonic elements, as compared with Alfarabi, and to intro-duce a far more deterministic outlook supported by much that was from Aristotle. The effect was ultimately a Neoplatonism more rigidly determined by Aristotelian concepts.

Central to the whole Avicennan system is his view of being: it governs equally the different facets of his outlook, logical, metaphysical, and theological. He regards the universe as composed of essences or natures; everything that exists is a distinct essence. Thus Socrates is a man; humanity is his essence which he shares with all other men, and it suffices to describe him as a man. The implication of this doctrine can be seen in the different branches of knowledge which are con-cerned with being. In logic, it enables Avicenna to employ the Aristotelian distinction between what we know of individual things (*intentio prima*) and our own mental constructions (*intentio secunda*) to establish the status of the universal. This was not only, as with Aristotle, a mental construction, but it corresponded to reality; it was *one* aspect of essences, and the one at which we arrive through intellectual processes. There were, he showed, three different states in which an essence could exist, each as real as the other. Firstly it could exist before the individuals in which it subsisted came into being (*ante rem*). In this state it existed in God's intellect as an immaterial archetype – an Idea. Only in this specific sense, as the form of individual things, could it be regarded as coming before the individual. Secondly, the essence could exist in individuals, embodied in their material existence (*in rebus*). They were as real here as in the first state. Finally, they could exist in our minds as the result of abstraction (*post rem*) by which they became once more separated into their pure state. The important point is that, in any case, the essence is still an essence, whether in God, in things, or in our minds; in itself it is neither universal nor singular, but what it is. As Avicenna himself said 'a horse is simply a horse'.

Now the deep significance of this view lies in regarding being as having a universal reality quite independently of its different modes. It asserts the Platonic belief in the primacy of essence as coming before all existence. Yet it differs from Plato's view in refusing to separate the essence from the individuals in which it subsists: for Avicenna expressly states that it would be erroneous to regard humanity as existing without individual men. This view is also important in accepting the correspondence between mental reality and reality itself: it acknowledges that intellectual knowledge is valid, and that for every logical distinction there must be a real distinction. Thus the universal which the mind apprehends in individuals is a reality, but not exclusive reality.

Let us examine each of these different states of being in turn. So far as God is concerned, Avicenna's doctrine has its starting-point in Alfarabi's distinction between necessary and possible being, though he reaches different conclusions. Being, Avicenna holds, is the most general concept available to the understanding; it is the first principle of all that exists. Now being, as common to everything, can itself be divided into necessary and possible being. Possible being is that which, in itself, can or cannot be; it has no inherent reason for existence, and therefore it is dependent upon another being for its existence. This view of possibility, as unable to cause itself, corresponds to the Aristotelian dictum that 'No being in potentiality can pass into act except by the influence of another being already in act'. It makes necessary being, alone actual and uncaused, the cause of possible being. Necessary being, in contrast to possible, must be by virtue of its own nature; it cannot not be. Thus since possible beings could not exist on their own, and since they do in fact exist, they must have a cause – necessary being. This is God, who by definition is first being, and whose essence is identical with His existence.

Avicenna has taken the distinction of Alfarabi between essence and existence to distinguish God's nature from that of all other beings. For everything other than God he made existence accidental to essence: the essence man, for example, does not involve the existence of the individual Socrates: Socrates's being was only the realization of one possibility among many, and humanity could remain without it, provided that there were other human beings. Avicenna was later to be criticized by Averroes and St Thomas for this notion of existence as an accident of essence. It was not directed to distinguishing different modes of being, but to distinguishing different *beings* – the necessary from the possible as they exist; it defines the possible as being which exists because of a necessary cause; its necessity lies in its cause, not in itself.

It has been important to emphasize Avicenna's meaning here because his entire view of the structure of the universe flows from it. Whereas, for Alfarabi, God, as necessary being, served to illustrate the radical contingency of the universe, Avicenna transfers His necessity to the whole of existence. Because God is necessary, all that He does is necessary. Thus He acts, not through His freely willing a certain effect, but because He could not do otherwise. This is to be the great gulf between Avicenna's philosophy and Christian thinkers; for, in Avicenna's eyes, to want something implies imperfection: a lack of wholeness, a dependence upon external support. Clearly, God, who is necessary and perfect, could not be actuated by motives. Avicenna, accordingly, refused Him any but necessary actions.

The effect of this was to destroy any contingency in existence; once in being, a thing followed inexorable laws. This meant that creation in the Christian sense did not exist: not only was there no initial act on the part of God by which the world was brought into being; God Himself did not, in the strict meaning of the term, create. The necessity of His own nature eternally transmitted being from Himself to the first Intelligence: any sudden creative act in time would have introduced change into God's nature and impaired His perfection. Moreover, with Plotinus, Avicenna was equally Neoplatonic in making God the cause only of His immediate effect, since one cause can have only one effect.

What we have, then, is, firstly, an eternal process of generation, in which a necessary being necessarily produces an effect, which in turn produces another effect, and so on. Secondly, each effect is superior to and the cause of its own subsequent effect: thus the first Intelligence itself gives rise to the second Intelligence together with the first celestial sphere; the second Intelligence in turn produces the third Intelligence and the second celestial sphere, until, finally, after the ninth Intelligence, the moon is reached, with the sub-lunar world of matter and the four elements below it. Thirdly, this means that God is only an indirect cause of all but the first Intelligence; the connexion between Him and the material world is through a series of intermediaries, in a strict order of precedence which precludes any direct contact with God. Consequently, in Avicenna's cosmology, there are at least five aspects which militate against Christianity: the inherent necessity of the universe; its eternity; the lack of anything that can properly be described as creation; the indirect power of God; and the subjection of the world to astral necessity. With Duns Scotus we shall see the culmination of the Christian reaction against these doctrines.

It is against this Neoplatonic background of a hierarchy of Intelligences (given an Aristotelian flavour as celestial spheres which rotate according to the laws of astronomy) that we must regard the actual existence of the sub-lunar world. Like the whole of the universe, it is regulated by two principles: the primacy of essence in all existence, and the dependence of potential being upon actual being. Essences, as we have suggested, contain all being as it is transmitted from God through the spheres to individual things. But in viewing material beings, Avicenna breaks with Neoplatonism and follows Aristotle: matter is not produced through the World Soul. It is eternal and the principle of multiplicity.

All bodies are composed of form and matter, but, in keeping with the dominion of essences, matter is itself dependent upon a form. Here we see the importance of the second principle, the division between potency and act, which is taken over by Avicenna to explain physical existence. For a body to be a body, it has to have a form which confers corporeity upon matter. This form of corporeity (*forma corporeitatis*) is, like every other essence, the *raison d'être* of that which it informs – bodies – and is, similarly, neither a universal nor an individual as such. It gives matter the necessary extension and dimensions which constitute bodies. To this basic form others are added, according to the nature (or essence) of the being embodied: every animal, for example, in addition to its bodily form has to have the form of animality in order to be an animal; in the case of man, the most complex of created beings, more is required, since he is distinguished from the animals by a soul. Finally, to these forms, individualized by matter, there are the characteristics peculiar to each individual – height, size, colour, etc. These accidents help to complete the individual which, in essence, is distinguished by the forms subsisting in it. This doctrine of the plurality of forms was to be one of the most marked traits of the Augustinian school of the thirteenth century. It gives an Aristotelian application to an originally Platonic conception, translating essences or Ideas into form and matter.

This same combination is apparent in man. Avicenna regarded man's soul as a spiritual substance existing independently of the body; but it also directs the body in a very real way. Even though Avicenna refuses to go the whole way with Aristotle, and to consider the soul as the body's form, he gives it the function of animating the body: it moved and perfected the body while retaining its own forms and existence. Avicenna distinguished the human soul from the vegetative and sensitive souls of plants and animals by its capacity for reflection and abstract thought. It was able to arrive at concepts and judgements and have a knowledge of properties outside material objects: as for example, that there is a first necessary being, or that number is a property of mathematics. Such knowledge, however, cannot be directly attained by the intellect (which Avicenna identifies with the soul); the intelligible and the immaterial can only come *via* the senses, through abstraction.

It is in this process of knowing that we can see clearly how important the distinction between potential and actual being is for Avicenna. The soul, although independent of the body and a spiritual being, is nevertheless dependent upon an external impulsion. In the first place, like all possible being, the soul is unable to act of itself. Therefore to know, it must be moved either by the senses or through divine emanation. So far as the general mode of knowing is concerned, it comes through the senses. The images presented by experience form the starting-point of knowledge. But, in the second place, before the soul, now partly in act, can reach an understanding of what has been presented to it, it needs to be brought fully into act. This can only come from a separate Intelligence, the active intellect, which, like Alfarabi's, is the last and ninth Intelligence in the hierarchy from God to the world. The active intellect illumines the possible intellect of man, enabling him to grasp the reality contained in experience. There is therefore a threefold progression in the attainment of knowledge: from the intellect as a *tabula rasa*, to the intellect possessing images drawn from the senses, to their final comprehension under the influence of the active intellect.

Thus, like Alfarabi, but along Aristotelian lines, Avicenna has reached the same conclusion: that there is a single active intellect for all humanity, which alone enables the possible intellects of individual men to know and to understand. Although for the very few, the holiest of men, there was direct contact with the divine, mankind as a whole was dependent upon the last Intelligence. It was the final affirmation of the dominion of actual being over possible being.

The importance of Avicenna's thought for the West cannot be overestimated. Both in its negative aspect, such as the necessity of everything (which we have already enumerated), and in its more sympathetic notions, it offered a stimulus to the West. It was *par excellence* a combination of Neoplatonism and Aristotle, transforming the One into a first mover from whom all existence ultimately sprang. For Christian thinkers it offered especial attraction in distinguishing God from His creatures, in terms of being; in holding essence to be the foundation of all existence; in making the effect dependent for both its being and its movement upon what was prior to it; and in regarding all knowledge as the result of illumination. But in each case, it involved their having to cut through Avicenna's proliferation of intermediaries, in order to establish God as immediate cause; it meant, above all, restoring to God the authority vested in the active intellect and the necessity of the spheres. Much of thirteenth-century thinking was directed to these ends.

The independence of Avicenna's speculation, and its reliance upon Greece rather than upon the Koran, brought in its train a not unexpected reaction. In this, the most prominent thinker was Algazali (1058–1111), also a Persian, who spent much of his life teaching at Bagdad and in Syria. His *Destruction of the Philosophers* was intended only as the preliminary to his attack upon the philosophy associated with Avicenna. It consisted very largely in an exposition of Avicenna's views; and unfortunately for him only this part – the *Intentions of the Philosophers* – reached the West, thereby propagating the very outlook he was opposing! His criticism of the peripatetics was directed against the necessity which had caught up God in its toils. His own attitude was the reassertion of divine liberty in defence of the faith: he supported such truths as creation of the world in time, and from nothing, and the omnipotence of God in everything. Conversely, he adopted an attitude of scepticism to philosophical speculation, undermining the Avicennan conception of causality by the unfettered sovereignty of God's will, which answered to no set laws. Algazali gave a foretaste of the main lines along which Christian theologians were to oppose Avicenna's determinism.

It was with Averroes (1126–1178) that Avicenna was met on his own ground of Greek peripateticism and his system challenged by a rival. During the later eleventh century, Spain had gradually become the intellectual centre of Islam, and it was there that the struggle over Aristotle was carried on in the twelfth century. Already Avempace (*d.* 1138) and Abubacer

(1100–1185) had confronted the problem of man's relation to spiritual reality. Avempace, in his *Guide to the Solitary*, started from the Neoplatonic hierarchy of Intelligences of Avicenna in describing the soul's return to the active intelligence by way of abstraction; it was able to disengage the immaterial forms from matter until it attained to reality. The same mystical approach was equally apparent in Abubacer, who also betrayed the influence of Avicenna's Neoplatonism. It was primarily in revolt against this predominance of Neoplatonism, as well as against the attacks of Algazali, that Averroes's thought was formulated. His aim was quite simply a return to the authentic Aristotle, and the greater part of his writings were either commentaries on Aristotle's works or the exposition of Aristotelian ideas. To the West he became known as the *Commentator*; his commentaries were in three series, the *Great Commentary*, a phrase by phrase discussion of the text, the *Middle Commentary*, and the *Paraphrases*. In addition, he wrote a reply to Algazali, the *Destruction of the Destruction*.

Averroes, like Avicenna and many other Islamic philosophers, was himself an orthodox Muslim, and not primarily a philosopher. He combined, with characteristic versatility, the pursuits of judge, astronomer, and physician (he was the Caliph's personal doctor). It is necessary to emphasize these extra-philosophical aspects of Averroes's life because his doctrine has been the subject of much misunderstanding which usually goes by the title of 'double truth'. This is apparently taken to mean that Averroes preached a doctrine that what was right for faith was not true in reality. It is indeed impossible to know the inner workings of Averroes's mind, but so far as the strict meaning of his words go, he was asserting something much more subtle. He was trying, as St Thomas Aquinas was to try later, to delimit the respective areas of faith and reason. This is one of his greatest contributions to the thirteenth century; his influence upon what was to become Thomism must be laid to his account, as well as his effect upon the Latin Averroists. Where he differed from St Thomas was in his refusal to reconcile what he regarded as irreconcilable. St Thomas accepted the primacy of faith;

Averroes not only rejected it but denied the ultimate harmony between faith and reason. Indeed, he saw the root of all the trouble between the philosophers and the theologians in their ignoring the different levels at which faith and reason operated. What was valid for faith was quite unsuited to philosophical understanding. It was not the Koran which was in dispute; it was the methods of dispute.

Averroes accordingly divided human understanding into three classes, corresponding to the different types of men. At the bottom of the scale were the simple and unenlightened for whom faith and the direct voice of authority sufficed. Next came the dialectical men who required probable arguments to convince them. Finally, there were those who needed absolute demonstration; and it was for these alone that philosophy was meant. The Koran, as divine revelation, was addressed to all three, and, therefore, only those who had attained to the highest state of wisdom could discard the precepts of simple faith in discussing truth.

Averroes's doctrine was, in effect, giving a *carte blanche* to philosophy independent of and in opposition to the tenets of faith. In doing so, he looked to Aristotle as the acme of all reason. 'I believe that this man (Aristotle) is a rule in nature and an example which nature has devised to demonstrate supreme human perfection.' He regarded Aristotle's doctrine as 'the highest truth, since his intellect was the summit of the human intellect. It is therefore well said that he was created and given to us by divine providence that we might know whatever can be known.' He set himself to extricate Aristotle from Neoplatonism, directing his main attack against Avicenna.

Avicenna's system was the repository for most of the violence done to Aristotle. Firstly, there was the distinction that Avicenna had made between essence and existence. This was to fly in the face of reality as upheld by Aristotle. To be real was to exist; there could be no separation of existence from essence or from accidents. Thus Averroes, like St Thomas after him, returned to existence as the primary term of being, refusing to separate a substance from the being by which it was a substance. Being extended to all that is, whether accident, quantity, or quality. This meant that, whatever the category of being, it bore analogy to all other states of being by virtue of having existence in common. Hence, with Aristotle, Averroes held that being was analogous. Moreover, again following Aristotle, he considered that all substance was individual; being did not exist apart from the individual things which existed. This, too, was a reversal of Avicenna's primacy of essences; and, in transferring it to individuals, Averroes returned to the Aristotelian view of the universal. The universal was not a thing; it existed in sensible things. If the universal had a separate existence, either each individual would possess only a part of it (different men would thus each contain a part of man) or it would reside entire in each individual. Neither was possible. In fact, the universal was the work of human understanding, by abstraction. It was 'that which can be predicated of several individuals' and corresponded to the forms making up each individual – the means by which matter was made actual.

This leads to the second aspect of Averroes's divergence from Avicenna. Avicenna had made God necessary being, as distinct from everything else which was possible. The latter therefore still remained possible as beings even though they existed, for they had come into being through an extrinsic cause. This, for Averroes, was meaningless: 'necessary does not designate an attribute added to being, as if it were outside the soul, but an attribute contained in the essence of the necessary being and which is not added to its substance'. In other words, Averroes saw necessity as inherent in being itself, not as a relation between beings already in existence. This inherent necessity was the difference between pure act and potentiality. Whatever was entirely realized, without any part of it still to be, was pure act, and so necessary. What, on the other hand, was unrealized and dependent for its being upon another, was not of itself necessary.

Averroes had transferred necessity and possibility to the mode of being itself. From this he was able to sweep away the Neoplatonic hierarchy of separate Intelligences and return to a first unmoved mover which, as pure act, contains the necessary Ideas of the potential beings of the sub-lunar world. The division between act and potency lies in form and matter; all that which contains matter is potential. Similarly what is pure act cannot be matter. Avicenna's mistake lay in regarding the One, alone necessary, as distinct from the first Intelligence which was only potential. This led to the separation of the One, as first cause, from its effects. On the contrary, God, as first cause, as pure act, is Himself the Intelligible; they are identical. This enabled Averroes to overcome the main limitation of Avicenna's Platonism: how could the One, the single cause of a single effect (the first Intelligence), be the cause of a multiplicity? Averroes was concerned to cut through the hierarchy of emanations, from Intelligence to Intelligence, which was independent of the One. With God Himself first Intelligence, He became the source of everything else; that which had previously resided in the separated first Intelligence was now annexed to God by virtue of His also being first Intelligence. He is no longer simply the One; He is the first uncaused cause.

This involved a further change from the Avicennan hierarchy: not only did God in knowing Himself know (and thereby create) everything else; He also necessarily produced *necessary* beings. His own necessary knowledge was inseparable from the necessity which was contained in His knowledge. Moreover, as pure act, God must always have existed, for to have had a beginning would have meant not always being – a contradiction. Therefore both He and His knowledge are eternal; therefore the world, as the result of His knowledge, is also eternal.

Springing directly from the first Intelligence are the celestial spheres; they, too, are pure act, for they are inseparable from the first pure act. They number thirty-eight in all, and their movement is governed by the love and knowledge that each has of its superior, culminating in the love and knowledge of God. Hence, in contrast to Avicenna's descending order of causality, Averroes reasserts the teleology of Aristotle: God is both unmoved mover and the final cause. God is not simply first in a series, as a remote cause; He is an active end directing the lower to the higher. The process of Neoplatonism is reversed and God Himself regains direction of His effects. The reason for this constant upward movement lay in Averroes's belief that each Intelligence knew only what was higher and nobler than itself. Similarly, God only knew other beings through Himself, as to turn for His knowledge to what was inferior would have been to demean Himself. This refusal to allow God direct knowledge of His creatures was to become a subject of much discussion in the fourteenth century.

Beyond the last of the Intelligences lay the moon and the sub-lunar world of matter. Here, again, Averroes came into conflict with Avicenna over the function of the active intellect, the last Intelligence in pure act. Avicenna had taken the active intellect as the source of all forms or essences in the created world. For Averroes, however, the function of the active intellect was not to create forms but to transform potential being into actual being. To follow Avicenna, complains Averroes, would be to break the unity of being by making it come from outside; in fact, being lies not in introducing essences but in passing from the state of potency to act, as fire derives not from the essence heat, but from actual heat. Now, since all form is actual and all matter potential, the work of the active intellect is to give form to matter, making it actual. Averroes has substituted an Aristotelian for a Neoplatonic conception; but he is nevertheless dependent upon something which approximates to a theory of Ideas for his view of human knowledge which follows.

As we have seen, Averroes regarded the universal as corresponding to the form embodied in an individual substance. In the case of man, this form was his soul, which, like all intelligences, strives upwards towards the active intellect, its source. Averroes is in harmony with Avicenna in holding that the human soul reaches knowledge by abstracting the immaterial form from its material composition; that to do this it is dependent upon the active intellect for bringing into act the potential forms in the human imagination; and that this engenders a material intellect by which the soul receives these forms. Where Averroes differed was in leaving the human soul no personal identity at all.

Avicenna had posited a possible soul in man which through contact with the active intellect produced the material intellect. The latter existed in its own right and could survive death. Averroes rejected the possible soul, replacing it instead with a purely passive intellect, which is simply a disposition to receive intelligible forms. This was corporeal, without separate identity, and perished with the body. Through its illumination by the active intellect, the material intellect was produced; but it had nothing to do with the human soul. It was rather like the rays from the active intellect in the human soul. Accordingly Averroes concluded, firstly, that the material soul was not corporeal; secondly, that it was not the property of the individual soul, but of the active intellect; thirdly, that intelligible knowledge is the property of the active intelligence, not of the human intellect; and finally, that there was no personal immortality. To the question whether, if all mankind shared the same intellect, all men did not think the same thoughts simultaneously, Averroes showed that individual knowledge differed because of different individual experiences; each individual, in the sensations peculiar to him, possessed one aspect of universal knowledge.

The importance of Averroes's doctrine of the human soul lay in its uniting the body with the soul and separating the soul from the understanding. This made the soul the body's form without which the latter could not exist and by which both became corporeal. In its total effect, Averroes's return to Aristotle both strengthened and weakened the theistic element in Avicenna's doctrine. It strengthened it by restoring to God His knowledge of His creatures and giving Him a much more direct influence upon their existence. It weakened it by closing the loophole between necessity and contingency, thereby strengthening the element of necessity in the universe. But it was above all in his decisive teaching on the mortality of the soul that Averroes flew in the face of revelation. His monopsychism was to be the single greatest danger to

Christian thinking. His influence on the West, however, was far from being negative; he raised the problem of the relation between faith and reason in a new way; his use of Aristotelian categories to denote God's being, and the relation of form to matter, were to be a fertile source of inspiration; while in uniting God's thinking with His being He overcame one of the greatest deficiencies in Neoplatonism.

(ii) Jewish Philosophy

Among the Jewish philosophers most influential on the West there were two, Ibn Gabirol (Avicebrol or Avicebron) and the rabbi Moses Maimonides. Both were born in Spain and both showed how greatly Jewish thought had been affected by Arabian thought. Yet it must not be supposed that the two were in any way synonymous: Arabian thought, as it reached the West, came primarily from its philosophers, who looked to Greek sources for their support and did not try to harmonize their findings with the teaching of the Koran. That was left to the theologians. With the Jewish thinkers, on the other hand, of the very small number known to the West, the most important were theologians. That is to say, they started from the tenets of the Jewish faith, contained in the Old Testament and their commentaries, especially the Talmud. Hence monotheism, creation *ex nihilo* and in time, God's sovereign freedom, were all accepted as axiomatic. There was never any attempt to by-pass them, in the way that Avicenna and Averroes could, say, deny creation from a strictly philosophical standpoint. Hence, also, the far less disturbing effect of Jewish thinking upon the West; indeed both Avicebrol and Maimonides were to have a formative rôle in Augustinianism and Thomism.

Avicebrol (*c.* 1020–1070), so called because he was regarded, through the Latin translations that came down to the West, as another Arabian thinker, was born at Malaga. His only philosophical work known to the scholastics was his *Source of Life*. Originally one of three treatises dealing with God, will, and matter and form, the *Source of Life* was primarily devoted to matter and form. There were, Avicebrol held, three great divisions in the universe: God, His will, and universal being composed of matter and form. God was alone free of matter, and this distinguished His being from that of everything else. This composition of form and matter (hylomorphism) extended to all beings, spiritual as well as corporeal. It constituted a universal essence 'which exists by itself, which is of a single essence, which is the subject of all diversity, which gives to every thing its essence and its name'. It comprises a universal form and a universal prime matter, each of which contains a hierarchy of forms – from the form and matter of the heavens to the form and matter of individual substances. The forms give matter actuality, and each different being, celestial or corporeal, has a plurality of forms, including that of its matter (which in bodies derives from a form of corporeity) and its own essential forms. So far as material things are concerned, their sensible forms contain such attributes as quantity, content, figure, colour, by which they are made corporeal.

We have here the classical Neoplatonic concept of Ideas, or forms, as the determinants of being, as well as the hierarchy by which they are graded from the heavens to the material world. Similarly, in regarding matter, both spiritual and corporeal, as the cause of individuation and form as the agent in making matter actual, Avicebrol was combining Neoplatonism with Aristotle in the manner so characteristic of Avicenna. Where he broke off sharply from them both was in making all being come from God's will.

Although he tends to treat God's will as an emanation, rather than an attribute, of His nature, he has no doubt that it is the creative cause, giving effect, through being, to the Ideas of form and matter which God knows in His intellect. 'That which joins matter to form, that which unites and conserves their union is the unity which is superior to them. The creative will is that which makes matter receive form, although matter does not receive being from that from which it receives form.' Avicebrol sees the forms as intermediaries between the divine will and God's creatures, for these provide the transition between God's infinite nature and the contingent beings of creation.

This break with the self-perpetuating hierarchy of Intelligences of Neoplatonism can also be seen in Avicebrol's theory of human knowledge. Man is no longer dependent, as with the Arabian thinkers, upon an external intelligence for his illumination; he is able to grasp the immaterial forms in things by his own powers; and by tracing these back he can ultimately arrive at their source in God's will. By this view, the whole of the material world provides evidence of God, and we are confronted with an outlook similar in some respects to that of Denys and John the Scot where nature is a mirror of the divine. It is not surprising that Avicebrol provided much that was germane to the more Platonic thought of the Augustinians, in his doctrine of the plurality of forms, the primacy of God's will, and the soul's ability to travel from the sensible world to the realm of intelligibility. His influence upon them was to be considerable.

There is a curious similarity between Arabian and Jewish thought in the sequence from the Neoplatonism of Avicenna and Avicebrol to the Aristotelianism of Averroes and Maimonides. Both the latter, writing in the twelfth century, were moved to substitute Aristotle for Plotinus. Moreover, like Averroes, Maimonides was particularly concerned over the relation of reason to faith. They differed in their solutions.

Moses ben Maimon (Maimonides) lived from 1135 to 1204. Born at Cordova, in Spain, he was a rabbi and a Talmudist. His entire emphasis, in contrast to, say, Averroes, was upon harmonizing faith with reason, and, where that was impossible, to accept the truths of revelation as beyond rational demonstration. This attitude was far more closely in keeping with that of the West, and his *Guide for the Perplexed* had a wide vogue, not least with St Thomas Aquinas. The *Guide* was designed for those who, in their knowledge of philosophy, were unable to reconcile it with the truth of God's law: 'This treatise has only been written for those who have studied philosophy.' He declared it his aim 'to explain the obscurities of the Law and to know the true sense of the allegories which

are above common understanding'. Thus, again, quite unlike Averroes, philosophy is the indispensable adjunct of
theology.

In philosophy, Maimonides looked to Aristotle as the one
who had attained to the highest in human knowledge. Thus
he rejected Avicebrol's hylomorphism, restoring the nine
Intelligences to pure act. But primarily he used rational arguments, drawn mainly from Aristotle, to support the funda-
mentals of faith: monotheism, God's nature as indefinable
(with the necessity of negating His attributes), creation *ex
nihilo*, and through His will, sin as coming from creatures, not
from God. These were all supported by a series of proofs,
numbering, in the case of monotheism, twenty-six. On the
eternity of the world, Maimonides anticipates St Thomas in
holding that although the creation of the world was philosophically probable it could not be demonstrated. This, as with
God's attributes, was a matter of following the Law. Its
importance lies in showing that for Maimonides, as for the
later scholastics, certain aspects of revelation remained inaccessible to reason. Only over the immortality of the human soul
did Maimonides align himself with the Arabs against faith:
for he took up a position, much like Avicenna's, of upholding
an active intellect, tenth in the hierarchy of Intelligences,
which distributes forms to the sub-lunar world of generation
and corruption. It is responsible for bringing the human
understanding into act.

The impact upon the West of these different systems, both
Arabian and Jewish, can be seen in all the main currents of its
thought in the thirteenth and indeed fourteenth centuries.
Apart from acting as intermediaries in giving the scholastics
their first extensive knowledge of Aristotle, they transmitted a
vast corpus of ideas which had to be assimilated. In the first
place, there was the employment of metaphysical categories to
distinguish God's existence from that of His creatures, whether
the possible and necessary being of Alfarabi and Avicenna, the
potency and act of Averroes, or the hylomorphism of
Avicebrol. These concepts provided the West with an arsenal
on which its thinkers could draw in their own discussions over

God's existence. Secondly, until St Thomas's return to the pure Aristotle, the different thinkers of Islam contrived to make his God an indirect mover. The different cosmogonies of Arabian and Jewish thinkers alike were given a Neoplatonic setting in the series of emanations or movements from Intelligence to Intelligence. Even Averroes had to turn the first mover of Aristotle into a creative cause, and his view of the active intellect owes not a little to a Neoplatonic theory of Ideas. Thirdly, it was in their view of the active intellect that the thinkers of Islam presented the West with so profound a problem: as it stood, it tended to deny the individuality of the soul; but it could be, and was, adapted to something approaching the Augustinian theory of illumination from God. By this means, as we shall see, the Augustinian school of the thirteenth century was able to make the active intellect correspond with divine illumination. Only in Averroes's denial of any independent (possible) intellect to man was the conflict irreconcilable. Fourthly, there was the specific Arabian legacy of determinism and necessity. This had two aspects: first, the lack of any theory of creation *ex nihilo* and in time from God's own untrammelled will; second, the eternity of the world. Both of these struck at the heart of Christianity and Judaism; and we have already seen the reaction of Avicebrol and Maimonides to them. In many ways, this was the most fundamental of all the issues between Islam and Christendom, for ultimately it put God's own nature at stake. The gradual revulsion in the West against the constrictions of determinism was to come to a head in the great Paris Condemnations of Averroism in 1277. Finally, we may mention some of the different concepts that the West took over from Islam, such as the distinctions between essence and existence, necessary and possible being, as well as hylomorphism and Aristotle's theory of abstraction, as means of tracing God's existence. What, however, all these notions required was that they be firmly set within a Christian framework if they were not to supplant the tenets of faith.

This indeed was the supreme challenge to Christendom in the thirteenth century. Could these non-Christian systems, similar to, and yet so different from, the outlook of the West, be assimilated? Or were they to overwhelm the tentative searchings of Christian thinkers? The greater part of the thirteenth century was given over to answering these questions.

CHAPTER 7

The Thirteenth Century: the Age of Syntheses

THREE circumstances dominated the thirteenth century: the recovery of Aristotle's works and the discovery of Islamic thought; the emergence of the universities as the main intellectual centres; the virtual monopoly of learning by the mendicant orders (the Friars), particularly the Dominicans and the Franciscans. Taken together, these different influences moulded the thirteenth century into a pattern very different from the twelfth.

This difference is apparent in a number of ways. The intellectual climate itself shows a marked change away from the humanism of the eleventh and twelfth centuries. The great breadth of interest, ranging from the classics to the sciences, the attention to style, the emphasis upon eloquence as inseparable from wisdom, all of which had characterized the outlook of the preceding two centuries, almost vanishes. In the eleventh and twelfth centuries, philosophy shared in but did not dominate the general reawakening in culture. It went together with the cultivation of classical literature: it was only one among the seven liberal arts. All branches of knowledge expressed a freshness that comes with discovery, even if they lacked an assured technique.

With the thirteenth century, the technical accomplishment is there, but partly at the cost of breadth of interest. There comes a gradual restriction of scope and enquiry: the first seeds of over-sophistication are being sown. This is very largely due to the dominance of dialectic, which had almost swallowed up the other liberal arts. Whereas, previously, the latter had been regarded as the starting-point for theology, now the arts course in the university consisted primarily of dialectic. This represented a revolution in the entire conception of learning. It meant that the *quadrivium* as well as the *trivium* was neglected; not only was the range of intellectual discussion narrowed, but the existing subjects were either ignored or transformed.

Roger Bacon in his laments for the times, to be found in his *Opus maius* and his *Opus tertium*, pointed to the declining knowledge of foreign languages as well as the widespread ignorance of mathematics. Both of these were good examples of what came of neglecting the seven liberal arts; and, even allowing for Bacon's exaggeration, they point to the preoccupation with logic and dialectic. At Paris university, philosopy and theology were studied virtually to exclusion of all mathematics; it was left to Robert Grosseteste and his disciples to make Oxford the great centre of science during the thirteenth and part of the fourteenth centuries.

Even more striking is the general change which this specialization wrought upon the *trivium*. Rhetoric virtually disappeared, and with it grammar, as a guide to literary expression. The study of grammar was now governed by its logical aspects; literary usage was subordinated, as incidental, to the discovery of universal laws regulating human thought. It became absorbed in philosophy, devoted to the language of logic (*grammatica speculativa*). The effect of this change can be seen on almost every page of scholastic writing in the thirteenth century and afterwards. Gone is the classical eloquence of St Bernard or the individuality of Abelard. Personal idiosyncrasies have been displaced by a uniform mode of expression, clear, technical, and syllogistic. Save for the likes and dislikes of Albert the Great, or the vehemence of Roger Bacon, it would be hard to point to any intrinsic stylistic differences between one writer and the next. They have attained to a degree of clarity and precision which in itself was an outstanding intellectual achievement, but it was at the expense of the expression of their personalities.

Another important difference was the changed position of theology itself. It was still the crown of all intellectual effort; but now it surmounted only dialectic and philosophy, not the full seven liberal arts. Even when we admit that, in practice, not all the subjects had received the same attention in the preceding centuries, the transformation is striking. So long as the *trivium* and the *quadrivium* had been allowed free scope, there was no single approach to theology. During the twelfth century the difference between, say, the school of Chartres and the Paris schools, or between the Victorines and individual thinkers like Alan of Lille, is clear to see, to say nothing of divisions in the schools themselves. Theories drawn from the *Timaeus* mingle with the theory of abstraction and the atomic theory. Diversity is the keynote. In the thirteenth century the philosophical aspect becomes uppermost: St Augustine is no longer treated simply for his spiritual value; his philosophical implications are brought out. Simple understanding, in the manner of St Anselm, gives way to a complex of techniques and enquiries subject to rigorous demonstration. In this way theology becomes a science which, like any other discipline, is governed by certain laws. These were largely taken from the categories of Aristotle's logic and metaphysics which, as we shall have further occasion to remark, came virtually to constitute the arts course in the universities and were preliminary to the study of theology. It led to the 'philosophizing' of theology; to the need to harmonize metaphysics with faith, or rather, to put theology upon a metaphysical foundation. Hence the thirteenth century is, *par excellence*, the age of syntheses. Its thinkers are, from early on, engaged in trying to provide a philosophical, or a natural, theology, largely under the impulse of Aristotle. It is the age of the great system and of the *summa*, with its comprehensive treatment of the full range of knowledge. From this point of view it can be regarded as the culmination of scholasticism.

In these circumstances it is not hard to see how the numerous rivulets of the twelfth century become merged in a few main streams of thought. To a great extent, the thirteenth century is the century of rival doctrinal schools. Most of the prominent thinkers can be associated with the Augustinians, the Aristotelians, or the 'Averroists'; similarly, the different groupings bear a fairly close resemblance to one or other of the main mendicant orders, especially the Franciscans and the Dominicans; and while hard and fast divisions are impossible, as the century progresses, the Franciscan outlook can be regarded as Augustinian, while most of the Aristotelians (except for the Averroists) are to be found among the Dominicans. Not only is the age of the individual master, like Abelard, a thing of the past, but the individual thinker who is not a friar is an exception.

The picture, then, that emerges of the thirteenth century is at once more sober and more mature than that of the twelfth. If it is less variegated than its predecessor it is more controlled; if it offers less profusion in its activities, they are better directed. The economy of its thought and expression give it a power which the twelfth century lacked. The measure of its effectiveness can be seen in the systems it achieved; beside them, previous centuries pale.

(i) The Introduction of Aristotle into the West

Aristotle's works first started to reach the West in the second third of the twelfth century. The peak period was from about 1130 until the last two decades of the twelfth century. The stream did not then dry up, but gradually changed its character, and from about 1240 there was an influx of new translations. The difference between the two phases is an important one. In the first phase a great part of Aristotle was translated from the Arabic and included much that was Neoplatonic as well as numerous Arabian writings. In the second phase, Aristotle was gradually freed from his Neoplatonic accretions, and the translations themselves were taken direct from the Greek. The effect on Western thought was great. It meant that for most of the twelfth century, and for the first third or so of the thirteenth, Aristotle is associated with an outlook which comes closer to Avicenna than anyone else. His thought becomes an inextricable medley of Neoplatonic emanations and separated intelligences, Arabian determinism and the rule of the active intellect, together with Aristotelian principles of being and movement. If these contrived to present the West with the first thoroughgoing explanation of the universe and the first complete analysis of nature, they did so in a distinctly non-Christian way.

Necessity, eternity, and pantheism were the most evident offspring of a cosmogony which saw God as an indirect first mover who did no more than set in motion a chain of effects, each responsible for the next. The prevalence of pantheism during the later twelfth century, among thinkers like Amaury of Bène and David of Dinant, not to mention William of Conches and Bernard Silvestris, was and can be directly attributed to this Arabian influence. Consequently, Aristotle was viewed with suspicion and hostility by the ecclesiastical authorities and the orthodox theologians. To them, his works seemed to be a threat to Christian belief – as indeed many of these ideas were. The result was a series of condemnations against the teaching of Aristotle.

The first was at Paris in 1210, when, under its Archbishop, the provincial synod of Sens forbade the scientific works of Aristotle together with those of Amaury of Bène and David of Dinant. This ban on Aristotle's natural philosophy was repeated five years later in the statutes for Paris university drawn up by Robert Courçon, the papal legate, who was thus voicing the official attitude of the Church. While Aristotle's logic was allowed, he reiterated the interdiction against the teaching, or commenting, of Aristotle's other works, either in public or in private. 'The books of Aristotle on metaphysics and natural philosophy may not be read, nor summae on them, or on the doctrine of David of Dinant or the heretic Almaric or Maurice of Spain.' This coupling of Aristotle with expressly declared heretics is clear evidence of how closely Aristotle was identified with his interpreters, both Islamic and Christian. Authority looked on Aristotle as a source of heresy and so tried to stamp him out. Moreover, the 'summae' which are mentioned in Robert Courçon's statutes almost certainly refer to Avicenna's philosophical encyclopedia, where it was his custom to incorporate Aristotle into his own system.

The ban on Aristotle was far from universal, and in 1229 we see the University of Toulouse openly specifying that 'the books on natural philosophy which were prohibited at Paris' can be used there 'to look into the very bosom of nature'. Moreover, the need to repeat the injunctions of 1210 and 1215 again in 1231, shows that they had not succeeded in stamping out the new ideas. Already in 1228 a ranging shot had been fired by Pope Gregory IX, when in a letter to Paris University he cautioned the theological faculty against the misapplication of philosophy. Three years later, in 1231, he issued a Bull for the university in which he confirmed previous condemnations. Shortly afterwards he set up a commission to purge Aristotle's *Physics*, after which it was to be allowed to circulate. Nothing came of this project, and in spite of two subsequent condemnations, by Innocent IV in 1245 directed against Toulouse, and by Urban IV in 1263 against Paris, no further action was taken.

Aristotle's works, like all ideas, could not be stamped out by decrees, and they steadily gained a momentum which finally culminated in the Thomist synthesis. When the great condemnations of 1277 were made, they were no longer solely against Aristotle but also aimed at the interpretation put on him by Averroes and his supporters at Paris.

Apart from the failure of the Church's bans on Aristotle, which were both ill-directed and ill-conceived, Aristotle survived for at least two reasons. The very opposition against him engendered a knowledge of his doctrine: to oppose, one must understand what is being opposed, and understanding involved study and propagation of his works. Ultimately, therefore, the attacks against him fanned the blaze rather than extinguished it. The second reason lies in the changed understanding of Aristotle which came with a gradual sifting of his works. The new translations of the middle decades of the thirteenth century, by Grosseteste and later that prince of translators, William Moerbeke, went to the true source; they therefore cut through the maze of Neoplatonism in which the true Aristotle had been imprisoned. This led to Aristotle becoming the main authority for the study of philosophy in the Arts faculties of the universities, and, together with the knowledge of Averroes's works, was to lead to fresh problems in the sixties and seventies of the century.

The earliest translations of Arabian and Aristotelian works had been by Adelard of Bath and Constantinus Africanus; they,

together with Hermann of Dalmatia and Robert of Rétines
had introduced the West to Greek and Arabian works of
science. It was the establishment of a school of translators at
Toledo, under Raymond its Archbishop, *circa* 1150, that
marked the real beginning of the process. Three of its most
outstanding names were Dominic Gundisalvi, John of Spain,
(the same as John Avendeath?) and Gerard of Cremona
(1114–1187). The first two, at the behest of Raymond, translated into Latin the works of Avicenna, including his *Logic*
and his *Metaphysics*, part of his *Physics* (taken from several
different works), Algazali's *Metaphysics*, Alfarabi's *De scientiis*,
and Avicebrol's *Source of Life*. Gerard of Cremona, who has
over seventy translations to his credit, in addition to translating numerous Arabian scientific writings, as well as the
works of Alkindi, Avicenna's *Canon* (his medical treatise), the
Book of Causes, Ptolemy's *Almagest*, also presented the West
with much of Aristotle. This included the *Posterior Analytics*,
the *Physics*, the *De caelo et mundo*, *De generatione et corruptione*,
and part of the *Meteors*. Other translations were made by the
Englishmen Alfred of Sareshel and Daniel of Morley.

Toledo continued to be the great centre of Arabic translation into the thirteenth century as well, and here the outstanding figure was Michael Scot (1180–1235), though he later
worked in Sicily. It was he who, more than anyone else, was
responsible for translating Averroes into Latin, and from the
1230s his works became increasingly in evidence at Paris and
elsewhere. They included Averroes's Commentaries on *De
caelo et mundo*, *De anima*, and perhaps also on *De generatione* and
others. Also responsible for translating Averroes was
Hermann the German, who in addition to his translations of
Aristotle's *Nicomachean Ethics*, *Rhetoric*, and *Poetics*, between
1240 and 1256, also transcribed Averroes's *Middle commentary*
on the *Ethics* and the *Poetics*, in 1240 and 1244. To Toledo,
then, the West owed not only its initial influx of Aristotle,
Arabian and neoplatonized in the twelfth century, but the
equally momentous introduction of Averroes in the thirteenth
century.

Sicily was another focus for translators, but these differed from Spain in going direct to the Greek sources. Particularly prominent was Henry Aristippus, Archdeacon of Catania (*d.* 1162), who translated the fourth book of the *Meteors*, Ptolemy's *Syntax* and *Optics*, Euclid's *Optics*, and Proclus's *Physical Elements*.

In addition to these *foci* a certain amount of translation went on in Constantinople, though it was too far divorced from the West ever to become a centre of the first rank. The names of James of Venice and Burgundio of Pisa are associated with it.

By 1200, a large part of Aristotle's works, in addition to translations of Greek and Arabian science and Arabian philosophy, had become available to the West: his 'new logic' (the first and second *Analytics*, the *Topics*, and the *Sophistical questions*) had been added to the 'old logic' of the *Categories* and the *Interpretation*, Porphyry's *Isagoge* and Boethius's commentaries. There were now also the *Metaphysics*, part of which was already in Latin, the 'natural books' of the *Physics*, *De generatione*, *De caelo*, and part of *De meteoris*; *De anima*; and books two and three (out of a total of ten) of the *Nicomachean Ethics*.

During the thirteenth century, in addition to the translations by Michael Scot and Hermann the German already mentioned, Robert Grosseteste translated or revised the whole of the *Ethics*, between 1240 and 1245, and Alfred Sareshel translated *De anima* and other works. But the greatest of all Aristotle's translators was William of Moerbeke (1215–1286), a Flemish Dominican, who was St Thomas Aquinas's collaborator and Archbishop of Corinth from 1277 until his death.

He undertook the direct translation from the Greek in order to supply St Thomas with proper texts. He was the first to translate Aristotle's *Politics* (1260) and his *Economics* (1267). In addition, he retranslated or revised most of the existing translations of Aristotle's works, and to him, more than anyone else, the thirteenth century owed a true and direct knowledge of Aristotle. He also rendered into Latin works by other authors, including Simplicius's commentary on *De caelo et mundo* and on the *Categories*, as well as commentaries by Alexander of Aphrodisias. His translation of Proclus's *Elements of Theology*, already translated by Gerard of Cremona, enabled St Thomas to recognize the provenance of the *Book of Causes*; he also translated a number of other works by Proclus, so helping to give a great impetus to Neoplatonism besides making it possible to distinguish ever more clearly between Aristotle and Neoplatonism.

It is not hard to gauge the shock which this tidal wave of new knowledge and strange thinking constituted for the West. Within a mere hundred years it had inundated its habits and outlook; and the problem of Aristotle becomes even starker when we recall that during this entire period only two of Plato's works, the *Phaedo* and the *Meno*, were introduced. Under this new impact, no aspect of thought and learning could remain unaffected.

(ii) The Universities

The emergence of the universities, although not the work of external influences, as with Aristotle, had a no less profound effect. If they did not confront Christendom with the same problem of assimilation which Aristotle presented, they were, in Paris especially, the cockpit of conflicting tendencies. These went beyond the simple question of Aristotle versus orthodoxy, to the struggle between a secular and a theocratic conception of life and learning. As such, they had a wider relevance – to Christian society itself.

This dualism can be seen even in the structure of the university. On the one hand, a *universitas* meant just another corporation; it was a term which could be applied to any body or grouping. In the case of the university, whose technical title during the middle ages was *studium generale*, it was a group distinguished by its craft, or skill, of learning. In structure, it was analogous to other craft gilds. It was made up of a number of qualified masters and doctors at the top and the mass of students, or apprentices, below. It betrayed gradations similar to the gild. The student, after several years of study and on passing his tests, became a bachelor, who like the journeymen had taken his 'degree' and who had to undergo a further period before he could be accepted by the masters as one of themselves. On the other hand, it was this very profession of learning which made a university so different from other gilds, and so important. The security of faith itself rested with the masters and scholars who studied there. Theology was but one of the four faculties, which embraced also medicine, canon and civil law, and the arts. The danger lay in following the latter regardless of theology, and in making them, not theology, the end. Thus the universities, especially in Paris, where theology was predominant, were particularly susceptible to the rival currents of heterodoxy and orthodoxy, of study for its own sake and of study with faith as its end. They marked a break in kind from the cathedral schools of the twelfth century, where the seven liberal arts had always been closely subordinated to the understanding of theology. This religious ideal was being challenged by an attitude which was primarily secular and which, as we shall see, lay at the heart of the struggles which went on at Paris.

The universities, however, were far from being uniform or homogeneous. In general, from the thirteenth century onwards, a *studium generale* became a place of study where the higher subjects of theology, medicine, law, and arts (Aristotle) were taught, and whose license to teach was universally recognized – 'the right of teaching everywhere'. In course of time, the universities became privileged corporations, exempt from outside interference and virtually self-governing, recognized by the Pope and secular rulers. But within these broad lines there were great divergences.

The greatest division, both in type and in time, was between Northern Europe and Italy. The three earliest universities were Salerno, Bologna, and Paris, each of which became a model for later foundations. Both Salerno and Bologna were primarily practical in their emphasis, and non-ecclesiastical in origin and in character. Salerno, the oldest university of any, had already reached its peak in the twelfth century, although it was not until 1234 that it was given official recognition by the king of Sicily, the Emperor Frederick II. As the meeting-place of Greek, Arabian, Jewish, and Latin civilizations, it had been able to maintain an unbroken connexion with ancient medical practice and theory, doubtless enhanced by its own qualities as a spa. It became the centre of medicine, until supplanted by Montpelier in the later thirteenth century, as well as one of the earliest centres for the translation of medical works.

In Bologna we have one of the two main archetypes of the medieval university. Founded almost certainly through the migration of jurists from Rome after its sack by the Normans in 1084, it remained the outstanding centre of law throughout the twelfth and thirteenth centuries. Its distinguishing features were twofold. From the first it was primarily practical in interest and urban in character. Theology or ecclesiastical authority played little part in its studies, in marked contrast to Paris and other northern universities. Secondly, in its organization it was a 'students' university': that is to say, the students, together with the bachelors, ran the university. Each of the different 'nations', into which the students were grouped, elected a rector, and the rectors presided over a council regulating the entire university. Only in the matter of examining did the masters have control, for which purpose they were grouped into colleges. Law, then, was its own justification, and the masters were regarded as paid teachers, not as members of a hierarchy. Until 1353 there was no faculty of theology at all. There could hardly be a clearer example of the utilitarian, non-theological concept of a university, and Bologna played little part in philosophy or theological speculation.

This was left to Paris, the great centre of logic, metaphysics, and theology, and the archetype of the 'masters' university'. This, in accordance with the normal gild, was ruled by its masters and doctors, with whom lay the acceptance of other masters as qualified teachers. Founded in 1200 by Philip II of France, Paris was recognized by Pope Innocent III whose legate, Robert Courçon, gave it its statutes in 1215. From the first, Paris was closely connected with the Church. It had sprung largely from the schools which had grown up on the left bank of the Seine, from the time of Abelard, together with the cathedral school where Peter Lombard had taught.

It had for long been a centre of student and intellectual life, and throughout the thirteenth century, and for part of the fourteenth, it was supreme. It contained, at one time or another, all the great thinkers of the epoch, none of whom, surprisingly, was French. It was, therefore, more than a university in the strict sense, and certainly more the concern of the international Church than of any individual king, as the constant intervention in its affairs by successive popes shows.

The university itself was divided into the four faculties of Arts, Law, Medicine, and Theology. Of these, arts and theology were by far the most important. Every student had to pass through the arts faculty before he could proceed to one of the other studies. The purpose of its course was to fulfil the rôle of the seven liberal arts by providing a grounding in the main branches of profane knowledge. This was usually preparatory to the study of theology; hence the close connexion between the two faculties. Although each was an independent discipline, one was designed as the completion of the other.

It was this fact which made for the great conflict at Paris during the thirteenth century; for as Aristotle's books became the mainstay of the arts course, there was an ever-growing tendency to regard philosophy as a self-sufficient discipline. Unlike the twelfth century, when for the most part Aristotle represented dialectic, the arts now had at their disposal a series of positive sciences, metaphysical, physical, and ethical. These could stand alone where dialectic could not; they could provide an alternative explanation to that given by faith, where dialectic, at best, could not go beyond elucidating faith. The seven liberal arts had become identical with Aristotle's system; they could either ignore theology as irrelevant or confront it as a rival. This threat to the established position of theology very largely explains both the papal attitude to Aristotle and the attempts by theologians to assimilate or disavow him. If 'Latin Averroism' was essentially the arts faculty's espousal of Aristotle as an end in himself, Thomism was the response of theology in harnessing him to faith.

The extent to which Aristotle had become the arts course can be seen from the list of prescribed texts for 1255. They included the *Logic*, *Physics*, *Metaphysics*, *Ethics*, as well as *De animalibus*, *De caelo et mundo*, *De anima*, *De generatione et corruptione*, *De sensu et sensato*, *De somno et vigilia*, *De memoria et reminiscentia*, to which were added works by Gilbert de la Porrée, Donatus, Boethius, and the *Book of Causes*. In view of this it is not hard to see how the seven liberal arts had given way to Aristotle's philosophy. Moreover, the emphasis of Paris upon logic, metaphysics, and theology led to the virtual exclusion of the more scientific subjects of the old *quadrivium* which now found a home in Oxford.

The courses in the arts and theological faculties both gave a marked impress to the mode of thought. Altogether a period of six years had to be passed in the arts faculty, the last two of which the student spent as a bachelor preparing for his master's degree. After that, it took a further eight years in the faculty of theology to become a master in theology. The first two years there were devoted to the study and commenting of Peter Lombard's *Book of Sentences*; the next two years to the Bible; and the last four years to teaching and disputation. The whole course, therefore, lasted fourteen years. Teaching was carried on mainly by reading (*lectio*), that is commenting the prescribed texts, and by disputation (*disputatio*). The latter were public discussions, held periodically and often lasting several days, presided over by a master. It would rest with the master, after the different arguments had been presented, to put them into logical order and to 'determine' them: that is, reach a conclusion. To determine a dispute was the final task of the bachelor before he could become a master. Hence most of the literature of the thirteenth century and after is in the form of commentaries and questions (*quaestiones quodlibetales* and *quaestiones disputatae*). The main works of thinkers like Bonaventure, Duns Scotus, William of Ockham were their commentaries on the *Sentences*, whilst a great part of St Thomas's writings was in the form of either questions or commentaries. These virtually superseded the literary and dialogue forms of the twelfth century, as well as the monograph. The style was almost invariably that of the *quaestio*, itself the embodiment of disputation. When we add to this the knowledge of Aristotle, we need not be surprised at the uniformly syllogistic nature of expression which predominated inside and outside the universities.

(iii) The Friars

The coming of the Friars to the universities, particularly Paris and Oxford, increased their importance still further. Not only did the Friars contribute almost all the great names in thought; they helped to define the different streams. Although it would be going too far to say that the Dominicans were Aristotelian in their outlook and the Franciscans Augustinian, this is where they tended: and their very cohesion as distinct and organized bodies helped towards each holding particular tenets. On the other hand, it must be stressed that, throughout the thirteenth century, and far more during the fourteenth, it is quite unreal to identify either order with any exclusive body of doctrine. This was never more apparent than in the reaction of St Thomas's own order to his assimilation of Aristotle. Both the orders reached Paris at about the same time, the Dominicans in 1217, the Franciscans in 1219. The Dominicans had from the first been organized as a body devoted to learning and theologically trained; but they had not intended to take part in the life of the university so much as to convert its students. Before long, however, they had been joined by distinguished masters who continued to hold their university posts as well. The Franciscans had been conceived by St Francis, their founder, as an order to preach the gospel in its direct simplicity without intellectual refinements; and although they never became a learned order in the sense of the Dominicans they, too, took up learning, entered the universities, and soon numbered some of the foremost thinkers among them.

The Dominicans and Franciscans were throughout distinct from the rest of the university. In the first place, as organized bodies, they had their own schools (provincial and general) independent of the universities. They, therefore, received a general education which gained them exemption from the arts course and allowed them to proceed direct to the faculty of theology. Secondly, they alone presented relatively compact and homogeneous groupings amidst the throng of university life. This contrast to the seculars inevitably led to rivalry and jealousies: they had their own doctors not subject to the Chancellor's approval, and they tended to keep aloof from the activities of the rest, as when they stayed put in 1229 during the strike of the seculars. They came to constitute the main strength of the theological faculty and thus, to a large extent, the struggle between philosophy and theology, especially at Paris, was the struggle between the seculars in the arts faculty and the Friars in theology.

(iv) The beginnings of thirteenth-century thought

Signs of Aristotle's influence on the thirteenth century were not for long wanting. Already it is apparent in the work of the important Toledan translator, Dominic Gundisalvi, to say nothing of the association (which we have already noted) of Amaury of Bène and David of Dinant with the doctrines of Aristotle. Gundisalvi, in his *On the Division of Nature* (*c.* 1150), his *Immortality of the Soul*, and other works, betrays the influence of Alfarabi and Avicenna. He holds to an unmoved mover; he regards God as the source of all forms, without which matter is only potential; he believes in a separated intelligence for all mankind. Gundisalvi's is only one aspect of a number of works, mostly anonymous, which point to this new universe of forms and separated Intelligences, the last of which is the cause of the sub-lunar world and the direct mover of the human soul. In this sense, Avicenna, or the outlook associated with him, was a far more formative influence on the early thirteenth century than Averroes ever was upon its later stages. He provided it with a cosmogony which could be, and was, adapted to Christianity, while Averroes largely remained a standing challenge to Christian belief.

With William of Auvergne (1180–1249) we come to the first important attempt to meet the threat of Aristotle's philosophy as well as to the last important French thinker

until the fifteenth century. He was not the first to have shown
an awareness of Aristotle; William of Auxerre, Archdeacon of
Beauvais and one of the members of the commission appointed
by Gregory IX to examine the *Physics*, showed in his *Golden
Summa* (on the Lombard's *Sentences*) an acquaintance with the
Ethics and *De anima*, while elsewhere he refers to the *Metaphysics*. Philip of Greve (*d.* 1236), Chancellor of Paris University, similarly, mentions certain of Aristotle's works. William
of Auvergne became bishop of Paris in 1228, at a time
when Aristotle was once more arousing the suspicions of
the Church. In his capacity as bishop of Paris, William had
control over the University through the Chancellor of Notre
Dame, one of its twelve professors in theology. He was
severely taken to task by Gregory IX, in 1229, for his laxity
in dealing with the problems of the university and in the same
letter the Pope also expressed his regret at William's election
as bishop. The most important among William's works was
his *De primo principio* (*De Trinitate*), *De anima*, and *De universo*.

Historians have sometimes found it difficult to know
whether to regard William as last in the line of twelfth-
century thinkers or as precursor of the new age. In one sense
he is both; his style, his lack of strictly syllogistic method, his
comparatively undeveloped view of being, all point to his
strong affinities with the past. On the other hand, and in my
view far more significant, his outlook is essentially the incor-
poration of peripateticism into an Augustinian framework. It
is not so much to christianize Aristotle, or rather Avicenna;
it is far more to refute his mistakes and to assimilate and adapt
what is of use. From this point of view, William sets the tone
for the Augustinian school which develops; unlike Thomism
it refuses to cede the traditional positions of St Augustine to
Aristotle and his followers, but reinterprets the latter in the
light of that tradition.

The main point of William's reaction to Aristotle and
Avicenna is over their view of God's workings and His effect
upon man. William accepts Alfarabi's and Avicenna's distinction between essence and existence. It enables him to prove
God's existence by showing that for a being's essence to

include its existence means that it is a first uncaused cause – in contrast to everything else, where existence is not inherent in essence, and so must come from another. It also enables him to show that this identity in God means that His nature is simple and indefinable. As such, we cannot know God save by the idea of being.* It is worth noting that this proof of God as being, rather than as God, is to become one of the foundations of Duns Scotus's system.

It is when he comes to God's creatures that William breaks off sharply from Avicenna: while, he, too, does not make the difference between essence and existence equivalent to that between form and matter, he at the same time refuses to regard it as possible being made necessary. God Himself acts completely freely, directly, and without intermediaries; His will is the immediate cause of all creation and the ever-present means of His creatures' existence. Hence created being is a participation in divine being. It is hardly necessary to stress that this is the reply of the Christian theologian to the infidel philosopher. It is a reversion to the creator of Christian faith, the rejection of the Neoplatonic One, who, because He is only responsible for one effect, sets into motion an eternal hierarchy of Intelligences emanating one from the other. With this rejection of such a view goes the dismissal of all intermediaries between God and His creatures. These William regards as absurd.

Thus when we come to man we have regained the ground of St Augustine and Plato. His soul is a purely spiritual substance without potentiality or matter. It does not depend upon an active intellect to set it in motion, nor is it purely passive. In order to reassert the unity of the soul, and to close the door to the doctrines of the active intellect, William denies that it is divided into different faculties, or that its will is distinguished from its knowledge. It is moved by its essence. This doctrine, too, was to become very important in the fourteenth century under Ockham's influence.

From this firm basis William is able to cope with the Avicennan doctrine of illumination by the active intelligence.

*See *De Trinitate*.

Firstly, he says, to hold that it is the active intelligence which moves the human intellect into abstracting from things their intelligible forms, is to misunderstand the true source of intelligibles. On the contrary, as St Augustine taught, we gain truth from within ourselves: 'There are certain things which the understanding cannot doubt, namely to be, to live, to be happy, sad, and so on' (*De anima*, III, 13). From the images presented to the imagination by abstraction we are able to gain only the most vague understanding. True knowledge of forms comes with a special illumination directly from God. What we gain from the senses is a knowledge of sensible things; but from the soul we have a direct intuition of the intelligible forms in individual things: 'according to the doctrine of Christians, which is necessarily true, it must be stated that the soul is like an horizon between two worlds. One of these worlds is the world of sensible things to which it is closely connected by its body; but the other is the creator, who is in Himself like the model and the mirror in which are reflected . . . the first intelligible [forms]' (*De anima*, V, 7). These true forms can only be known through the gift of grace, and immediately. Thus, as with St Augustine, truth is supernatural, even though for William it is not *via* Ideas (as it is for St Augustine) but by a direct intuition. Here we have one of the most marked traits of Augustinianism. It is that we can know the sensible world, but *only* as the sensible world. There can be no unbroken line through abstraction from the natural to the supernatural. For this we need a quite different source, in the soul, independent of the material world. The gulf between nature and God can be bridged only by grace. This is the governing principle of Augustinianism; as taken up by William it is flung back at the Aristotelians: the first direct challenge in the long duel between them.

While William of Auvergne was responding to Aristotle's influence in theology, Robert Grosseteste (1175–1253) was laying the groundwork of a new outlook in science. Already there was ample evidence of the stimulus which scientific thinking had received from the translations of Arabian and Greek writings. Alexander Neckham (1157–1217) and Alfred of Sareshel, the translator, had written on different aspects of natural history, often with the strangest results; so also had another important translator, Michael Scot. But it was left to Grosseteste to leave the realm of fantasy. He was born in England, and it was in England that he passed most of his eventful life as Regent Master and Chancellor of Oxford University, first master to the Franciscan school at Oxford, and Bishop of Lincoln from 1253 until his death.

Like William of Auvergne, Grosseteste was one of the handful of outstanding thinkers who did not belong to any of the religious orders, and despite his close contact with, and great influence upon, the Franciscans he remained a secular. Grosseteste can also be compared with William of Auvergne in helping to leave his impress upon subsequent Augustinian thinking; indeed, Grosseteste, far more than William, was the initiator of an entirely new school of thinking which came to be associated with Oxford. This, in marked contrast to Paris, placed foremost emphasis upon scientific and mathematical studies. Treatises on optics and mathematics became for Oxford what logic and metaphysics were to Paris. Where Paris did not go beyond the old *trivium*, Oxford took up the *quadrivium*. There could be no clearer example of the way in which the traditional conception of education through the seven liberal arts had been displaced by specialization.

There was, also, another characteristic peculiar to Oxford: the preponderating influence of Platonism both in thought and in science. The two went hand in hand, each helping to inspire the other. They constituted an outlook which was at once *a priori* and deductive; which regarded knowledge, not as deriving from empirical observation, as with Aristotle and his followers like Albert the Great, but as exemplified in mathematics. It dealt with intelligible (i.e. non-sensory) principles, whose laws were ascertainable in the light of pure reason. The idea not the individual, the mental rather than the physical, formed the basis of its calculations. It owed everything to the Augustinian, Neoplatonic conception of truth as residing in the soul, to be reached through intellectual illumination: this provided its thinkers not only with a defence against Aristotle but with a full-fledged cosmogony, which came to be known as the 'light-metaphysic'.

Thus, neither in thought nor in science did Aristotle leave the same mark upon Oxford as upon Paris. Whilst the latter, in spite of constant struggles, became the main focus of Aristotelianism, Oxford held fast to Augustinianism as developed by Grosseteste and his disciples. Consequently, although in no way immune from the currents of the time, at Oxford they tended to be channelled into a separate stream which was ultimately to become as important as that at Paris.

Grosseteste personified this Oxford tradition. In theology he was conservative, in that he followed the old biblical school and upheld St Augustine's teaching; it was in his application of science to his beliefs that he innovated. In common with William of Auvergne, the main stimulus to his thinking came from the Islamic philosophers, especially Avicenna and Avicebrol, rather than from Aristotle. Similarly, their effect was to foster his reassertion of the traditional theology, not to embrace the new.

Grosseteste was in an almost unique position to respond to the challenge of Aristotle, in having a knowledge of Greek; and a great deal of his work was devoted to commenting and translating a number of Aristotle's writings. These, in addition to the *Ethics* (already mentioned) included both *Analytics*, the *Sophistical Questions*, and the *Physics*; he also did the same for several of the writings of the Pseudo-Denys. His own works extended over astronomy, meteorology, optics, physics, linguistics, metaphysics, free will, and the soul, not all of which have yet been published.

Grosseteste's position was founded upon St Augustine's conception of truth as in the mind. 'Therefore the truth of beings is their being as they should be and their conformity and accordance with the Word by which they are eternally spoken . . . truth was appropriately defined by Anselm, when he called it righteousness only perceptible to the mind' (*De veritate*, 135, 4). The lineage of Grosseteste's thought can be seen in his view that all knowledge originated as reason in God's intellect and is known to us by the forms in things.

It is when he comes to the working out of these divine Ideas that Grosseteste introduces the new conception of the 'light metaphysic'. Given fullest expression in his *De luce*, this regarded light as the stuff of the universe, at once the first form and the first matter. Already Avicebrol had put forward a similar view of the unity of form and matter, with light as a universal form. With Grosseteste, however, it was made the object of a scientific analysis, which traced all being to light. Light had been created by God to be the bearer of all matter and form; for its properties were not only a fineness of substance which made it almost incorporeal, but a capacity to generate itself. Thus in order to create the universe it sufficed for God to create a single point of light, in itself without dimensions, from which all being would spring. 'Light of its very nature diffuses itself in every direction in such a way that a point of light will produce instantaneously a sphere of light of any size whatsoever, unless some opaque object stands in its way' (*De luce*, 51, 11). Since matter is inherent in light, as soon as the point of light (which has no magnitude) has engendered a sphere (which has) it will also engender dimensions, that is, a material body extended in space. Thus we are able to attribute the whole of the physical universe to the workings of light. When light has finally reached the limit of rarefaction, the limit of the universe (as a sphere) is reached. From its limits, light is then reflected back to what becomes the centre of the earth, above which it engenders the nine celestial spheres and the four spheres of the material elements (air, fire, earth, and water). All these thirteen spheres combine to inform the earth.

Now the importance of Grosseteste's light metaphysic is twofold. In the first place, it is derived from a Neoplatonic metaphysic. Its starting-point is form as the foundation of being. Light provides this 'form of corporeity' which, joined to matter, gives rise to a body; only through this form can a body come into being and in turn receive other forms which determine its nature. We have met this concept of a plurality of forms before in Avicenna, and it becomes one of the hall-marks of Augustinianism. In contrast with Aristotle's view of matter, as without form and of itself undefined, Grosseteste regards the form of corporeity as the noblest of all: 'It is the most dignified of all the subsequent forms; it surpasses them in vigour; it is a more noble essence; it is the one which bears most resemblance to the immutable and separated forms'.

In the second place, Grosseteste makes mathematics, especially geometry and optics, a *sine qua non* for an understanding of nature; without science, knowledge is impossible. 'All the causes of natural effects should be reached by lines, angles, and figures; otherwise it is impossible to know their cause' (*ibid.* 60, 14). This is especially important in the case of spherical figures, since all activity develops in spheres. Lines, angles, and figures as the foundation of knowledge: how different from the syllogistic methods of Paris. They constituted another realm of reality and truth; reason lay in intelligible knowledge, not in grammar.

This is very apparent in Grosseteste's theory of knowledge. It takes the same Augustinian principle of divine illumination, which William of Auvergne took, to be the source of all our knowledge. With St Augustine, Grosseteste held that the soul, as more noble than the body, could not derive its knowledge through the senses; nor, except for a few privileged men, could it attain to truth directly. Through the repeated impact of sensations, the intelligence, the superior element in the soul, can distinguish the forms in things. In turning from sensation, it is illumined by a spiritual light which is from God and which enables it to see divine Ideas. God's Word is the form of all creatures, and knowledge of Him is, as with St Augustine, immediately apparent in the soul.

Grosseteste in his theory of knowledge, therefore, is close to William of Auvergne in seeing the individual itself as the object of universal knowledge; there is no need for abstraction to reach the form, since the individual is its essence. Here, too, we are in the universe of essences which both Avicenna and Duns Scotus also made so central to their outlook. In the treatise on *Free Will*, attributed to Grosseteste and which Bradwardine was to cite so fully, the author combats Averroes's view that God cannot know individual things.

Similarly, in the *Summa of Philosophy*, which, it has been established, was influenced but not written by Grosseteste, there is equal emphasis upon the singular as the object of understanding.

Grosseteste's influence was to continue down the middle ages, especially at Oxford. He provided an alternative to Aristotle's *Weltanschauung*; his scientific system was independent both of Aristotelian physics and metaphysics; it inaugurated a school of science. His work is testimony to the fact that Aristotle's influence not only was not all-pervasive, but that much of its fruitfulness lay in the reactions against it.

Grosseteste's immediate pupil and collaborator was, according to Roger Bacon, Adam Marsh (*d.* 1258), Master of the Franciscans and later Regent Master at Oxford. Adam's pupil, Thomas of York (*d.* 1260) particularly, showed the influence of Aristotle and his Arabian and Jewish commentators, above all Avicebrol. His metaphysics was primarily concerned with the nature of matter, which he regarded under three different aspects: corruptible, spiritual, and universal. In addition to its being the substance of all material bodies, matter also made up angels and spiritual natures, while, as universal, it was the condition for the existence of all eternal substances. Thomas regarded knowledge as coming through illumination, where, following William of Auvergne, he held that the intelligible could be directly seen in the individual. Although he did not achieve a synthesis of the old and the new, Thomas was a further example of the awareness of the new knowledge and the desire to relate it to established principles.

(v) Augustinianism

We are now in a position to identify that complex of thought which goes by the name of Augustinianism. In doing so, it must be emphasized, firstly, that this does not imply a compact body of doctrine or thinkers in any way approximating to an organized party; and secondly, that the term must not be taken to mean the rejection or disavowal of everything connected with Aristotle. On the contrary, the

Augustinians expressed one of three possible alternatives open to the West in dealing with the new knowledge: to accept what was in harmony with the tradition of St Augustine while rejecting the tenets of peripateticism; to incorporate Aristotle's metaphysics into Christianity; to accept Aristotle as he stood, regardless of the consequences to faith. The Augustinians took the first alternative which, in effect, meant filtering off the Neoplatonic elements and leaving Aristotle himself on one side; the Thomists followed the second and christianized Aristotle; the 'Averroists' adopted the third and severed faith from reason.

Augustinianism, then, was far more an attitude than a technique, although, as we shall mention, it had certain elements peculiar to it. It took its stand on the primacy of faith; and in this sense was essentially the response of Christian theology to a largely pagan philosophy. It regarded faith as containing its own justification (as the anonymous *Summa of Philosophy* asserted); it conceived truth as inseparable from revelation and its comprehension as dependent upon grace. It therefore preserved the essential tenets of St Augustine in refusing to divorce understanding from illumination, knowledge from will, will from inclination, and inclination from grace. These could not start with the senses; they belonged to the realm of the supernatural.

What we see, then, in Augustinianism is a philosophical justification of traditional positions, which, in great measure, had been also those of Anselm and St Augustine. It reasserts the primacy of faith not simply in having the last word, but in governing reason. That is why we often find a similar tendency to apply reason to faith in the manner of Anselm: faith was so inherent in reason, that it must be its starting-point. Such an attitude is particularly apparent with Bonaventure.

In itself Augustinianism could in no way be called anti-dialectical; its exponents all made full use of the logic and new knowledge, just as William of Auvergne and Grosseteste did. They helped to transform theology into a full-fledged science like any other, with its own laws and methods. They discussed and enquired where a century earlier most theologians would have accepted: the nature of the soul, the meaning of illumination, the place of sensory experience, the elements of matter, were all given much more precise examination. Much that was not pure St Augustine came to be included: it could not have failed to be, if Augustinianism was to survive. Thus within the context of faith there was virtually no limit to ratiocination. It was sensory knowledge that had no part to play.

This attitude to truth as the property of the Idea, or the intelligible, dominated all Augustinian thinking. From it sprang two tenets held in common by all its members. The first was that of divine illumination, which, as we have seen already, played such an important part with William of Auvergne and Robert Grosseteste. It is the hall-mark of Augustinian thought and a direct legacy from St Augustine. More than anything else, it expresses the essentially supernatural, ideal nature of truth and reality, which can only come through God's aid. This illumination differed from Neoplatonism and Arabian determinism in being the direct gift of God; ultimately, therefore, it depended less on intellectual clarity than on the inclination of the soul. Intuition of the truth was, as with St Augustine, part of a way of life.

We have already seen the close connexion between illumination and the 'light metaphysic'; its importance lay not so much in identifying knowledge with light, which was common enough, but in the analysis of light itself, to which it gave rise at Oxford. Optics and mathematics, as such, remained mainly the preserve of Grosseteste's disciples.

The second trait of Augustinianism was inherent in, though not inseparable from, the first: a plurality of forms in each individual. It became particularly important in the controversies with Thomism, over the relation of the human soul to the body. For the Augustinians, as we have had frequent cause to remark, reality lay with the forms or essences or Ideas which originated in God. These were the source of all intelligibility as revealed in the Word. Accordingly, everything that existed did so by virtue of the forms which subsisted in it. This essentially Platonic notion was held by nearly every important Christian thinker until Ockham; for without Ideas there could be no intelligible world over and above the world of the senses. The difference came over the precise way in which forms and their relation to matter were understood. The Augustinian universe was a universe of essences and Ideas; they made up not only each individual but inhered in each distinct aspect of it. Starting with the form of corporeity, transforming matter from the mere potentiality of Aristotle's view into a distinct quality, a series of forms were added which combined to determine the nature of a given individual: thus a man was made up of his bodily form, his animal form, and his human form. Without the first two he could not become a man. In each case he was what he was through his forms. Here, too, we recall William of Auvergne and Grosseteste's contention that the individual revealed his own essence, without their having to construct a separate theory of universals. The great difference between this view and Thomism was that it refused matter any part in the make-up of an individual: this depended entirely upon its forms; and matter, far from individuating forms, as St Thomas was to hold, was itself made individual by them. Reality was therefore synonymous with Ideas and could be grasped directly in the individual.

The other traits of Augustinianism were not necessarily all present in the same thinker; indeed they were more adjuncts to its fundamental position than its essential constituents. Among these was hylomorphism, which was a corollary of the plurality of forms in its rejection of the Aristotelian concept of prime matter as sheer potency, awaiting the actions of pure form. Hylomorphism was essentially a reaction against the Arabian separated Intelligence, the justification for which had been that it provided the forms for the material world of pure potentiality. The combination of matter and form eliminated this dependence upon a separated intelligence. This doctrine did not itself come from St Augustine but was taken over from Avicebrol. Other additions to the Augustinian corpus were St Augustine's seminal ideas, which again struck against the sheer formlessness of matter, as held by Aristotle;

instead, matter had within it germinal tendencies to receive particular forms. Finally, the Augustinians' emphasis upon the soul as the means to true knowledge went with their assertion that it was a self-subsisting being, with its own composite structure. It was therefore entirely independent of the body, not compounded with it as the Aristotelians held. In contrast to the latter, they denied the definition of the soul as the body's form.

This complex of doctrine was not confined to any one university or to any order. Certainly until about 1270 it was to be found among both the Franciscans and the Dominicans as well as secular thinkers. After that, as the impact of St Thomas Aquinas was coming to be felt, it tended to be associated primarily with the Franciscans. At Oxford, particularly, there was always a Franciscan tradition dating from Grosseteste. At Paris, the leading Franciscan teachers, like Alexander of Hales and Bonaventure, gave clearest expression to Augustinianism; and in this sense we can say that the Franciscans until the time of Duns Scotus were, as an order, Augustinian in outlook. The Dominicans, on the other hand, while not all going over to St Thomas, officially embraced Thomism in 1309.

(vi) The Franciscan school

When the Franciscans arrived at Paris in 1219, two years after the Dominicans, they met with the same influx of recruits, from both masters and scholars. Consequently, the two orders soon possessed teaching positions; and when in about 1231 Alexander of Hales, who had been a secular master for some years, joined the Franciscan order he brought them their first chair in theology. He continued as first Franciscan master at Paris until 1238. Born in England between 1170 and 1180, Alexander had studied in the arts faculty before he graduated to theology. His own work consisted of a *Commentary on the Sentences*; but he is known for the *Summa theologica* associated with his name. This was not, in fact, written by him, though his influence upon it was doubtless very great. It is a compilation by diverse hands, including

Alexander's pupil and successor John de la Rochelle, St Bonaventure, and William Meliton. Roger Bacon in his *Opus minus*
described it as 'that great summa, heavier than a horse, which
was not done by him but by others'.

Its great interest for us is that it is an outstanding example
of the reaction of the traditional theology to Aristotle and the
Arabian thinkers. Furthermore, it expresses clearly the main
positions of the Franciscan school before 1250, by which date
it must have been written, since St Bonaventure cites it. In
method the *Summa* adopted the dialectical approach of the *Sic
et Non*. This may well have been due to the direct influence of
Alexander of Hales, for in his *Commentary on the Sentences* his
distinctions were along the same syllogistic line: the question
was posed, the arguments for and against given, the solution
arrived at, and the objections answered. Secondly, the sources
of the *Summa* showed a knowledge of the full Aristotelian
corpus; and here again Alexander's *Commentary* may well have
set the tone. With Aristotle's works went the works of the
Augustinian tradition, by Augustine himself, Boethius, the
Pseudo-Denys, St Bernard, Gilbert de la Porrée, Alan of Lille,
and others.

The main features of the *Summa* were, firstly, that it upheld
divine Ideas as the source of all being. These, in contrast to
Avicenna and Avicebrol, were not through a separated Intelligence but directly from God. 'The first essence has no need
of a model; there is no other model but itself.' These Ideas
are the forms of the things in which they subsist. Hence we
have a strongly Platonic view of reality, but in a Christian
setting, with God as the immediate cause. Secondly, the
Arabian teaching of an active intellect separated from the
passive intellect is rejected, and in its place the two are joined
together in a single soul. 'The active intellect and the passive
intellect are two different intellects in the same soul.' Knowledge is derived from the active intellect working upon the
images presented to it and illumined by God. Thus we see
forcibly how Augustinianism was modified by the new knowledge. The concepts of an active intellect and abstraction,
which came with Aristotle, were incorporated into the

Augustinian principle of divine illumination: God Himself replaces the separated intellect as the cause of intellectual understanding, and abstraction is introduced to describe the way in which the human soul operates under God's influence. The danger to the individual soul which the separated intellect presented has been nullified by endowing the soul with its own active intellect.

We see the same interaction of Jewish thought upon the West in the *Summa's* adoption of hylomorphism. This is not the universal matter of Avicebrol, but a separate form and matter for all beings, spiritual as well as corporeal. 'It must be declared that although, according to certain philosophers, the intelligence which is an angel is a form without matter, it seems that it should be said to be composed of matter and form.' This spiritual form and matter in angels corresponded to the active and passive intellects in the soul.

The *Summa* hardly leaves us in doubt that there was an Augustinian outlook before 1250 and that it was very largely in response to Aristotle and Islam. Some historians have questioned the existence of an Augustinian school at this time, while others have been unwilling to recognize it as Augustinian but rather as Aristotle neoplatonized. The first position seems untenable if by Augustinian is meant adherence to the primacy of faith in knowledge, with the soul as the recipient of divine truth. The second view leads to the most arid approach to thought by dissecting and labelling the constituents of an outlook while neglecting to judge it in its totality. From a strictly philosophical point of view it is hard to attribute one concept to any medieval thinker, from St Augustine onwards, which is not to be found in Plato, Aristotle, the Stoics, or Boethius. Their originality lies in the application which they were given. While it is certainly true that Alexander's *Summa* did not distinguish the *Book of Causes* from genuine Aristotle, the Christian interpretation of its Neoplatonism is apparent as soon as we recall the treatment given to the active intellect, or to illumination, or to divine Ideas.

The relevance of the *Summa* to Augustinianism, and particularly to Franciscan thought, is seen with St Bonaventure (1221–1274). Already John de la Rochelle (*c.* 1200–1245), Alexander's pupil and colleague at Paris, had incorporated Aristotle's theory of knowledge into divine illumination. Rather in the manner of Alexander of Hales's *Summa*, he regarded both the possible and active intellects as faculties of the human soul, with the active intellect as the highest. There was a similar division between sensible and intelligible knowledge. Knowledge of sensible things was by abstraction, the active intellect illuminating the sensible forms in the imagination. Knowledge of pure truth, first principles, and of God was dependent upon an outside illumination which came from God. 'Therefore in regard to the highest truth and its intelligibles which are beyond the human intellect, God is called the active intellect.'

St Bonaventure (John of Fidanza) was born near Viterbo in Tuscany in 1221 and entered the Franciscan order when he was seventeen years old; he subsequently studied at Paris, where for two years he was the pupil of Alexander of Hales. From 1248 until 1255 he taught theology there, occupying the chair which Alexander had first gained for the Franciscans. In 1255 the great struggle at Paris between the Friars and the seculars broke out, and there was an interruption to teaching. The attempt of the secular masters under William of St Amour to drive out the mendicant teachers, however, failed; and in 1257 the Pope appointed Bonaventure and Thomas Aquinas to the Franciscan and Dominican chairs respectively. But already for Bonaventure the years of study and learning were past: he had been elected general of his order, and until his death in 1274 he was involved in the world of affairs. St Bonaventure, therefore, was only thirty when he wrote his main work, his *Commentary on the Sentences*. Unlike St Thomas, he was never in a position to take the full measure of Aristotle's growing importance, although he shows a wide acquaintance with the philosopher's works. In addition to his *Commentary*, Bonaventure's other main writing was his mystical treatise on *The Journey of the Soul into God*.

The name of St Bonaventure is usually coupled with that

of St Thomas Aquinas as one of twin peaks in medieval thought; and to a great degree the association is justified. They were the foremost exponents of the divergent ways of tradition and innovation; their works were the fullest expression of Augustinianism, on the one hand, and Christian Aristotelianism on the other; they showed the different responses which were possible to the same challenge. Yet when all this has been said, it remains equally true that St Bonaventure and St Thomas defy comparison in almost every respect; their approach, their methods, their assumptions, their purposes, were so far apart, that we are really confronted with two different species of thought.

A great deal of controversy has been raised over the nature of St Bonaventure's outlook; it has been regarded as so theological that it contains no philosophy worthy of the name, while, again, its primarily theological preoccupations have been made the occasion for abstracting its more directly philosophical aspects. This great emphasis upon Bonaventure as a theologian seems to be misplaced when it is used to mark him off, in some way, from his Franciscan contemporaries. It is hard to see where Bonaventure, either in his notions or in his attitude, is so strikingly at variance with those displayed in, say, the *Summa* of Alexander Hales. He, rather, gives greater point to the common outlook of his school, which goes back through thinkers like William of Auvergne, the Victorines, St Bernard, St Anselm, to St Augustine himself.

This outlook can be simply described as the primacy of faith. It makes all knowledge, in the intelligible meaning of the term, dependent upon revealed truth which is from the divine gift of grace. As a result, all wisdom, the awareness of first principles, and above all of God, lies outside the sensible world and can come only to those who believe. Such is the declaration of faith which characterizes all Augustinianism; it differs from Thomism in making truth *ipso facto* revealed truth, and knowing conditional upon grace. This refusal to recognize the aid of things natural in reaching God is, *par excellence*, theological, and, in that sense, to look for a separate philosophical level is to do violence to the greater part of medieval thinking.

What we can expect to find, in Bonaventure no less than in St Thomas, is the rational elaboration of these positions. But they remain elaborations; they have no meaning when taken in themselves, for they are essentially attempts to explain man and the world in theological terms.

St Bonaventure is outstanding for the pitch to which he brings this all-pervading theological approach. He subordinates all ideas to the overriding end of loving God; the arguments he uses in its support are not in themselves strikingly new; and, doctrinally, we can best describe his outlook as the culmination of the Augustinianism which we have already encountered in Alexander of Hales and John de la Rochelle. Indeed, for his part, Bonaventure regarded himself first and foremost as the disciple of Alexander of Hales. In his preface to the second book of his *Commentary on the Sentences* he wrote: 'Just as in the first book I adhered to the general judgements and opinions of the masters, especially my well-remembered master and father, brother Alexander, so in the following books I shall not turn back from their path . . . I do not, moreover, wish to combat new opinions, but to develop old ones.' Faith is his starting-point in a threefold progression towards knowledge of God: 'The order is to begin from the stability of faith through the serenity of reason to contemplation.' Therefore reason at a philosophical level, of natural knowledge unenlightened by faith, cannot reach truth. In neglecting to start with faith, the philosophers have failed to achieve contemplation. 'This truth [revelation], so open and luminous for the faithful, has escaped the wisdom of the philosopher' (*Sentences*, Bk. II, 1). Lack of faith is the root of the mistakes of Plato, Aristotle, and the other pagan philosophers. Bonaventure's reply, like Grosseteste's before him, was that of the Christian believer, not the philosopher. Through Adam's sin man had lost his capacity to contemplate God directly; it now needed an effort of will which could only be sustained by grace. Thus, as with St Augustine, to know the truth was a condition of the will; it needed supernatural help. There was in the will a natural inclination towards the good; this 'innate light' or disposition did not of itself suffice to discern the good from the bad; to transcend the moral limits of this world, grace was required; only by its agency could the supernatural life be reached, and without it 'the works of man are vain'. It was 'the root, form, and end of virtues joining everything to a final end . . . it keeps order in the diversity of things to be loved and itself possesses unity in leading to a single end and the first object of love' (*Sentences*, II, 25). In short, truth was love and love was supernatural.

Now the whole of St Bonaventure's outlook is governed by what has been called exemplarism. That is to say, all creation was a sign of God. This in itself was not confined to Bonaventure; in a very different way it was also true of St Thomas. The difference, however, was that for St Bonaventure a creature was to be regarded only insofar as it provided a trace of God; it was to be considered not in itself but in divine terms. This supernatural approach to truth led to the same neglect of the validity of the sensible objects as that which characterized St Augustine. Nature in itself can confirm our belief inasmuch as it is open testimony to God's work; when seen with the eyes of faith, its beauty and its order redound to God's glory: 'things are made in view of the glory of God, not to acquire or augment it, but to display it' (*Ibid*.). But so far as truth and knowledge of God are concerned we have to look elsewhere – to the immaterial principles and Ideas residing in the soul.

Bonaventure proceeds along the same lines as St Augustine and St Anselm in finding direct knowledge of God in the soul. He adopts, as they did, the Platonic notion that reality rests with Ideas. The very fact that we have a knowledge of being must mean that it exists; we can only judge the state of particular beings through having absolute being as our reference: 'Unless, then, being in itself is known, the definition of any substance cannot fully be known.' 'How would the intellect know that a being was deficient and incomplete if it had no knowledge of a being without any deficiency?' (*Itinerarium*, 3, 3). This argument of an absolute standard recalls Anselm; and Bonaventure follows Richard of St Victor and Alexander of Hales in accepting the ontological proof of

God's existence, drawing upon Richard to counter the objections of Gaunilo and in his own day of St Thomas.

The lineage of St Bonaventure's thought, then, is plain: it is that all truth is immaterial, borne by the divine Ideas which reside in God. They are the expression of God's own essence, which, in opposition to the pagans, is the cause of all multiplicity; while He remains 'the most pure, most actual, most complete and absolute' being. The divine Ideas manifest God's creative will, whose actions, again contrary to the Neoplatonists, are completely free: 'The Idea in God, according to its reality, is divine Truth, and in accordance with our mode of knowing, the resemblance of the thing known; this resemblance is the direct cause of the act of knowing the universal or the individual, though in itself it is no more universal or singular than God' (*In Hexameron*, XII, 11).

So far, we are in a world of Ideas or essences which are the bearers of all reality as communicated by God. It is to these ideas that we must turn for knowledge of the truth, or as Bonaventure calls it, wisdom. 'This wisdom is transmitted to everything, because a thing, insofar as it is, by virtue of the property which it is contains the rule of divine wisdom and manifests it' (*ibid.*, XII, 20 and 21). To reach this wisdom it is necessary to turn away from things to their Ideas as found in the soul.

It is in the working out of this path to wisdom that Bonaventure has to go beyond Augustine and Anselm, and it is in doing so that we are able to recognize his differences from them. Unlike his predecessors he cannot stop at intelligible reality and turn away from the sensible world; he has to account for the new philosophical aspects of knowledge, even while holding to the primacy of faith. His thought displays that same dualism between the intelligible and the sensible which characterized all Augustinianism in the thirteenth century. It involves the elaboration of theological positions in order to account for natural processes; this makes the world of Bonaventure very different from that of St Augustine or Aquinas.

In the first place, Bonaventure held to the principle that all beings were hylomorphic. Being is made up of a common form and matter which, following Grosseteste, he identifies with light. Light is not in itself corporeal but represents the form of matter, by which matter comes into being; as it is common to being, all bodies participate in light: 'Light strictly and abstractly speaking is not a body but the form of the body.' 'Truly light is the most noble form among corporeal things ... and all bodies naturally participate in light' (*Sentences*, II, 13, 2, 2). Every creature, spiritual beings included, is made up of matter and form; only by their union can a creature exist. But, as with all the Augustinians, he ascribes a very different rôle to matter from that of Aristotle. Where Aristotle made matter the cause of individuation, the specific embodiment of the form by which it became individual, with Bonaventure matter is individuated by its own form. From this follow two conclusions. Firstly, it is the forms which impose individuation: 'The property of being an individual does not come from accidents, but from an actual union of principles, and it is in itself something substantial' (*Sentences*, II, 3, 1). Secondly, this leads to the doctrine of the plurality of forms; there must be the universal form of light before matter can come into being at all; it is then able to receive the determinations of other forms by which the individual becomes a distinct entity: ' ... there is a double aspect to corporeal matter, general and special: general by the form common to all bodies, and this form is light; special by other forms, or elements of composition' (*Sentences*, II, 13).

In addition to the determining rôle which he ascribed to forms, Bonaventure also takes up the concept of seminal reasons which St Augustine had adopted from the Stoics. This enables him to move even farther away from the Aristotelian view of matter; far from being purely formless, matter has within it a disposition to receive certain forms, and when it does so these forms come into existence. 'Other natural forms are not produced from nothing, but there is a certain active power from which they come, as from a seed plot' (*Sentences*, II, 15, 1, 1). St Bonaventure's metaphysics, then, follow his predecessors' closely, and they have an important bearing upon his view of the soul, and the manner in which it knows. Firstly, the principle of hylomorphism differentiates God, as pure act, from His creatures, as act and potency (or matter and form). This was one of the most telling points in favour of hylomorphism – the means of distinguishing between divine and created being. Secondly, the soul itself (as well as angels) was an independent substance in its own right. Like Alexander of Hales, St Bonaventure recognized explicitly the hylomorphic nature of spiritual beings. Consequently, the relationship of the soul to the body was not one of form to matter but the union of two complete beings each with its own form and matter. Not only did this mean a plurality of forms in man, but the soul itself, although directing the body, was in no way dependent upon it for its knowledge or its existence. This enabled Bonaventure to counter the Aristotelian view of the senses as the source of all knowledge, and to hold to St Augustine's concept of the soul as animating the body. 'Although the rational soul is composed of matter and form it has the desire to perfect the natural body, just as the body composed of matter and form has the desire to follow the soul' (*Sentences*, II, 17, 1, 2). Although he cedes to Aristotle that the soul receives the body's sensations, he regards this only as the signal for the soul to pass judgement on what the body has experienced; this is the way to sensible knowledge.

It is when dealing with the soul that we see clearly Bonaventure's need to take Aristotle into account, while remaining faithful to St Augustine. He is forced to recognize sensible knowledge as well as that experienced by the soul. The soul, itself, says St Bonaventure, while a single substance, is divided into faculties: a possible and an active intellect. But it is neither purely passive, like the Arabian possible intellect, nor completely active, like their separated active intellect. 'The possible intellect is not purely passive, for its has the power to turn towards the species which is found in the imagination, and, in turning towards it, to receive it through the aid of the active intellect and to judge it; and the active intellect is not entirely in act; for it can understand nothing of itself, if it is not helped by a species, which, separated from the image, can be united with it' (*Sentences*, II, 24, 1). In common with his forerunners, Bonaventure has taken the active intellect to be individual to each soul; he rejected the Arabian concept of a separated Intelligence as contrary to Catholic faith. He also makes the distinction between sensible and intelligible knowledge, which we have already noticed. So far as the former is concerned, all knowledge is by abstraction. The images which the possible intellect receives from sensible things are then made intelligible by the active intellect. But when we come to the knowledge of God and eternal truths, the senses and abstraction have no place. Aristotle is forsaken and we return to Augustine.

Bonaventure's theory of internal illumination differs from that of Alexander of Hales and John de la Rochelle in making divine Ideas, rather than God, the direct source of the soul's knowledge. ' . . . God, although the principal agent in the action of any creature, yet gives it an active faculty, by which it may carry out its own action.' The soul sees truth in and by these divine Ideas, and has no need to look beyond them. Through them it is able to know God 'without the support of the external senses'.

Supernatural knowledge, then, has to be infused, not abstracted. While the moral laws of this world can be known in the natural light of the soul, all that pertains to eternal truth comes only through divine Ideas: 'For certain knowledge the intellect has to be ruled by immutable and eternal rules, not by the state of its own intellect, but by those which are above it in eternal truth' (*De scientia Christi*, v, 23). We have returned to the initial position, that truth comes by grace; it is dependent upon God Himself, not the senses; for the latter can bear no resemblance to the eternal truths which represent 'an impression of the supreme truth upon the soul'. The highest point to which our knowledge of God can attain, contemplation, is reached only by turning away from this world of the senses until the soul is united with God. The six stages in this ascent to God, which he traces in his *Journey of the Soul*, follow the same progression, from the senses to pure intelligence, which animated his whole outlook.

Bonaventure's great achievement was in annexing Aristotle to Augustine. Unlike St Thomas's synthesis, however, his outlook retained a dualism which refused any independent rôle to sensory experience. Much of the fascination of Bonaventure's thought lies in the way in which he used Aristotle to supplement St Augustine's concepts; he is the first to make a systematic attempt to provide them with the detailed arguments which they had previously lacked. The essentially supernatural, ideal world of St Augustine is given a metaphysical support, itself largely Augustinian; the relationship between sensible and intelligible knowledge is made much more exact; philosophy, in the broadest sense, is incorporated into theology.

In all this we can see how formative Islamic and Aristotelian thought was upon the West: indeed the difference between, say, Anselm and Bonaventure is very largely the difference between Western thought before and after the entry of Aristotle. But it is also the measure of how constant Augustinianism remained to its basic tenets. As striking as Bonaventure's use of Aristotle is his subordination of him to traditional concepts: Bonaventure has no use for the Aristotelian corpus *per se*; indeed it has been said, not without truth, that, in common with all the Augustinians, he mainly took from Aristotle what was Neoplatonic. In any case, the influence of Aristotle in no way modifies the Augustinian conceptions of truth; they still see Ideas and the soul as the realm of reality; they still make all truth supernatural in its inspiration and absolute in its validity. This is particularly apparent in Bonaventure's proof for the eternity of the world in which, by calculation, he attempts to show that it must be finite and created in time. Only one for whom reason was indistinguishable from revelation would have undertaken a task which was beyond the scope of reason. St Thomas's treatment of the same question was to emphasize this. Thus, as with Anselm, Bonaventure displayed the common Augustinian tendency to regulate all knowledge by faith, to judge everything in theological terms, and to deny material sensible experience any rôle in the attainment of truth.

St Bonaventure did for Augustinianism what St Thomas was shortly to do for Aristotelianism: he welded it into a coherent body of doctrine which took account of the new philosophical knowledge and which had its own distinctive tenets. Under his influence it became general throughout the Franciscan order, prevailing until the appearance of Duns Scotus, at the end of the thirteenth century. It was largely from the positions established by Bonaventure that the struggle against the innovations of St Thomas was waged, and it is to these that we must now turn.

(vii) Christian Aristotelianism:
Albert the Great and St Thomas Aquinas

We have already mentioned that the body of doctrine known as Augustinianism was essentially one response of Christian theologians to the new knowledge. It was not in itself a self-contained or coherent system: certainly nothing that could be called a philosophy in any way distinct from faith. It did not constitute an Augustinian as opposed to an Aristotelian outlook, for the simple reason that so far no one had attempted to take over Aristotle as a distinct body of thought and contrapose it to tradition. Throughout, Christian theologians were attempting only to incorporate those aspects of Aristotle (or more frequently Avicenna) which harmonized with faith.

It is necessary to emphasize this theological adaptation of Aristotle and the Arabian thinkers if we are not to lose sight of the common framework in which all medieval thinkers, except for the 'Latin Averroists', worked. It will also help us to place the innovations which St Thomas introduced. The early Dominicans were no more inclined to adopt Aristotle wholesale than the Franciscans; nor were they any more clear over what was genuine Aristotle and what was Arabian, Jewish, or Neoplatonic Aristotle. Indeed the Dominicans, although from the first an order devoted to learning, had as late as 1228 banned the study of Aristotle in their constitutions.

Members of the order veered between acceptance of much that was new and suspicion of it. The first holder of the

Dominican chair at Paris, Roland of Cremona (who kept it for one year, from 1229 to 1230), showed the liveliest sympathy with and knowledge of Aristotle's works. But his successors, John of St Giles, Hugh of St Cher, Guerric of St Quentin, did not share his sympathies and showed strong leanings to the old theological tradition.

It is with Albert, known to his contemporaries as the Great (1206 or 7–1280), that Aristotle takes firm root in the Dominican order. He was of a noble Swabian family, and studied first in Italy and then at the Dominican school at Cologne, spending the next twelve years (1228–1240) in teaching theology at various Rhineland Dominican houses. He went to Paris in 1240 where he remained as Regent Master until 1248. It was during this time that he had St Thomas Aquinas as his pupil. Thenceforth, the greater part of his life was spent in Germany in full spate of activity.

Albert has so often been joined with Thomas Aquinas as creator of a Christian Aristotelianism that we run the risk of confusing their vast differences. His life was dedicated to making 'all parts of [Aristotle's works] intelligible to the Latin world'. 'Our intention, in natural science,' he wrote, 'is to satisfy, as far as we can, the brothers of our Order who have for many years asked us to compose such a book on Physics in which they would have both perfect natural knowledge and the means by which they could properly understand Aristotle's books.' The greater part of his work was devoted to commenting, explaining, and editing Aristotle's work with this intent. He was essentially the critical glossator rather than the original synthesizer; and his voluminous output is far more a vast compilation than a system; its value lay in the emphasis it put on Aristotle and the storehouse it provided for others, such as St Thomas, to draw upon.

Albert as a thinker is disappointing and muddled, and we do him no credit if we either judge him, or try to compare him, with Aquinas. His interests lay in observation, where, especially in zoology and botany, he made notable original contributions. He believed in the importance of experiment, and above all he upheld natural science as something different from revealed truth. This, indeed, is where Albert marks the break with his contemporaries and with tradition. He is the first Christian who is prepared to accept a rational treatment of natural phenomena; the first in the West to take over Maimonides's distinction between faith and reason. In doing so, he introduced a new approach which he did not himself exploit to anywhere near its full potential. That was to be the achievement of St Thomas.

Albert, in turning to Aristotle for his physics, metaphysics, and science, turned also from faith to reason to explain nature. He began by taking what he found rather than by accounting for it in divine terms. Theology and philosophy, he held, were two different pursuits: theology dealt with revelation, philosophy with natural experience. This meant that neither could act as the explanation for the other. It struck at the Augustinian attempt to employ reason in what lay beyond it. The truths of dogma could not of themselves be reached from ordinary human understanding, for it had no direct experience of them: 'the human soul has no knowledge of anything except of that principle which it contains within it' (*Summa Theologica*, I, iii, 13, 3). Accordingly 'from a purely natural light no one can attain to knowledge of the Trinity, the Incarnation, and the Resurrection' (*ibid.*, I, i, 1). This delimitation of knowledge is the first and most important principle of the new outlook; for it gave reason an accepted place and safeguarded faith from speculation. It therefore raised the dignity of both, in respecting what belonged to each; neither was to ride roughshod over the other, as had frequently happened in the past, from theology as well as from dialectic.

We must not, however, exaggerate the achievement of Albert's rôle here; his own philosophy is not only very hard to disengage from his writings, but he nowhere achieved the balance he advocated. He came closest to doing so in refusing to pronounce decisively on the creation of the world, its eternity, or the necessity of the spheres. All these lay outside the scope of demonstration, and, rationally, they could be, at most, only probable. Similarly, when arguing with Averroes over the unity of the human intellect, he gives thirty arguments in favour and thirty-six against,* recalling the treatment that we met in Maimonides. Elsewhere, however, Albert's world is far from Aristotelian, or rationally ascertainable; and for this reason it is with the greatest caution that he can be bracketed with St Thomas. In the first place, he works largely within a Neoplatonic universe in which he follows Avicenna more closely than any other thinker. In the second place, when the full balance has been struck, his outlook shows little difference from that of the Augustinians: his Aristotle is largely Neoplatonic and is made to harmonize with traditional concepts. Albert is still the theologian attempting to fit Aristotle within an existing structure; his thought is an eclecticism of Christian principles mingled with Jewish, Arabian, and Aristotelian concepts. To judge Albert doctrinally would be to put him among the great majority of his contemporaries, who made Aristotle an additional ingredient in an already prepared mixture.

Albert regarded the universe as a series of ten concentric spheres on the Ptolemaic model, although he recognized that this could not be proved. In many respects, Albert's universe was the substitution of God for the Arabian separated intellect. He was the source of all creation; His divine Ideas conferred distinct forms on everything and so brought matter from potency into act. These forms were the images of the divine Ideas in God. They, therefore, following Avicenna, had three aspects: as the Idea in God prior to all things (*ante rem*); as the form in things, the universal by which it can be known (*in re*); and as the form in the soul which the latter abstracts from the individual (*post rem*). This leads him to accept the conclusion that individuation is through the impress of form upon matter, since matter is the bearer of forms. 'Matter is present in everything which is determined, for it is the principle which confers its individuation on a thing' (*Metaphysica*, XI, i, vii), but 'form is the universal being, not matter' (*De intellectu*, I, 2, 3). He is not, however, clear whether there is more than one form in each individual, though he opposes hylomorphism.

* *De unitate intellectus contra Averroistas*, v, 185.

So far as man is concerned, Albert holds to Avicenna's view that soul is a spiritual substance, in its own right; although it is the form of the body, this refers to its function and not to its own nature. By this means, Albert considers that he has resolved the opinions of Plato and Aristotle wherein lies the highest attainment possible to wisdom. 'Considering the soul in itself, we agree with Plato; but considering it as the form of animation which it gives to the body, we agree with Aristotle.' As a spiritual being, the soul is itself composed of its own principles of individuation: this he explains from Boethius's distinction between the substance (*quod est*) and the form by which it is (*quo est*). Following William of Auvergne, he holds that God actualizes the *quod est* already existing by conferring upon it the *quo est* by which it becomes a soul. We are therefore back at Avicenna's original concept of necessary and possible being: since all that is not God is dependent upon a form to make it actual, this is the function of the *quo est*.

It is over the unity of the soul that Albert sharply separates himself from the Arabian thinkers. Again, like William of Auvergne, Alexander of Hales, Bonaventure, and others, he attributes both a possible and an active intellect to each individual. The soul, as we have just seen, is a separate substance; therefore, it is self-directing and independent of an external intelligence. Moreover, as the image of God, through the forms received from Him, the soul is illumined by God's Ideas. 'There is an absolutely separated Intellect, the Intellect of the Intelligence, of which the human intelligence is a certain image' (*Metaphysica*, XI, i, ix). Having once established God as the cause of the soul's knowledge, Albert is able to take over the Arabian explanation of abstraction by which the possible intellect, in itself a *tabula rasa*, is able to understand the images abstracted from sensible objects in the light of the active intellect. In this way, the sensible forms are rendered intelligible. All knowledge, therefore, is from abstraction and consists in a progression from things to understanding, which transcends them, to knowledge of God Himself.

Albert, consequently, rejects all separation between the illumination in the soul and the experiences of the senses, without rejecting illumination itself. He keeps the way open for an ascending order of knowledge in the light of the knowledge given by God, although he rejects the ontological proof for His existence. Thus it is not surprising that Albert gave rise to a distinct stream of thought: for all his attempts to incorporate Aristotle he had remained much closer to Neoplatonism. It was upon the German mystics, Hugh and Ulrich of Strasbourg and Dietrich of Freiburg, that his most direct influence was to be felt.

With Thomas Aquinas (1226–1274) we come to the real watershed between the old and the new. What Albert had hinted at, St Thomas achieved. He took the two decisive steps that meant the substitution of Christian Aristotelianism for Augustinianism. The first was the separation of faith from reason: the second was to make the senses the source of all human knowledge. Now it was St Thomas's readiness to accept the senses as sovereign for man in his human state that made this achievement possible. Until he appeared, every theologian had boggled at the thought of Aristotle because they could not reconcile the transitoriness of this world with the eternity in God. Terms such as form and matter, act and potentiality, all invoked movement and change, coming into being and going out of existence; they represented a world of becoming. How could they, then, have any application to God? At the most, Aristotle's descriptions were conceded for this world, but they could have no bearing on the reality beyond it. Nor was this all: we must remember that Aristotle's cosmology meant a world without a creator and man without a soul. These, too, were very real threats to a Christian outlook. It is not surprising, then, that Aristotle was not very readily taken to the hearts of Christian thinkers. The depth of the opposition to him is to be seen in the reactions to St Thomas.

Yet it is easy to exaggerate the gulf between Thomism and tradition. Both he and Albert the Great have been regarded as the liberators of mankind, the precursors of Descartes, the revivers of philosophy and reason as independent pursuits. Were they, in fact, so different in their aims or conclusions from their contemporaries? In the first place, we can all agree that for the first time reason became endowed with its own domain, and that, as a result, both faith and reason benefited. We have already stressed that the lack of demarcation between faith and reason, on the part of the Augustinians, put both in peril, with each at the mercy of the other. But this is not the same as saying that reason now became either independent or sovereign.

The foundation of Thomism was that reason supplemented faith, not denied it. St Thomas's own system is the most lasting testimony to knowledge in the service of belief. But it was not knowledge in its own right or for itself. It was directed to proving the truth of revelation. Indeed the safety-valve of Thomism was his refusal to stretch reason beyond its limits: hence when two arguments seemed equally probable, there could be no final judgement by reason. It then was left as a matter for faith. In the same way, it was a purely Christian interpretation to endow the first mover with the attributes of God as creator; from the point of view of pure reason, there is no more *evidence* for seeing Him as God than as first cause. St Thomas's Christian purpose can be seen equally in his theory of analogy, by which the creature bore resemblance to the creator. This is not to deny the validity of St Thomas's discussions on these subjects; but it is to deny that they come from the sheer undirected play of rational concepts, without assumptions or intentions. They are as much from a Christian theologian seeking to harness knowledge to faith as the arguments of Bonaventure or Augustine.

This brings us to the second point: St Thomas did not stand for the sudden inundation of philosophy into what had previously been theology; on the contrary he was for a separation of their two streams so that each could follow its own course the better. He was first and foremost a theologian giving a theological response to non-theological knowledge. He differed from his contemporaries in method, not as a philosopher amongst theologians.

Finally, when we come to the pure philosophers of the arts faculty – the 'Averroists' – we can see how impossible it was to have an independent philosophy without endangering faith. The gulf between St Thomas and Descartes is the Paris Condemnations of 1270 and 1277, where reason had to accede to the dictates of faith or be damned. St Thomas never showed the least inclination to cross it.

Nonetheless, St Thomas was the clearest thinker and the boldest innovator in scholasticism: his range and his phenomenal capacity for synthesis give his system a harmony and a sweep which for sheer intellectual achievement have a beauty all their own. St Thomas's thought has often been likened to a Gothic cathedral, and, at the risk of banality, their common sweep and proportion, balance and harmony, may be reiterated.

St Thomas was born of a noble family at Aquino, near Naples in 1225 or 1226; for nine years (1230–1239) he lived in the monastery at Monte Cassino, but did not become a monk. He first studied at Naples University, and in 1244 entered the Dominican order. After being held captive by his brothers for over a year, on his way to Paris, he eventually reached the University there in 1245. He studied theology under Albert the Great, with whom he went to Cologne in 1248. In 1252 he returned to Paris to teach theology, becoming a regent master in 1256 at the same time as Bonaventure. He had already been initiated into Aristotle when a student at Naples, but it was when he went back to Italy, in 1259, that his study of the philosopher really began. During the ten years he was there (1259–1268), he undertook, with the aid of the translations of his confrère, William Moerbeke, to comment Aristotle's works. These commentaries included the *Interpretation*, *Posterior Analytics*, *Physics*, *Metaphysics*, *Ethics*, the *Soul*, the *Meteors*, the *Heavens*, the *Generation*, the *Politics*. He then spent another three years as regent in Paris until 1272, from where he was once more recalled to the papal court in Italy. He died in 1274.

St Thomas's writings, in addition to his Commentaries on Aristotle, on Proclus, and the Pseudo-Denys, and a series of *Questions* on fundamental topics, comprised three great works: his *Commentary on the Sentences*, which dates from his second stay at Paris (1253); his *Summa against the gentiles*, written while in Italy (1259–1264), and his *Summa theologica*, started in 1266 and never completed. His *Sentences* were the fruit of his early studies in theology, when his ideas were still in formation; his *Summa against the gentiles* is his most complete exposition of his system in rational terms: for, as its title tells us, it was a work of apology, to explain the Catholic faith. His *Summa theologica* was a synthesis of his whole work designed as an introduction to it; it therefore lacked the intricacy of argument, and proof, over positions which had already been established in his *Summa against the gentiles*. In addition to these, St Thomas, by having a clear understanding of what was not Aristotle, was the first to identify the so-called *Book of Causes* with Proclus's *Elements of Theology*. He also wrote treatises against the Averroists, *On the unity of the intellect*; against the Augustinian opposition to his own doctrines; *Against the Murmurers*; and against William of St Amour, *Contra impugnantes Dei cultum*.

St Thomas's system is too complex and too individual to be described as simply Aristotle Christianized, even though Aristotle was undoubtedly the most formative influence in Thomism. Not only were there other important elements, especially from St Augustine and Neoplatonism, but, in our search for categories, we risk missing what is new. Perhaps we can best describe St Thomas's outlook by saying that, whereas all Christian thinkers before him had sought to explain the effect by the cause, he started with the effect: that is, instead of trying to explain God in His own transcendent terms, he began with what could be known from His creatures. He did not dismiss the sensible world as a shadow and its existence as unreal; but as the surest evidence open to us of reality. He turned the Augustinian world upside down, working from the individual to the universal, from effect to cause. In this sense he was the first medieval thinker really to act upon the Christian truth that God had created the world, for he took it as God's work and man's surest evidence of Him.

We have already stressed that for St Thomas theology and reason were both distinct and yet complementary; and this indeed was the clearest expression of his outlook. The identity of reason sprang from the separate identity of sensible reality; its subordination to, and ultimate harmony with, revelation expressed God's sovereignty as creator. The relation between faith and reason, therefore, marked at once the essential difference and the inherent unity between God and His creatures. Accordingly, St Thomas, like Albert, made a sharp distinction between the two: faith came from revelation, and dealt with divine truths which were not accessible to reason; reason, on the other hand, had to start with what could be known through experience and demonstration.*

Now it has often been implied that the difference between faith and reason was also that between philosophy as such, on the one hand, and theology, on the other. But the two cases are not the same, and their confusion has probably been the main cause of the false distinction that many historians have made between medieval philosophy and medieval theology. A believer who uses reason to support revelation is doing so with a theological, not a philosophical, end in view. He is not following reason for its own sake, but to support certain particular assumptions. He is in fact building up a natural theology, a theology based upon rational argument.

This is where St Thomas made his great contribution to medieval thought; for, although he also completed and clarified much of St Augustine's positions in dogma, he did so as a theologian, accepting the validity of revealed truth. As a natural theologian, however, St Thomas utilized reason to support revelation. He himself recognized the distinction between 'the philosopher [who] considers creatures in that which relates to their own nature, as for example fire', and 'the believer [who] considers them in so far as they are related to God, as for example, that they are created by Him' (*Contra Gentiles*, II, 4). As a pure philosopher, interested in nature for itself, St Thomas followed Aristotle very closely. It was when he turned to it as creation that he took his own path.

The whole of Thomist thinking is governed by the primacy

*See *Summa Theologica*, 1ᵃ, q.32, a.1.

of being, and this, for St Thomas, meant sensible reality. This was the starting-point in all knowledge: 'First in the intellect's conception is being, because by it everything knowable exists in so far as it is in act; hence being is the proper object of the intellect; and thus is the first intelligible, just as sound is the first audible' (*Summa Theol.*, 1ᵃ, q. v, a.2). This has two very important consequences: the first is that from being we are able to arrive at certain guiding principles; and, secondly, only through being can we come to knowledge.

In the first case, St Thomas is able to formulate a number of axioms which govern all our thinking: the principle of contradiction: 'that being cannot be non-being', so that we cannot 'at once affirm and deny'; the principle of *raison d'être*, 'that everything which is has its justification in itself, if it exists in itself, in another if it does not exist by itself'; the principle of substance where 'all that which exists as the subject of existence is substance' and is distinguished from its accidents; the principle of efficient causality by which every contingent being (that is, one dependent upon another) has an efficient cause; the principle of finality by which 'everything acts on account of an end', and which, expressed in ethics, means to do good and avoid evil. St Thomas therefore founded all intelligibility upon being: its principles and the laws of reason sprang from the experience of reality. In his own words 'nothing exists in the intellect unless first in the senses'. His entire natural theology derived from applying concepts taken from sensible reality.

The greatness of the revolution that this constituted can be seen in his solution to the nature of being itself. From the time of Parmenides and Heraclitus the contradiction between the flux of the sensible world and the stability of our ideas had called forth varying answers. Medieval thinkers, as we have seen, had in general followed St Augustine in upholding Plato's interpretation, suitably modified. It made reality correspond to Ideas. This outlook had guided the majority of Augustinian thinkers, especially Anselm and Bonaventure. For St Thomas, however, the solution lay in Aristotle's analysis of being as made up of potency and act. Although we have had cause to discuss these concepts frequently, they had never been given the central position which St Thomas attributed to them. He resolved the antinomy between non-being, or imperfect being, and actual being, into different states of being: potency was still undetermined being, which had not received a form. It was therefore in a state of becoming, neither nothing nor imperfect being, but unrealized.

The importance of this outlook on all St Thomas's thought can hardly be exaggerated. In the first place, it made being the act of the form; the form transformed what was in potentiality into actuality. 'The form gives being to the thing.' In the second place, St Thomas conceives being as hylomorphic, made up of form and matter combined; for since the form gives being, there must be something to receive it, something to bring into act. 'Those which agree as species but differ in number, agree in form, but are distinguished materially' (*Summa Theol.*, 1ᵃ, q. L., a.4). Matter, therefore, is the principle of individuation in so far as it defines and delimits the forms which it contains. It is 'the principle of diversity among individuals of the same species'. This is not to say that matter and form are the same; on the contrary, they are really distinct, corresponding to the distinction between potency and act; and 'matter of itself has neither being, nor is knowable' (*Summa Theol.*, 1ᵃ, q. xv, a.3).

The reintroduction of Aristotle's view of individuation by matter was of the first importance for Thomism; it showed that the individual thing was a distinct entity in its own right, which, without matter, would not exist. It struck a blow at the Neoplatonic view of the individual as the ultimate reflection of the universal, and of matter with its own form. Moreover, St Thomas, in making existence come through the union of matter and form, rejected a plurality of forms. Instead, like Aristotle, he held to the unity of the substantial form. 'Therefore every created substance is composed of potentiality and act, that is of that by which it is and being [form] . . . in the way that white is composed of that which is white and whiteness' (*Quodlibet*, III, a.20).

This view rested upon regarding form as the act which

determines being; to have more than one form is to invite one of two alternatives: either to destroy the unity of an individual by giving it several essences, or to posit a series of forms none of which is in itself sufficiently perfect to bestow being, and which are capped by a substantial form – as humanity in man is added to animality, corporeity, and so on. The latter had been the solution given by the Augustinians, usually implicitly. For St Thomas, however, this was the essence of Platonism in its identification of abstractions with independent reality. As we shall see, it made for a very different interpretation of the human soul.

Thirdly, the difference between potency and act led to the difference between God and His creatures; and it is here, if anywhere, that we can see the striking novelty of St Thomas's approach. It will be remembered that Avicenna had first put forward the difference between essence and existence to show that, while the two were the same in God, in His creatures existence was but an accident of essence, since it need not be included in essence. Averroes had combated Avicenna's view by holding that it went against Aristotle's dictum, that 'the substance of anything whatever is the existence of that thing'. Clearly, in a very real sense, to adopt Avicenna's formulation was to open the way to a world of essences, whose existence was independent of whether or not they subsisted in sensible things; on the other hand, Averroes saw no difference between the two states.

St Thomas, as so often, found a mean. He followed Averroes in seeing existence as inseparable from essence so far as individuals were concerned; but he in turn made existence the actuality of essence. That is to say, essence was to existence as matter is to form: the individual was the result of their union. 'Being is an accident, not as an accident in itself, but as the actuality of any substance' (*Quodlibet*, II, a.3). Anything, therefore, must have a cause if it is to come into being. Now this involves either passing from potency into act, and hence having an efficient cause, or moving oneself, that is, to be self-caused. Everything created must have an external cause, from which it receives its existence, passing from potency to act. For the creator, on the other hand, as first cause, existence is included in His essence: for otherwise He in turn would be dependent upon another cause. Thus all that of which we have experience, since it is a composition of form and matter, potency and act, must be contingent being. This means it must have a cause from which it holds its existence. In other words, the distinction between essence and existence leads us to God by way of analogy and causality.

So far as analogy is concerned, all things, St Thomas held, had being in common. Although there could be no direct comparison between a substance and its accidents, they both shared the common state of existence. All things, therefore, in so far as they exist, are analogous as beings, even though their degrees of being vary. Being is not a nature, or a genus, but a resemblance in a diversity of aspects. The contrast between this and Duns Scotus's view of being, as univocal, will be an important one. By analogy, we are able to define God Himself: for if He is both essence and existence, He must be without potentiality – pure act. As pure act He must be self-subsisting, independent of all determinations or additions. Therefore, He may be described as Being itself.* We shall discuss the implications of this definition shortly. First, however, we must examine causality.

We have already mentioned that the distinction between essence and existence means that a being is contingent, dependent upon an efficient cause. It is upon this principle of causality that St Thomas puts forward his five proofs for the existence of God (*Summa Theol.*, 1ᵃ, q. 11, a.3). Despite their differences, they all have in common the two traits we have just noted: they start from being, and from contingency; they therefore approach God from His effects in the sensible world. The first proof elaborates the axiom, 'that all that is moved is moved by another', to show that this must imply either an infinite chain of cause and effect or a first cause. Since there cannot be a regression to infinity, there must be a first cause, which is God. The second proof starts from the existence of efficient causes, each necessary to the other (such as a hand to

*See *Summa Theol.*, 1ᵃ, q. VII. a.1 and 1ᵃ, q. XIV and XIX.

push a stick). These, too, must have a supreme cause to maintain their essential sequence: this is God. The third proof
follows from Avicenna's distinction between necessary being
and contingent being. As we have already seen, while necessary being has no cause but itself, contingent being is
dependent upon an external cause. This necessary being must
be God. The fourth proof makes use of analogous qualities
in things, which they hold in varying degrees, and which presuppose an absolute standard. Thus goodness, beauty, truth
all have an ultimate source, which is God. The fifth proof
returns to Aristotle's final cause, where all things, quite
spontaneously, seek an end which can only be God, their
maker.

As we have remarked, the sequence has been from the
finite and imperfect being to the infinite and perfect being.
St Thomas's God is very different from Aristotle's 'Thought
of Thought'. He is firstly Being in its plenitude, 'I am that
I am' of the Bible. He is active creative being, and strictly
speaking creation is the conferring of being upon what is
outside Him. Secondly, then, God and His creatures are
linked by their participation in being: a creature is by virtue
of receiving from God what pre-exists in Him. Accordingly,
God as first act is in all things, moving His creatures from
potentiality to actuality; and it is in this sense that their being
is analogous to His. There is, therefore, a far more marked
degree of divine determinism in St Thomas's system than we
have so far encountered. For the first time the relationship between God and His creatures has been ordered as one of
direct cause and effect, with God, as first cause, included in
every action of His creatures.

It is here that we reach the Platonic elements of St Thomas's
thought. We have already mentioned that the analogy between
God and His creatures comes from the latter's participation
in His being. This not only enables us to gain a faint glimmer-
ing of God's attributes, His will, perfection, goodness,
omniscience, omnipotence, and so on; but it means that God's
creatures must be the result of the archetypes which He has
of them. They can only come about by His willing them.

Once more, St Thomas takes a mean way between the Aristotelians and the Platonists. For Aristotle, as for Averroes, God
knew only Himself, since to know anything outside Himself
would imply imperfection. The Neoplatonists, on the other
hand, including Avicenna, separated the first Intelligence from
God, making it the source of all forms. St Thomas accepts the
Neoplatonic view of Ideas as the archetypes of all things, but
follows St Augustine in making them inseparable from the
divine essence. 'God does not see things in themselves, but
inasmuch as His essence contains the resemblance of other
things.' He further marks himself off from the Neoplatonists
by holding, with William of Auvergne, that divine Ideas are
in no way independent spiritual substances: 'Universals do
not have being in the nature of things as universals, but only
in so far as they are individuated' (*De Anima*, art. 1 and 2).
They are in the Word through God's self-knowledge; for by
knowing Himself He knows all things, past, present, and
future, eternally. He even knows free future actions without
determining them, since they are ever-present in Him. Thus
'all things must pre-exist in the Word of God before they
exist in their own nature. That which is in a thing is in it
according to the mode of that thing and not according to its
own: the house exists in the architect intelligibly and
immaterially; and so must be understood things pre-existing
in the Word according to the mode of the Word' (*Contra
Gentiles*, IV, xiii). God's knowledge, therefore, is the ultimate
source of being as given effect by His will, freely and immu-
tably. His simplicity is preserved and yet His omni-causality
is assured.

We are now in a position to examine the application of
St Thomas's metaphysics to the higher intelligences and to
man. For St Thomas, the angels are the higher intelligences:
unlike material beings, they are pure form without any
material composition – the highest created beings. They are
distinguished both from God and from material creatures: so
far as God is concerned, they differ in the distinction between
their essence and existence; although they are in act, they are
still dependent upon God for their being. Hence, the safeguard

between God's being, where essence and existence are one, and that of immaterial creatures is maintained. 'In intellectual substances there is a composition of act and potency; not of form and matter but from form and participated being' (*Summa Theol.*, 1ª, q. 75, a.5). In comparison with other creatures, therefore, the angels differ as beings without matter and so without individuation. Strictly speaking, then, each angel is a species. Moreover, as spiritual beings, they are able to have a direct knowledge of reality without the need of discursive thought.

Man, on the other hand, is both a material and spiritual being, composed of a body and a soul. His soul is his form and thereby the act of his being. It was here that St Thomas's theory of potency and act created greatest opposition, for, in this world, it made the soul no longer an independent spiritual being, with its own spiritual form and matter, but the form of the body – actively united with matter. St Thomas saw the soul as dependent upon the body for its experience and for its knowledge, thus closing the Augustinian path of direct spiritual illumination by God. 'I say that there is no other substantial form in man than the intellective soul, and that as it contains virtually the sensitive and vegetative souls, so it contains virtually all inferior forms' (*Summa Theol.*, 1ª, q. 75, a.4). Thus the substantial form is sovereign, subsuming all inferior faculties. As St Thomas has said, 'the form gives being to the thing'.

The human soul, then, was very different for St Thomas as compared with, say, Bonaventure. It was dependent upon the body, its knowledge was from sensibles, and it was in itself devoid of innate ideas. The object of man's intellect was, as we have already said, being – things as they existed. Man's understanding was not, therefore, spontaneously directed towards God; he was dependent upon abstraction for his knowledge of immaterial forms. The latter, as we have seen, exist only in things, as their act, and in disengaging them from their individuals we are able to reach intelligible knowledge. This is the rôle of the active intellect, the highest faculty in the soul. In its light, the sensible species, already in the possible intellect, are made intelligible. Thus the soul itself is in potency when the sensible objects are presented to it; only when it has received their images (in the possible intellect) can the active intellect disengage them of all their individual properties and so render them intelligible. 'And this is to abstract the universal from the particular, or intelligible species from the images, namely, to consider the nature of the species without considering the individual principles which are represented by the image' (*Summa Theol.*, 1ª, q. 85, a.1).

The mode of man's knowledge has a very real bearing upon his nature and his place in creation. He is last in the spiritual hierarchy passing from angel to angel. His own soul still links him with the spiritual beings, but it is also joined with a material body. It cannot, therefore, share the angels' immediate participation in the divine light. Man's own active intellect, which is the faintest glimmer of God's illumination, can only function by means of sensible experience. Yet, by its agency, he has the power to trace intelligible reality along the path back to God. Hence man's understanding shows his intermediate position between the spiritual and the material. It is evidence both of the soul's spirituality and of its immortality, joined though it is to a corruptible body in this world. 'That which operates independently of matter correspondingly exists and comes into being (or, rather, is produced) independently of matter.' This in turn means that it must be immortal. 'The intellect apprehends itself absolutely for all time. Wherefore everything having an intellect desires always to exist. But this natural desire cannot be in vain. Therefore every intellectual substance is incorruptible' (*Summa Theol.*, 1ª, q. 75, a.6).

Man's nature, then, prevents him from direct contact with intelligible reality or with God, but he can, as we have seen, attain to first principles through sensible reality. St Thomas's moderate realism – the existence of the universal in things, not in itself – is very different from Abelard's; it is founded upon reality, while Abelard's came from logic. Moreover, it provided real criteria for what could be and could not be known. Not only did it lead to St Thomas's rejection of Anselm's ontological argument, but also to Bonaventure's proofs for the

creation of the world in time. Whilst St Thomas was prepared
to accept the evidence for its creation, its duration was beyond
the scope of metaphysical reality. It could only be believed as
a matter of faith. 'It is [a matter] for belief that the world had a
beginning, but it is not demonstrable or knowable' (*Summa
Theol.*, 1ª, q. 46, a.2).

In man's moral judgements, we have already mentioned
St Thomas's principle that good is to be done and evil
shunned. The object of the will is good as such, and it tends
spontaneously towards it. Man's reason is the cause of his free
will, for only by the intellect can he act from free judgement.
Accordingly 'the radical cause of all liberty is reason' (*De
Veritate*, q. 24, a.2); in it lies his power to choose freely. But
to remain free from sin, to believe, to love God, and to achieve
meritorious actions it is necessary to be infused with grace.
'Grace does not abolish nature, but perfects it.' St Thomas
follows the same balance between morally attainable virtues,
such as prudence and temperance, and the supernaturally
infused virtues of faith, hope, and charity.* All these constitute habits, or states, which dispose their bearers towards their
particular object. Man in his state of sin, although he can
acquire certain natural habits for good, is dependent upon
supernaturally infused habits if he is to transcend the limits of
this world. Similarly, he can also acquire evil habits; and sin
itself St Thomas regards 'as an act or a word or a desire contrary to the eternal law'. Original sin, however, is distinguished as being transmitted by human nature; 'it is a lack of
original justice by which the will is substituted for God'
(*Summa Theol.*, 1ª 11ᵃᵉ, q. 82, a.3). Thus, like all sin, it is a privation, strictly speaking non-being, and, far from coming from
God, it is the measure of the gulf between His infinite
perfection and His imperfect creatures.

(viii) Philosophy and the Arts Faculty

How far removed Thomism was from philosophy can be
seen when we examine the pure philosophers of the arts

*See *Summa Theol.*, 1ª 11ᵃᵉ. q. 63.

faculty and the culmination of their doctrines in heresy. In order to do so, it is important to have some understanding of the way in which the arts faculty, above all at Paris, was developing. We have already mentioned that the arts course was the preparation for theology and the higher studies; that by the middle of the century it had come to consist mainly of Aristotle's works, philosophical as well as logical; and that its members therefore could study these works, with their doctrines, without needing immediately to relate them to theology. Consequently, throughout the thirteenth century we have the paradox of a group of masters and students who, although subordinate to theology, were in fact pursuing a non-theological discipline. This was the latent cause of the conflict which was to break out in 1270, though it did not in itself entail it.

The conflict came about through the changed subject-matter of the arts course. While it had remained confined to Aristotle's logical works, it could not confront theology with a rival outlook; for dialectic depended upon explaining what was already there; it was not a 'real science', independent in the way that metaphysics was. Left to itself, it could only transform grammar, not theology, and this is what it did in the hands of the dialecticians.

During the middle years of the century, a series of logical treatises was written which introduced a new form of logic: the logic of the various 'ways of signifying' (*modi significandi*). It had for its purpose to formulate the different properties in words and the differing ways in which they could be used. It tended, therefore, to reduce all grammar to a series of universal laws of meaning; it was an art, a body of rules by which understanding could be reached. The most outstanding examples of this new logic of the properties of terms were William Shyreswood (*d.* 1267), Lambert of Auxerre (*c.* 1250), and Peter of Spain (*d.* 1278). Although both William's *Introduction to Logic* and Lambert's *Dialectics* dealt with similar topics, it was the *Summulae logicales* of Peter of Spain (later Pope John XXI) which gained the greatest vogue. They were commented by a wide range of thinkers, and for the next three centuries were in universal use.

Now the work of the logicians shows two things: first, its independence of theology; it constituted as great a separation from the tenets as faith as pure Aristotle was to constitute. Secondly, its greatest threat was to language, not theology; speculative logic meant the death of style and humanism in writing, just because it regarded words in their symbolic, and not in their affective, nature. Expression as such was an accident which played no part in the functions of grammar. The prevalence of this attitude among the Artists inevitably led to the decline of style during the thirteenth century, as we have already noted. The repository of the seven liberal arts had become the home of logic and dialectic alone.

The change away from the dominance of logic comes with Aristotle's works and with the displacement of purely logical speculation by metaphysics and philosophy. To allow the latter to stand side by side with theology was to invite comparison, and conflict, with theology. The non-theological attitude of the master in arts becomes fully apparent only with philosophy.

The growth of a purely philosophical attitude was not in itself the work of unbelievers or heretics; nor were all the masters in the arts faculty supporters of the autonomy of philosophy. The masters themselves, though neither theologians nor Friars, were clerics whose task it was to teach the syllabus. They did not have to agree with Aristotle when teaching him any more than any teacher has to identify his own views with those he has to explain; and even at the height of the controversy over Aristotle, only a minority of the arts masters were pure Aristotelians. Yet, inevitably, as the course stood, Aristotle and his Arabian commentators could be regarded in their own light, independently of theology. This is what happened, with what has been called 'Latin Averroism' as its consequence.

The term 'Latin Averroism' is proving more unsatisfactory, the more the period at Paris from c. 1265 to 1277 is examined. It used to be held that the pure philosophers in the faculty of arts were the disciples of Averroes, whose interpretation of Aristotle they regarded as the only true one. Now it is clear,

both from the doctrines put forward by the leading Averroists, Siger of Brabant and Boethius of Dacia, as well as those
for which they were condemned, that these were not specifically Averroist; but rather an amalgam of the more deterministic aspects of Aristotle common to Arabian thought
generally. Where there was a very real influence from
Averroes was in the so-called 'double truth' by which the
philosophers defended their views as true for philosophy but
not for theology. Yet even this only becomes apparent after
the first condemnation of 1270, and we therefore run the risk
of narrowing down what was essentially the challenge of all
Aristotelianism into that of a single commentator.

There are two distinct but connected aspects to the growth
of an Aristotelian philosophy. The first was its connexion
with faith; the second was the doctrines themselves. In the
first case, it is important to note that the Aristotelians (or
'Averroists') were doing something very different from
St Thomas. Although St Thomas himself had followed
Averroes in dividing faith from reason, he had done so the
better to build their unity. The ultimate purpose of reason was
to support faith; it was but another route to the same destination, and if it failed to reach it, this showed that the route was
wrong, not the destination. Averroes, and those who accepted
his division, made no attempt to harmonize reason with faith.
Philosophy was to be taken at its own value, wheresoever it
might lead. Thus, in the hands of the pure philosophers,
Aristotle was an open challenge to faith. Where St Thomas
had sought to forge a link between philosophy and theology,
the pure Aristotelians snapped it.

It is not surprising, then, that Thomism itself should pass
under a cloud in view of the full implications of Aristotle's
doctrine. These doctrines had started to gain currency sometime between St Thomas's departure from Paris in 1259 and
his return there in 1269. When he left there was no suggestion
of a movement specifically associated with Arabian and
Aristotelian thought. He and Albert the Great had both
opposed Averroes in their earlier works, but from the point
of view of his errors generally rather than as a special menace.

But in 1270 St Thomas wrote *De unitate contra Averroistas*: which was especially directed at what he described as the growing error of the Averroists – a single intellect for all mankind. St Bonaventure had already in 1267 delivered the first of a series of attacks upon errors which contradicted faith. Meanwhile in the same year as St Thomas's attack Giles of Lessines, a Flemish Dominican, sent to Albert, for refutation, a series of fifteen propositions that 'the most eminent masters teach in the schools of Paris'. Thirteen of these coincided with the propositions which made up the first condemnation by the Bishop of Paris in 1270.

These may be grouped under five main heads: a single intellect for all humanity; the subjection of the human will to astral determinism; the eternity of the world; God's ignorance of individual things; and the denial of divine providence. We have met most of these before, not only in Averroes and Aristotle but in Avicenna. They constituted a denial of the fundamental tenets of Christianity: creation, in time and *ex nihilo*; God as the immediate cause of creation; the immortality of the human soul. Not all of these condemned propositions can be found in Siger of Brabant's writings, which are far from being intact; but his main positions corresponded with them.

Siger of Brabant (?1240–?1284) seems undoubtedly to have been the leader of the small band of pure philosophers. His doctrine was not simply Averroist, although he upheld its most marked trait: that the possible intellect was part of the separated active intellect, outside man; so that, strictly speaking, man's own understanding was passive, material, and corruptible – hence without personal immortality. He rejected St Thomas's distinction between essence and existence in favour of a being's capacity for existence; that is to say, once something was in being there was no means of distinguishing its essence from its existence: it simply existed. In common with the peripatetics, Siger taught the necessity of the Intelligences, the eternity of matter, and of the world, and the subjection of the human will to them.

In order to defend these views he distinguished between

the truth of revelation and the findings of the philosophers. By this means he could reserve truth for all that belonged to faith, while still expounding purely philosophical conclusions. His aim, he said, was 'to discover simply what the philosophers and especially Aristotle have thought, even if by chance the thought of philosophy did not conform with truth [revelation], and if revelation had provided our soul with conclusions which natural reason could not demonstrate'. There is no way of knowing whether Siger was sincere in his protestations of faith; in any case, they would in no way alter the undisputed distinction that he was compelled to make between faith and reason, not simply as different pursuits but as different truths. This is where the conflict lay.

The initial condemnations of the thirteen propositions in 1270 had no effect, and the growth of heterodoxy continued. The increasing vehemence of Bonaventure's denunciations, especially in his *Hexameron* (1277), the attacks written against the 'philosophers' by Giles of Rome in the *Errors of the Philosophers* and the *Purification of the Possible Intellect*, Albert the Great's rather ineffectual replies to the Averroists, in *On the Fifteen Questions* (addressed by Giles of Lessines), all bear witness to the prevailing ferment. It finally erupted in a second and decisive condemnation in 1277 by the same Bishop of Paris, Étienne Tempier.

This time 219 theses, covering every aspect of pagan philosophy, and also including courtly love, were censured. This was more than simply an attack upon Averroism, but upon the separate existence of a non-Christian philosophy; it extended to all the main theses of Arabian thinking and to several of Thomism, especially that matter was the principle of individuation; that spiritual beings were species, without matter; that the body participated in the intellectual operations of the soul; that the will was controlled by the intellect. Many of the opinions condemned were no doubt spoken rather than written: for example, 'that the sayings of theologians are based on myths'; 'that no one knows more for knowing theology'; 'that the wise men of the world are the philosophers'; 'that there is no state superior to the practice of philosophy'. But they echo the prevailing tone – the denial of supernatural truth. This can be seen in the proposition 'that no other virtues are possible than those acquired or innate'. Above all, there was the rejection of the indirect nature of God's power, which, as we have so often seen, came from restricting His own capacity for creation to that which was immediately outside Him. From this, there had grown up the characteristic Arabian systems of a hierarchy of separated Intelligences, all in eternal motion, reaching down to the world, no less eternal.

This horror of astral determinism, of eternity, and of God's indirect power, was among the most important legacies of the Great Condemnation. Nor did it stop there: eleven days later, on 18 March, Robert Kilwardby, a Dominican and Archbishop of Canterbury, carried out his own condemnation of thirty propositions at Oxford. These differed from those at Paris in being extended to St Thomas's unity of the substantial form: that is, a single form for each being. As we shall see, this, especially as it affected the soul, was to be one of the most bitter issues in the succeeding years.

The importance of these two condemnations hardly needs to be stressed. They were more than a local retaliation by the conservative theologians who made up the secular clergy. They were at once a revulsion against the pollution of Christian faith with alien elements, and a confession of failure to treat pagan philosophy as an ally of revelation. St Thomas Aquinas himself had been the one theologian who had established a balance between them; but it was too difficult to maintain for any but the most scrupulous observers of its rules. It was attacked on both wings: for the theologians, it opened the way to material explanations; to the philosophers, it followed Aristotle only to lead where he himself had never trodden. Consequently, one of the most immediate results of the Condemnation was the series of disputes over Thomism. As for 'Averroism', it did not survive the second attack and Siger himself died before 1284, probably in prison. From this time onwards the emphasis in thought began to change from synthesis to separation. There was the progressive attempt to disengage what belonged to faith from what could be known by reason. The conclusions of St Thomas's own analysis of the scope of reason were taken to heart, but with a very different end: their separation, not their union. Never again, after 1277, shall we see quite the same confidence in reason's ability to know that which was a matter of belief. Full tide had been reached and now it was slowly on the ebb.

(ix) The reaction to Thomism

One of the most common fallacies about thirteenth-century thought has been to regard it as the age of Thomism. In reality, far from meeting with immediate success, St Thomas encountered widespread opposition and above all consternation. For the last fourth of the thirteenth century, and into the first two decades of the next, Thomism was less a body of doctrine to be accepted than a series of propositions to be discussed. Its own novelty was immeasurably complicated by the dangers of Aristotelianism generally. Thus what would, in any case, have been a difficult matter of assimilation was worse confounded by the condemnations. Consequently, many of St Thomas's views were regarded not simply in their own light but for their possible implication in heterodoxy; with the fear that they might reopen the door to Arabian determinism or to the monopsychism of Averroes. In this sense, the questions at issue were judged primarily by theological criteria.

It would be wrong to regard every thinker as reacting for or against Aristotle, or Thomism, during the last three decades of the thirteenth century; and even more wrong to imagine that there were two firm and distinct alinements of Augustinianism and Thomism. What appears to have happened is that while Augustinianism still continued as a complex of doctrines until Duns Scotus, discussion became increasingly centred on certain topics raised by Thomism and the condemnations. These were largely interpreted in opposition to St Thomas's conclusions, with the majority of Franciscans, and secular thinkers like Henry of Ghent, taking the side of tradition. There was a similar reaction to St Thomas amongst certain Dominicans, such as Robert Kilwardby. On the other side, Thomist views were defended in whole or in part by individual thinkers like Giles of Rome and Godfrey of Fontaines, without our really being able to talk of a Thomist school as such. Thus we can say that from about 1265 all thinking bears witness to Thomism and the growth of heterodoxy, and that to a large extent the discussion is governed by them.

There were four questions in particular which became increasingly prominent. First, the principle of individuation and with it the plurality of forms; second, the Thomist distinction between essence and existence; third, the nature of divine illumination; fourth, the relation of the human will to the human intellect.

The first was in some ways the most searching, for bound up with it were the vital questions of the nature of the soul and the relationship of form to matter. St Thomas, in making a single form the act of individual being, had done two things: he had thereby made matter the principle of individuation; and he had made the soul the form of the body and so the act of an individual man. These went against two of the most cherished tenets of Augustinian thought. The latter had, in greater or lesser degree, always upheld the Platonic view that form was the source of all reality; hence form not matter determined being, and matter was itself the subject of its own form. To make matter the individuating factor was to deny this. Over the human soul, the Thomist view was an equally flagrant breach with the tradition of St Augustine, for it transformed it from a spiritual being, in its own right and with its own distinct forms, into the act of the material body. It made it dependent upon the body for its earthly existence and for its knowledge. This was a threat to the soul's spirituality, and could mean that, in place of its direct connexions with the intelligible, it was dependent for all spiritual knowledge upon an external intellect. Accordingly, the Thomist view of a single substantial form in any being aroused the most heated opposition.

The second argument over the distinction between essence and existence was bound up with hylomorphism. The Augustinians had almost all adopted Avicebrol's view that matter and form were common to spiritual as well as to material beings. It had enabled them to distinguish sharply between God's existence as pure form, and the composite being of all his creatures; St Thomas's twofold substitution of essence and existence in all created beings, as well as form and matter in material beings, was opposed and very largely misunderstood. It denied that pure essence was of itself synonymous with being, in contrast to the transcendental view of the Augustinians, who identified essence with being. Similarly, as against pure Aristotle, it introduced a division that Aristotle had never made. Often the meanings became highly confused: St Thomas had never made a real distinction between essence and existence; he had rather spoken of them as a composition in which, in Boethius's terms, that which is (the *quod est*) and the form which makes it what it is (*quo est*) are what they are by the act of being, given by the form. A great deal of the difficulty therefore came from making existence and essence distinct things where St Thomas had not done so.

The problem of illumination was one that confronted the Augustinians throughout the thirteenth century. It was not so much a specific concept as an attitude – more concerned with making intelligible knowledge independent of sensible experience than with any given mode of operation.

The two main adjuncts to simple illumination of the soul by uncreated light had been abstraction and the active intellect. We have already seen the different combinations in which they could be used: William of Auvergne had upheld the active intellect as the source of divine illumination, but had differed from Avicenna in indentifying it with God: Bonaventure had recognized abstraction for sensible knowledge while making wisdom the province of divine Ideas. What all the Augustinians, after St Thomas, had to face was the relationship of illumination to abstraction and the nature of this illumination – was it divine or was it natural? A more precise mechanism of the way in which the essence of things was grasped was required, and we shall see thinkers like Matthew of Aquasparta, Roger Marston, and Richard of Middleton all concerned to provide the metaphysical explanation lacking in St Augustine and St Anselm.

Concurrently with this reassertion of internal illumination, which had been so strongly held by Bonaventure, went the reaffirmation of Anselm's ontological proof, also invoked by Bonaventure. The succession of Augustinian, especially Franciscan, thinkers who utilized Anselm is as much a testimony to the influence of Bonaventure as to that of St Thomas.

Finally, there was the question of the relationship of reason to will. Now this was more than a mere quibble; it had a very real bearing on the condition needed for right doing and for right knowing. St Thomas's view, as we have seen, was that the will was subordinated to the intellect: 'nothing is willed unless known'. This preponderating rôle of the intellect had already been attacked in the Paris condemnation of 1277. It suggested that the intellect sufficed for a knowledge of truth and beatitude, thereby dispensing with the need for grace. Thus it reversed the Augustinian order which, from the days of St Augustine, had made the disposition of the will the prerequisite to understanding. Many thinkers, and Duns Scotus in particular, were to revert to this emphasis.

Not all these questions were treated by every thinker, while a few, like Henry of Ghent and Richard of Middleton, continued to search for their own synthesis. But for the great majority of theologians these constituted the most important matters to be solved.

(a) *The Franciscans*. These preoccupations are very apparent among the Franciscans and, especially Matthew of Aquasparta (1235 or 40–1302), General of the Franciscans from 1282 to 1288 and St Bonaventure's most important pupil. Born in Italy, like Bonaventure, Matthew devoted himself, in his *Commentary on the Sentences* and *Questions*, to underlining Bonaventure's positions; he shows an awareness of the need for precision in the presence of strong opposing views. In his defence of hylomorphism he denies that a simple distinction between essence and existence is enough to define God from His creatures.

Similarly, he upholds individuation by matter and form, as against matter alone, together with seminal forms. On divine illumination, especially, Matthew goes into great detail. He is particularly concerned to show that illumination is the source of knowledge and that it consists in an uncreated (divine) light. 'When the intellect attains to a first species it is not by reasoning or abstracting that it grasps it, but by transforming it within itself. The cognitive virtue unites the particular images and shows them to the intellect, which creates in itself the concepts of universals' (*Questiones de fide*, p. 291).

This view is characteristic of many Augustinian thinkers after Bonaventure: it posits a parallelism between the essences in things and the Ideas of these essences in the soul. By this means they avoid the need for abstraction, because knowing becomes less a matter of intellection than of recognition; indeed, we are near a Platonic concept of knowledge as reminiscence – the calling up of Ideas within the soul by which we are able to identify the corresponding images in things. The universal 'is the quiddity itself conceived by our intellect but related to the art or eternal exemplar, inasmuch as, touching our soul, it acts upon it as a mover'. It leads to grasping directly the individual for what it is. We can see here the great development from William of Auvergne, who also very largely took the same solution, but without the technical elaborateness of Matthew. Similarly, when we reach the second aspect of illumination – its natural or supernatural nature – Matthew is true to his antecedents in opting for the latter. Our knowledge of eternal truth can only be known through an eternal light: 'But this [natural] light is not enough ... unless controlled and connected to this eternal light, which is the perfect and sufficient reason of knowing' (*ibid.*, 253). 'Therefore I say that whatever is known certainly by intellectual knowledge is known in the eternal reasons in the light of the first truth' (*ibid.*, 261). Matthew attacked St Thomas for 'upsetting all the foundations of the thought of St Augustine'. Sensible experience is necessary for sensible knowledge and comes through abstraction by the soul's active intellect, itself illumined by God. Like Bonaventure, Matthew refuses to extend it to intelligible truth. We have, then, in response to St Thomas's division of faith and reason, the reassertion of faith and the indispensability of supernatural knowledge in the most emphatic manner, which is capped by Matthew's support for Anselm's ontological proof.

Others among Bonaventure's pupils, Eustace of Arras (d. 1291) and Walter of Bruges (d. 1307), were also faithful to the main Augustinian positions of hylomorphism for all creatures and direct knowledge by illumination of the soul. Roger Marston, who studied at Paris in 1270 and taught at Oxford and later at Cambridge, tried to combine the active intellect of the Arabian thinkers with Augustinian illumination. Like his confrères, he regarded knowledge as coming through the 'uncreated light in which we see with certainty all true things'. In addition to the separated active intellect, which is God, each soul has its own active intellect illumined by Him. Roger, also, denied the need for abstraction in knowing the individual essence: 'Whence it is necessary to posit something in the intellect beyond the phantasm or species abstracted, by which we attain to completely immutable truths. . . . For eternal light, irradiating the human intellect, makes a certain active impression upon it, from which is left passive in it a certain impression which is the formal principle of knowing immutable truths.' By this means there is a correspondence between knowledge in the soul and the essence in the individual. He also attacks St Thomas for having used St Augustine's name in his own theory of knowledge, where the light of the soul's active intellect derives from God. Similarly, he reverts to St Anselm's ontological proof as the ultimate attainment of illumination. Already, in the direct knowledge of individuals, we can see the germ of Duns Scotus's theory of knowledge.

Two of the strongest exponents of the Augustinian way were John Peckham and Peter John Olivi. John Peckham (1240–1292) succeeded Robert Kilwardby (see below) as Archbishop of Canterbury in 1279. He maintained Kilwardby's opposition to Thomism, renewing the former's condemnation of 1277 in 1284 and 1286.

Peckham expresses more openly than anyone else the deep hostility which St Thomas had aroused. Not only did he use his episcopal authority to condemn the Thomist thesis of the soul as man's form, but he personally opposed St Thomas in a disputation at Paris on the same subject. In a letter written in 1292 he speaks of the gulf that separated the Franciscans from the Dominicans: 'We do not reprove philosophical studies in so far as they serve the theological mysteries, but we do reprove the profane novelties of language [i.e. St Thomas's use of Aristotelian terms] introduced twenty years ago into the profundities of theology against philosophical truth and to the detriment of the Fathers whose positions are disdained and openly despised. Which doctrine is the sounder and more healthy, that of the sons of St Francis, that is, brother Alexander, of holy memory, of brother Bonaventure and others, which is founded upon the Fathers ... or that doctrine, entirely recent and almost entirely contrary, which fills the entire world with quarrels and words, weakening and destroying all that which St Augustine teaches on eternal rules and immutable light, ... let God judge and apply the remedy.' Doctrinally, his main opposition was, as we have noted, over the place of the human soul. In addition, he followed Bonaventure and Matthew of Aquasparta in seeing knowledge as the immediate result of divine illumination. The act of knowing involved three concurrent operations, 'the created but imperfect light of the intellect, the uncreated light illumining [it], and the possible intellect apprehending the intelligible species'. Peckham also utilized Anselm's ontological proof.

Peter John Olivi (1248/9–1298), who became the leader of the Spiritual Franciscans, accepted the full array of the Augustinian complex, including hylomorphism, plurality of forms, and illumination. He was so concerned to keep the soul separate from the body that he divorced the intellectual soul from the vegetative and sensitive souls, making the latter alone the body's form. This doctrine was condemned at the Council of Vienne in 1311. He also reasserted St Augustine's proposition that the soul could not be acted upon by the body.

William de la Mare's *Correctorium Fratis Thomae* written in 1278 shows the degree to which St Thomas's doctrines were judged and condemned on theological grounds. Throughout, he was concerned with how they harmonized with the traditional teachings of St Augustine, and there was no real attempt to work back from St Thomas's conclusions to his initial positions. The *Corrective* was adopted by the Augustinians as their official doctrine in 1282, to be appended to St Thomas's writings. This in turn called forth a corrective of the *Corrective* by Richard Clapwell the Dominican, and thus the conflict raged – over essence and existence, the plurality of forms, the soul, hylomorphism.

One of the most novel defences of the traditional theology was by Raymond Lull (1235–1315); or rather it was an attack, in the form of an apology, on Averroism and for the conversion of the infidel. Lull had spent a great part of his life as a missionary, and in his *Ars generalis* he tried to evolve a method of making the faith intelligible to unbelievers. It consisted in an elaborate mechanism for relating concepts to one another which, when rightly followed, would lead to the conclusions of faith. This desire to show the concord between reason and faith was not a new one, and had been behind the *Summa against the Gentiles* of St Thomas. What was striking was the precision with which philosophy and theology were reduced to a common outcome. There was to be 'a general science for all the sciences, so that in the general principles would be contained the principles of all particular sciences, as the particular [is contained] in the universal'. Unfortunately, the difficulty lay in deciding on these general principles, and the nine that Lull chose in his *Ars magna* were inevitably arbitrary. In his conviction that all creation was the expression of God, he was in the line of Bonaventure and St Francis himself. Lull's work was to have widespread influence, extending to Leibniz, whose *Dissertation on the Art of Combination* was written with a similar intent.

The thinkers we have examined here have so far all displayed an accentuated Augustinianism, mainly in their theory of illumination. But there were also among the Franciscans growing signs, towards the end of the thirteenth century, of an acceptance of much of Thomism, or, at least, a modification of Augustinianism. Two of the main representatives of this path were Richard of Middleton and William of Ware.

Richard of Middleton (*d.* ?1307) studied at both Oxford and Paris, where he was censor of Peter John Olivi's teachings. His outlook may be summed up as follows: rejection of intuitive knowledge for abstraction by the soul in the light of its own active intellect; illumination as nothing but the natural light of the intellect ('We can say that we can understand naturally any created truth in eternal truth . . . by means of the natural light impressed in us by God.'); no innate knowledge of God in the manner of Anselm's ontological proof. On the other hand, he upheld direct knowledge of the individual, which yielded the knowledge of first principles; he supported the Augustinian primacy of the will over the intellect; he rejected the Thomist view of essence and existence; and held fast to hylomorphism in spiritual beings and to a plurality of forms. We can also see the impact of the Paris condemnations in his theory of the universe which he said was capable of expansion or contraction. This ultimately fruitful scientific notion was not due to scientific calculation but to a reaction against the eternal necessity which governed the Greco-Arabian world. Like Duns Scotus after him, Richard retaliated with the radical contingency of all creation. We see also the same attitude in Kilwardby.

William of Ware (*d.* 1300) taught at Paris towards the end of the thirteenth century. He, too, believed that knowledge was through intellectual abstraction, rather than through divine illumination: 'thus the soul, since it is more noble, should much rather have its own instruments by which it can elicit its own natural action, which is to understand'. For this, it did not require any supernatural aid. He also abandoned hylomorphism in spiritual beings: but held to the primacy of the will over the intellect.

(*b*) *The Dominicans*. The Dominicans showed a marked lack of agreement in their attitude to Thomism. This ranged from open hostility to support often based upon an incomplete understanding. The foremost opponent of St Thomas, among his own order, was Robert Kilwardby (*d.* 1279), who held the Dominican chair at Oxford from 1248 to 1261, after studying at Paris. He became Archbishop of Canterbury in 1272 and Cardinal in 1278.

Kilwardby's predecessor at Oxford, Richard Fishacre (*d.* 1248), had also been conservative in outlook, and in this sense Kilwardby was not going against precedent in upholding Augustinianism. The difference was that, while Richard had not fully grasped Aristotle, Kilwardby had commented a great number of his writings and he opposed him from full knowledge. His disapproval of Thomism culminated in his own condemnation of it at Oxford on 18 March 1277. This differed from that at Paris in being less the action of authority than a general censure by many of the theologians. It also concentrated more on St Thomas's notion of the human soul. In his own work, Kilwardby held to the plurality of forms, seminal reasons, hylomorphism in spiritual beings. His view of individuation was an elaborate one: first, there is matter and form; next, the determination of the form; and then the individual itself. This proliferation of forms applied equally to the soul of which 'the vegetative, sensitive, and intellective parts are essentially different'. Hence it is not surprising that the twelfth proposition in his condemnation was directed against those who held to the contrary viewpoint. He also took up an attitude similar to Richard of Middleton on the universe.

Giles of Lessines (*d.* 1304), in his *On the Unity of the Form*, wrote a reply to Kilwardby, who had thought to give the *coup de grâce* to St Thomas's view by arguing that if there were a single form for each being there would be only one form for everything. Giles is notable for his faithful exposition of St Thomas's views. John Quidort also came to St Thomas's support, but without the clarity of Giles; while previously Richard Clapwell had answered the attack of William de la Mare already noted.

(*c*) *The Seculars and others.* Three of the most outstanding thinkers during the later thirteenth and early fourteenth centuries were neither Dominican nor Franciscan. The greatest of these was undoubtedly Henry of Ghent (*d.* 1293) whose system as found in his *Quodlibet* and his *Summa theologica* put him in the first rank of thirteenth-century minds. His was an essentially independent outlook, but he had drunk deeply of the troubled waters of the time. As master of theology at Paris from 1276 to 1292, he was at the centre of the events of 1277. He was as aware of the dangers of Aristotelianism as he was of the limitations of the classical Augustinianism; and while he followed the latter in most of its basic assumptions he was unwilling to entrust himself to it completely.

The most marked feature of Henry's system is the overriding primacy of essence. Like Avicenna, he regards being, which is the first object of knowledge, as prior to all categories. From the notion of being can be deduced the distinction between necessary and possible existence, and this in turn can lead to the proof of God's existence as first being. Thus, in common with Avicenna and in contrast to St Thomas, Henry makes the idea of God come from the abstract notion of being and not from sensible things. But no one could be more aware than he of the dangers of Avicenna's determinism, by which God cannot help transmitting the essences of potential being through the first Intelligence. It may well be that this accounted for Henry's refusal to go the whole way with Avicenna, as Duns was to go when he posited a universal being common both to God and His creatures. Henry, on the contrary, was content to see it analogically, as a *resemblance* common to them.

Henry's awareness of the essentially contingent nature of created being can be seen in two respects. From the notion of God's infinity, while like all Christians recognizing it as negative (the absence of limit), he drew a positive conclusion: infinity affirms God's power to transcend all limitations (*Summa*, II, 44, 2). He is thereby in no way bound to do anything, and the existence of His creatures is solely through the free working of His will, not from necessity. The second is the nature of created being, which arises from God's free choice. Through His own essence, God has knowledge of all possible beings in divine Ideas. The act of creation therefore consists in realizing the existence of these possible beings.

Now in order to maintain the distinction between God's essence and created essences, Henry was forced to distinguish between the divine Ideas in God and the actual essences which they produced. Otherwise he ran the same danger as Erigena – of making divine Ideas at once creators and created. Like Duns Scotus after him, Henry felt compelled to duplicate the ideal existence of each divine Idea in God with an actual essence in a created being. He distinguished the latter from the former by calling it the existence of the essence (*esse essentiae*) (*Quodlibet*, III, 9). Henry, then, followed William of Auvergne and many other Augustinians in making the being of essence correspond to an intelligible Idea. Where he innovated was in giving the concept full precision – a precision which was primarily to avoid the necessity of Avicenna's system: for unless Henry could mark off possible being as an essence distinct from divine Ideas, there could be no way of showing that it is the direct effect of God's willing. God's will has to break the chain of eternal emanations which dominated the Arabian systems; there therefore has to be a radical difference between His Ideas and created being. We shall see a similar solution with Duns Scotus.

We are now in a position to examine the working out of Henry's system. Let us first observe that his is an essentially transcendental notion of existence, where reality resides in the essences, or in the intelligible, as opposed to the sensible. This, in the first place, means that Henry rejects St Thomas's view of essence and existence as composing all created being; instead we have the *esse essentiae* to distinguish each creature, as possible, from God as necessary. Henry devoted much attention to combating Giles of Rome on this point. (*Quodlibet*, I, 9). In the second place, Henry regarded individuation not by matter alone, but by form as well. Matter, as something created, has its own Idea in God; it is not the sheer potentiality of Aristotle and St Thomas. 'With God Himself conserving what He is able in Himself to create without the action of any form, His own nature can enable anything to be in act, although it is not in perfect act' (*Quodlibet*, I, 10). Finite beings, therefore, are made up of essences in partial or imperfect state of being which join with other such beings to make up an individual. This is what Henry means when he talks of an individual as a double negation: internally, it negates difference (that is, it is a unity); externally, it negates identity, that is, it is distinguished from other beings which are not it. 'It is therefore to be said that in specific created forms, as they are specific, the reason of their individuation by which they are determined ... is negation ... this is not simple but double, because it removes, from within itself, all plurality and diversity, and from outside, all identity' (*Quodlibet*, v, 8). Thus we have a plurality of forms in anything beyond a simple body.

So far as the soul and human knowledge are concerned, Henry held to Augustinianism. The soul itself, as we can easily deduce, is its own substance, not the form of the body, which has for its form the form of corporeity. There is in man a double source of knowledge – by abstraction through the senses, and by illumination in the soul – corresponding to the dualism of body and soul. By abstraction we are able to know sensible things, but not intelligibles; not even the essence of the thing we are contemplating. For certain knowledge, we are dependent upon a divine illumination by the active intelligence, which is God.

Knowledge therefore resides in the divine Ideas which God's illumination enables us to see. It is 'this uncreated, created truth which impresses itself into our conception, which it transforms according to its nature, and which informs our soul by the model that the thing to be known has in the first truth. Therefore, if all illumination is excluded, man cannot know the truth from his natural powers; of themselves they cannot reach the rules of eternal light, so that they see them in genuine truth ... God gives it to those He wills and raises those He wills' (*Summa*, 1, 2, 1). Thus Henry places knowledge upon an intermediate footing: while sensory knowledge is necessary to the soul in its present condition, it does not need to know an essence by abstraction. For this, it is enough for the 'possible intellect, at once informed of the species of the intelligibles in the immediate light of the active intellect', to grasp the intelligible without actual knowledge. There is the same correspondence between the models in the soul and the essences in things that we have already noted; Platonic reminiscence, rather than Aristotelian abstraction, provides the means of knowing. Henry's theory of knowledge can therefore be regarded as one of illumination, on the model of Bonaventure and Matthew of Aquasparta; with the latter, he has made perception a very much more direct process of recognition.

Henry also showed his strong Augustinianism in the primacy which he gives to the human will in human actions. 'The act of knowing is only an indispensable condition and not the cause of the act of the will; the will is in no way passive; it is a faculty which determines itself without being determined by any other' (*Quodlibet*, III, 17). As we have seen before, it goes with the theory of illumination, which inevitably throws the onus of knowing upon the disposition (*habitus*) of the knower.

On all the main issues, then, Henry of Ghent gives an Augustinian response. We might almost say that his doctrine was the most comprehensive attempt to reorientate Augustinianism in the light of Arabian thought, particularly Avicenna's. It accepts, and meets, all the basic challenges which the 1277 condemnations threw down to Christian faith, not by reasserting what Bonaventure had already taught, but in providing faith with a full-fledged metaphysic. This enabled him to meet Aristotelianism as well as Thomism on a metaphysical, not simply a theological, footing. Indeed the more one considers Henry of Ghent the more one is bound to conclude that he, more than anyone, provided the most impressive Augustinian synthesis and that it deserves to be ranked as one of the main alternatives to Thomism.

Godfrey of Fontaines (*d.* 1302), the other important secular theologian of the later thirteenth century, devoted himself to clarifying some of the more pressing matters of dispute which arose out of Thomism. In contrast to Henry of Ghent, he was a supporter of Thomism, though an independent one; by the same token, he opposed Henry of Ghent himself. Godfrey differed from St Thomas over the composition of essence and existence; but his attack was directed less against St Thomas than against Giles of Rome, who had regarded them as two different things (*res*).

He followed St Thomas in upholding abstraction against illumination, but he accentuated the passive rôle of intellect, by making the intelligible essence of the individual immediately perceptible to it. The illumination of the active intellect enables the 'quiddity' of the image to be grasped. He adopts a corresponding passivity for the will which, like the intellect, is dependent upon an object to move it. The desirability of the object is in turn determined by the intellect. Hence, like St Thomas, and in opposition to Henry of Ghent, the intellect is the source of freedom.

Giles of Rome (1247–1316) has often been regarded as the direct disciple of St Thomas, but his doctrine, in so far as it is yet known, shows great divergences. He entered the Augustinian order in 1260 and may have studied under St Thomas between 1269 and 1272. Giles's defence of St Thomas's doctrine of the unity of the substantial form, in his *Against Grades and the Plurality of Form*, written in reply to the 1277 condemnation, brought down upon him the wrath of Étienne Tempier; he was forced to leave Paris and had to wait until 1285 before becoming a master of theology there. From 1285 to 1291 he was the first holder of the Augustinian chair at the University, his outlook becoming the official doctrine of his order in 1287. In 1292 he was made Archbishop of Bourges.

Like Godfrey of Fontaines, Giles was not a mere exponent of Thomism; his independent outlook is particularly apparent in his view of essence and existence, which, in contrast to St Thomas, he regards not as inseparate elements in a single being but as distinct things (*res*). He viewed the problem from the actual condition of real beings, whereas St Thomas had done so as part of the notion of God. Giles's attempt to prove the real distinction between essence and existence led him into a long polemic with Henry of Ghent. Altogether, Giles's outlook seems to have been strongly influenced by the Neoplatonism of Proclus.

(x) Science in the thirteenth century

One of the seeming paradoxes of the thirteenth century is that the greatest development in mathematics, optics, and astronomy went with the most transcendental outlooks. Augustinians like Grosseteste, Richard of Middleton, Roger Bacon, John Peckham, all combined their Neoplatonic beliefs with scientific activity. Even a man like Kilwardby gave what was, unwittingly, a more scientific answer to questions on the universe than St Thomas. The reason perhaps lies in their belief in non-sensory truth, which led them to mathematics rather than to zoology, and to light and optics rather than the metaphysical properties of being. Similarly, their rejection of Aristotle's determinism saved them from a closed view of the universe, as we have noted with Richard of Middleton: if God could act as He willed, as opposed to following a constant order, changes in the universe could not be ruled out: it was possible for it to expand or contract or even to be transformed.

Undoubtedly, after Grosseteste, the most fertile scientific mind was Roger Bacon (born between 1210 and 1214; died after 1292). He was an Englishman who studied at Oxford under Grosseteste and Adam Marsh, and then |in the arts faculty at Paris, before returning to Oxford to teach. He joined the Franciscan order probably in 1257. He was never a master of theology, and his whole career was a revulsion against the scholastic methods current. His original turn of thought and his outspoken attacks upon his contemporaries earned him many enemies; only during the brief pontificate of his friend and protector Clement IV (1265–1268) did his ideas find acceptance. Some of his own theories on astronomy were included in the Paris condemnation of 1277; he was imprisoned in 1278, and he remained in captivity until about 1292. The date of his death is unknown.

Bacon's most striking ideas on theology, science, and learning in general are to be found in his *Opus maius*, *Opus minor*, and *Opus tertium*. These were to have culminated in his *Opus principale*, a universal encylopedia, but it was never written.

Perhaps the first thing to be emphasized about Bacon is that, far from being a free thinker or a man born out of his time, he was very much a child of his age. At a time when St Thomas was trying to make a distinction between faith and reason, Bacon was asserting the subordination of all knowledge to theology. He did not differ from his contemporaries over aims or beliefs so much as over method. Bacon's main opposition to men like Alexander of Hales, Albert the Great, and St Thomas was over their neglect of positive studies and their ignorance of Greek and oriental languages and mathematics. Theologically, Bacon's views were largely those of the traditional Augustinianism, in keeping with his order; he upheld the universal form of matter, hylomorphism in spiritual beings, seminal reasons, the identity of essence and existence, and divine illumination. The latter he regarded in much the same way as William of Auvergne, who had adapted Avicenna's view of illumination by an active intellect to mean illumination by God. 'The wisdom of philosophy is completely revealed by God and given to philosophers, and it is He who illumines the souls of men in all wisdom; and because that which illumines our minds is now called by theologians the active intellect . . . I show that this active intellect is principally God . . . ' (*Opus tertium*, 74). In order to know, therefore, there must be illumination from God.

Where Bacon differed from the majority of his confrères was in the other aspect of knowledge. Whilst on the one hand there was the inner experience which came with illumination, on the other there was empirical knowledge which derived from external sources. Together they made up experience. Now external knowledge was an added means of gaining understanding; but, even with Bacon, it was not an end in itself. Rather, natural knowledge was to play the traditional rôle of the seven liberal arts; to provide a better understanding of the truths which belonged alone to theology, as the fount of all wisdom: 'One science is the mistress of all others, theology.' Thus all other knowledge (philosophy) was to be reduced to theological truth. He attacked his contemporaries just because they lacked the means of doing so. It could come about only through a proper knowledge of science and of languages.

This is where Bacon shows his indebtedness to Grosseteste and also to Peter de Mauricourt. Like Grosseteste, he makes mathematics all-important, indeed indispensable, to an understanding of any science: lines, angles, and figures are the key to knowledge. 'Every science needs mathematics.' 'In mathematics we can come to full truth without error and to the certainty of all things without doubt.' To Peter de Mauricourt (fl. 1270) Bacon owed the idea of experiment. Mauricourt in his work on magnetism had advocated experiment in order to attain the correct results. 'It behoves us to use the skill of the hand, which, as this work shows, has wonderful results.'

Bacon himself did not engage directly in experiment so much as advocate it as a method of verification which gave certitude and furthered a knowledge of nature: 'There are two ways of knowing, reason and experiment. Theory concludes and we must accept the conclusions, but it does not give that assurance freed from all doubt where the soul reposes in the intuition of the truth. . . . If a man, who has never seen fire, proved by conclusive arguments that fire burns, that it destroys and ruins things, the mind of his hearer would not be satisfied and he would not avoid fire before having put his hand or a combustible object into it to prove by experience what theory taught. But once the experience of combustion is made, the mind is convinced and knows in the evidence of the truth.' Logic itself, then, should not be based upon Aristotle, but derive from experience, dealing with concrete individuals; for this reason Bacon rejected universals completely: 'individuals are nobler than universals' (*Metaphysics*, 11, 95), and knowledge should deal with individuals.

Bacon ranged over the whole field of science, covering optics, astronomy, alchemy, and physics. These were all germane to the prosecution of knowledge, not autonomous in themselves. In one sense, Bacon was giving only a more sustained and widespread application to the fundamental Neoplatonic doctrine that the world was a theophany. The truths that were discovered by science could not stand on their own; they were indissolubly connected with the principles which emanated from God, and, as we have seen, they could only be understood in the light of divine illumination. Bacon followed the Victorines in positing a series of stages in the ascent from natural knowledge to knowledge of God, culminating in ecstasy. Thus, like all the Augustinians, Bacon refused to accept sensory knowledge as the means to the truth: 'it cannot show us the truth of the physical world because it cannot reveal anything of sacred truth which governs it; truth of the supernatural order can only be revealed to man internally.' Ultimately, verification itself was the confirmation of principles which lie beyond things and in intelligible Ideas. Experiment is to reinforce them, not to discover them.

Another example of the influence of Neoplatonism in science is to be found in the work of the Polish scientist Witelo (*b. c.*1220–1230). His *Perspective*, although in no way concerned with theology, was governed by the light metaphysic. Light was the universal corporeal form, besides being diffused in the higher forms. Witelo was strongly influenced by the Arabian scientist, Alacens, and by Greek scientists, like Euclid. He bears witness to the growing interest in astronomy, particularly the rotation of the earth. The view that it did so was also mentioned by Francis of Mayronnes in his *Commentary on the Sentences* in 1322. Already, then, there was a movement away from the Ptolemaic system towards what was one day to be the theory of Copernicus. This was to be even more marked in the next century with Nicholas of Oresme.

(*xi*) *Political theories*

The greatest impetus to political theory during the eleventh and twelfth centuries came from the struggle between Emperor and Papacy. The tone had already been set by such Church reformers as Peter Damian, and it was progressively strengthened by the growing impetus of the reform movement itself. Moreover, the conflicting views were heightened by the renewed study of law, Roman and canon, providing both Emperor and the Pope with legal arguments which had previously been neglected. For the Pope, the most influential was the donation of Constantine, a forgery which had been incorporated into canon law and which asserted that the Emperor Constantine had handed over all the western part of the Roman Empire to the Pope. This gave him primacy over all other powers and princes. On the Emperor's side there was the much more authoritarian interpretation of princely power to be found in Roman law: it gave a ruler's will the force of law, and this, too, went far towards disturbing the balance of the Gelasian doctrine.

Under Pope Gregory VII the papalists went over to the offensive and claimed ultimate jurisdiction over the political powers. The main points at issue were not over the nature of the State itself but over the division of its authority. Granted that there was a spiritual as well as a temporal aspect to society, with corresponding rulers, what was the character of the monarchy? what was its origin? what its scope? how could it be opposed? The papalists affirmed that as the monarchy was the result of sin, it lacked a divine origin, unlike the Church. The king himself, far from having any jurisdiction over the Church, was subject to it. Moreover, both Manegold of Lautenbach and John of Salisbury went so far as to say that the King could be deposed if he misruled his people. This element of popular sovereignty was expressed by Manegold when he compared the King to a swineherd who was responsible for his flock: if he failed in his duties he had invalidated his contract with them.

The contractual theory attacked the whole idea of medieval kingship, not least its priestly element. John of Salisbury in his *Policraticus* carried this freedom to depose the sovereign to the point of tyrannicide. Ultimately, however, this idea failed to prosper; from the first it met a resolute counter-offensive by Imperial supporters like Peter Crassus, who reinforced his views with arguments drawn from Roman law, and the anonymous author of the York tracts.* Moreover, king-

* In fact, probably of Rouen.

ship was becoming too established in its own right to be denied. Hence, during the thirteenth century denigration of secular authority had died down, St Augustine's view of the sinful origin of the State was being replaced by Aristotle's – that the State was natural to man.

This changed attitude was given fullest expression in St Thomas Aquinas's political views, where, as with his metaphysics and theology, he put Aristotle in a Christian setting. Just as he regarded reason as having an independent status, so he saw the State as its own justification. It was not primarily the result of sin but man's highest achievement in this world, and natural to him. He differed from Aristotle in the interpretation he gave to natural law. It not only provided man with a pattern of conduct, based upon an eternal rational order, but it was the bridge between the created and the divine; it enabled him to know naturally what was right, even if, as the result of original sin, he could not fulfil it. Thus politics ultimately rested upon ethics. There was no need to seek an historical justification for the State: it was organically part of man: sin became merely a by-product of human imperfection to explain injustice, not the State itself.

The difference between St Thomas's outlook and St Augustine's is the difference between a settled society and social upheaval. Where St Augustine cast desperately around to explain evil, St Thomas could return to the classificatory method of Aristotle: he made the State part of the eternal order of reason where St Augustine had seen it as punishment for an erring will.

PART III

SCEPTICISM

(*c.* 1300–1350)

CHAPTER 8

Introduction to the Period

THE changes that came with the fourteenth century were of a different order from those of the preceding periods. They were not from innovations so much as from a regrouping of existing elements. They can perhaps best be described as the waning of hierarchy and universal order. From the first decades of the fourteenth century it is possible to notice a growing differentiation within most walks of society and no less in thought. It made for new relationships between spiritual and secular power, seigneur and tenant, faith and reason. Ultimately, this division, where previously there had been union, if not unity, was to mark the end of the middle ages.

The core of medieval society was its series of carefully defined gradations embracing nearly all men and maintained from generation to generation. Although there were exceptions, especially in the towns, it was predominantly a world where authority went with status, and where it was perilous, if not completely impossible, to change one's hereditary station from unfreedom to freedom. The belief in the divine dispensation of this order was part of the cement of society. The endemic struggle for primacy between successive Emperors and Popes had been a very real expression of the order of things.

Gradually, however, this was changing. To take the papacy first, we find little of the universalism which had marked it at its height. A succession of worldly popes during the thirteenth century had culminated in the humiliation of the most worldly of all, Boniface VIII, by Philip IV of France. It had led to the Pope's leaving Rome and settling at Avignon in 1305, where he remained for the next seventy years, largely under the tutelage of the French crown. The so-called 'Babylonish captivity' opened a new phase for the papacy; while it would be untrue to say that it meant the loss of its ecumenical position,

255

its international character was certainly weakened. It fell largely under French domination, and its very change of location from Rome, the centre of Christendom, could not but point to the change since the days of Innocent III. The succession of new troubles that came with the Great Schism and the Conciliar Movement (1378 to 1415) was a further step away from universalism.

The same can be said of the Church in general. The inevitable slackening of religious fervour after each of the successive reforming movements, by the monks and the friars, led to fresh demands for reform. But where previously these had operated within the Church or had consisted in the creation of new orders, there was now a demand for the reform of existing institutions. The great wealth and privileges of the Church and of its orders were the main target: and already during the thirteenth century the spiritual wing of the Franciscans had demanded absolute poverty. This protest, coloured by the apocalyptic views taken from Joachim of Flora, led to their persecution under John XXI in 1318 and the final condemnation of the doctrine of Poverty in 1323. The subsequent revolt of some of the Franciscans under their general Michael of Cesena and William of Ockham led the latter to join forces with the Emperor in attacking the Pope. The extremity of Ockham's doctrines, both philosophical and political, were matched by those of Marsilius of Padua and opened a new era in political theory. The same discontent with the condition of the Church is evident in the direct attacks upon it made by Wyclif in England and Huss in Bohemia, in the later fourteenth and the fifteenth centuries. It is also apparent in the spread of mysticism, not purely as a personal outlook but as a social ideal (among the Béguines in Flanders) and as a standard of revolt (in Languedoc).

Thus, at both its upper and lower reaches, the Church was in travail; and for the most part it could reply only with persecution – against the Lollards in England (though Wyclif was left unmolested), against the Hussites, with Huss himself burned at the stake, against the heretics in southern France. Luther had many forerunners.

Within secular society there was an equally marked shift in emphasis. Politically, the days of the Empire were irrevocably past; it had been on the wane from the time of Frederick II, and with his death, and the interregnum that followed, went the substance of Imperial power. Germany had for long been an agglomeration of principalities under independent princes, and was to remain so until the nineteenth century. The dominating struggle of the fourteenth century was no longer that between Pope and Emperor, though this still flared up under Louis IV of Bavaria, but the Hundred Years War between England and France; although it was not continuous, and indeed was largely made up of pauses, it was a constant strain upon both, particularly France, as most of the fighting was on French soil. It took toll both of her resources and her greatness, and France, in the fourteenth and much of the fifteenth century, was a shadow of what she had been in the thirteenth century. Paris itself lost its universality as the centre of learning, and the interchange between English and French thinkers was seriously impaired by the periodic expulsions which went with the state of war. England, too, found her wealth gradually drained by the fighting. The persistence of the war was something new in medieval history, although we should be chary of seeing it as a struggle between nations.

Economically and socially, there were similar signs of disturbance: from about the third decade of the fourteenth century there seems to have been a definite decline in population, in the area under cultivation, and in trade, while the international power of Italian financiers suffered heavily from their being made bankrupt by the inability of English and French kings to pay their debts. These developments were no doubt aggravated by the Black Death in 1348–9; but in any case changes were taking place in the very structure of society. During the fourteenth century there were increasing signs of unrest, and a growing tendency for the lord's demesne to be leased out among the wealthier peasants. Although the shortages of labour caused by the Black Death retarded this process it also increased many of the difficulties; and the fourteenth century is marked by a series of peasant risings, the *Jacquerie* in France and the Peasants' Revolt in England, as well as recurrent disturbances in the urban areas of Flanders and elsewhere.

The atmosphere of fourteenth century thought catches these changes: much of the self-confidence in the powers of reason has evaporated by the second and third decades. There is a similar differentiation between faith and natural knowledge to that developing between secular and spiritual authority; there is a growing distrust of an ordered hierarchy between the tenets of revelation and rational demonstration, at a time of mounting discontent with a fixed social order. The union between understanding and belief is under attack, together with much else in Christendom.

There are three dominating traits in the thought of the fourteenth century. The first is the desire to disengage faith from reason. The revulsion against determinism that marked the 1277 condemnations gradually spread to the attempt to trace God from His creatures. It was felt that to describe God in terms of a first cause was to regulate His actions; that to attribute to Him a constant mode of operation impaired His absolute sovereignty. Accordingly, emphasis was coming to be placed upon the infinite freedom of His will which defied analysis or explanation. Henry of Ghent, as we have seen, was particularly at pains to stress the free and unconstrained nature of divine will. Duns Scotus was to establish this view, which was given new application by Ockham and his followers. It made for a redefinition of what could be known about God. The distinction between faith and reason, to which St Thomas had so firmly held, was taken to make each self-contained; the natural and the supernatural were not merely on different planes but without a meeting-point; since they dealt with different truths they could not inform one another.

This led to the second trait: the growth of rival outlooks founded upon either faith or reason. On one side, there was an attitude which, as developed by Ockham, can best be described as empiricism; fact became the touchstone; and to move beyond its boundaries was to enter the realm of speculation and leave certainty. Matters of belief, and God Himself, could not be a subject for reason, but for faith alone. To discuss them was to conjure up possibilities, not to assert the truth.

Such an attitude induced scepticism towards faith; it meant that so far as reason was concerned, the rulings of revelation had no validity; to try to impose them could only mean the undermining of faith. On the other side, faith took on an increasingly independent attitude. It looked to revelation and authority for its support, rather than to ratiocination. This was the other side of the coin: if reason could not reach faith and faith could not illumine reason, the one must be as independent as the other. The tenets of faith were a matter of revealed truth – to be believed and not to be proved. Accordingly faith tended more and more towards a régime for worship, which, founded upon dogma and revelation, was independent of any rational support: to believe in God was the only criterion for knowing Him; evidence for His existence came from Scripture, not from demonstration. These twin attitudes of scepticism and authority go together; hence it is not surprising to see them often held by the same thinker. The demarcation between faith and reason had made what was formerly one outlook two.

The third trait was a marked change in the lines of thought. It is usually common to regard the fourteenth century as the period of the second struggle between realism and nominalism, with Duns Scotus and William of Ockham as the leading actors. Consequently, there has been a misleading habit of equating Scotism with realism and Ockhamism with nominalism and making their opposition govern the intellectual history of the period. Yet the more this view is examined, the more untenable it becomes.

To begin with, we tend to fall into the trap which modern historians have been so keen to avoid, of regarding medieval thought as the struggle between nominalism and realism. Although it is true that Ockham, at least, adopted what could be called an extreme nominalist view towards universals, he was far more concerned with the validity of our concepts and their relation to faith, than taken in themselves. Both he and

Duns Scotus lived in very different circumstances from Abelard and William of Champeaux – in the aftermath of the 1277 condemnations and the conflict over Thomism. Though Duns and Ockham worked from opposite poles, they devoted themselves to realigning faith and reason rather than to any single problem of cognition. Both, moreover, in their attempt to free God from human calculations, discounted the causality of Thomism and Aristotle, and placed all emphasis upon the unconstrained play of God's will: it was a supreme law unto itself and permitted no order or prediction.

A glance at their contemporaries and successors will show that the issue was not realism versus nominalism, but the problem of how much reason could know of faith. Often, indeed, one finds the names of Scotus and Ockham coupled together, as with Adam of Woodham, in mutual support for an opinion – especially over God's will or His absolute power. This is particularly apparent in the questions at issue in the fourteenth century. These show very clearly the effects of the division between faith and reason.

Firstly, hardly any thinker accepted an overall framework embracing both faith and reason. This meant a drastic limitation in the scope of the discussion. The *Commentaries on the Sentences*, by most thinkers after Ockham, no longer followed the full range of questions raised by Peter Lombard and his commentators previously. Much was excluded, while many matters that had occupied separate 'distinctions' in the original *Sentences* were now grouped under a single 'question'. This shrinkage is largely attributable, it would seem, to Ockham's denial of the validity of many of the traditional questions raised. Consequently, much was omitted that could not be founded in direct evidence and fact. In the commentaries of, say, Holcot, Buckingham, Halifax, Woodham, many of the questions most fundamental to scholasticism are absent: universals, proofs of God's existence, His nature, His attributes. Only the directly personal ontological proof is accepted, for it is independent of sensory experience – itself an indication of the new trend.

Secondly, these shadows of the classical commentaries of

the thirteenth century were centred mainly on such topics as the relationship between the different persons of the Trinity and the faculties in man's soul; the place of grace and its connexion with merit and free will; the possibility and the effects of God's future knowledge upon the actions of free will (future contingents); the nature of the sacraments; and matters of physics – such as the possibility of the existence of infinite bodies – which were very largely the result of the growing belief in indeterminacy, and which we have already noted in Richard of Middleton and Kilwardby. Some of the greatest disputes were directly over grace and future contingents, for it was there that faith and reason came into direct conflict.

Thirdly, beside this narrowing of the field of speculation there is a renewed interest in humanism, particularly, classical learning, and even mythology. These often go together in the same thinker, as for example Robert Holcot or Thomas Waleys. There is also at the same time a great interest in mathematics, astronomy, and physics, which, freed from any theological suppositions, followed their own course: John Buridan, Albert of Saxony, and Nicholas of Oresme, at Paris, Bradwardine, at Oxford, are among the more prominent names. The close interest in the problem of the remission and the intensification of forms is often to be seen in its application to theological forms like grace.

The fourteenth century, then, carries no direct impress of the thirteenth. It is not, like the latter, an age of syntheses, or of dominant schools of thought. It is preoccupied with the limits, rather than the scope, of reason; its thinkers devoted themselves to definition rather than to construction. Above all, it is a time of eclecticism and shifting currents. One would be hard put to it to identify anything approaching pure Thomism or Augustinianism among the majority of the thinkers: men like Durandus of St Pourçain and Holcot, both Dominicans, have as little in common as Pierre Aureole and William of Ockham, who were both Franciscans. If ever an age defied pigeon-holes and categories it is the fourteenth century.

CHAPTER 9

The Fourteenth Century: Scepticism versus Authority

(i) The Precursors: Duns Scotus

The dividing line between the outlooks of the thirteenth and fourteenth centuries cannot be fixed by any single date; and as with all human pursuits, much of the old remained after the new had become established. Men like Giles of Rome continued to write after the man most responsible for the change was dead – Duns Scotus. It was with Duns Scotus (*c.* 1266 or 1270–1308) above all that the seal of reaction against Thomism and Arabian determinism was firmly set. Duns directed his system to disengaging what belonged to theology from what was accessible to reason. In his desire for a more direct and simple way of viewing God, unencumbered by human calculations, he turned against both St Thomas and much that was Augustinian. He led the first general retreat of reason from faith; henceforth scholasticism was irreparably weakened from the positions thus lost.

John Duns Scotus was born at Maxton, Roxburgh, Scotland, and early entered the Franciscan order. He studied at Oxford and Paris, writing *Commentaries on the Sentences* in both universities. He was among the Englishmen expelled from Paris in 1305 by Philip the Fair. He was sent to Cologne in 1307, where he died in the following year, being at most little more than forty years of age. His main works were his two *Commentaries on the Sentences*, known from their place-names as the *Opus Oxoniense* and the *Reportata Parisiensia*. The *Opus Oxoniense* is his most important writing and the source of his main doctrines. He also wrote a series of Questions on metaphysics and Free Questions (*Quodlibeta*) which altogether formed an abundant output for his comparatively short lifetime.

Duns Scotus was one of the most remarkable of medieval

thinkers; his qualities were a highly critical and subtle mind (he was called the subtle doctor), which enabled him to cut through the jungle of concepts and terms, combined with an audaciousness that is the property of great intelligences. His originality is of a comparable order with St Thomas's though he lacked the latter's harmony and clarity. Duns's thought has laboured under certain handicaps: his early death, before he had fully formulated his ideas, makes him often difficult to grasp; in addition his manuscripts have been transmitted in such a faulty state that it is only now that they are in the process of thorough editing. Consequently both in himself and through his circumstances Duns is one of the most complex thinkers of the middle ages.

Duns's system cannot be described in traditional terms: he owed perhaps more to Henry of Ghent than anyone, but less in detail than in spirit. As a Franciscan, he spoke with the voice of the Augustinian tradition; but as a thinker, living in the afterglow of Thomist synthesis and the 1277 condemnations, he had to redefine the relations of faith and reason. Thus he marked a break with Augustinianism; for while rejecting St Thomas's use of Aristotelian terms to describe God, he equally cast aside divine illumination as a means to reach Him. Duns was so intent on restoring God to His own devices that he refused any explanation of divine actions. His outlook is dominated by two overriding considerations: the first is the limitation of reason; the second is the absolute freedom of God. He therefore carries on where Henry of Ghent left off; but his very ruthlessness of purpose leads him to a far more individually defined system.

In these aims Duns has constantly the image of St Thomas Aquinas before him; his arguments, his topics, his use of Aristotelian concepts are largely framed as answers to their treatment by St Thomas. Indeed, we might go so far as to say that, in origin, Scotism is a counterblast to Thomism. Both outlooks raise the same questions only to give diametrically opposite replies; they both draw widely upon Aristotle; they both recognize that the relation of faith and reason is the central problem; they both acknowledge the impossibility of discussing God except from His effects. In the process two entirely different systems emerge.

The point of departure for Duns as for St Thomas is to define the respective realms of theology and philosophy. Philosophy, or, more strictly, metaphysics, dealt with being and its attributes; theology with God and His attributes. Where he differed from St Thomas was in not regarding them as complementary; reason cannot confirm what is revealed by God, because all revelation is a matter of faith and not of natural experience. It was one of Duns's most emphatic assertions that the theologian and the philosopher are not, and never can be, the same. This virtually excluded theology from being a science, with its own laws, and gave it instead a far more directly practical nature: 'Its knowledge should be described as practical' (*Opus Ox. Prol.* 4, 31). Its truths lie outside the evidence of things, and so do not lend themselves to proof drawn from natural perceptions. Metaphysics, in turn, could not transcend being, and was therefore unable to describe God except in so far as He was being. All our knowledge of God could be only through the notion that we have of being.

Now the importance of Duns's use of being to prove God's existence was twofold: first, it cut at the only two modes of knowing God: St Thomas's proofs drawn from sense experience and Augustinian divine illumination. So far as Thomism was concerned, Duns held that proof taken from the physical world could not go beyond the physical world: to deduce God as pure act, from sensible beings, was to describe God in sensible terms; it meant enclosing God in the contingent world of finite beings, and so could not reach Him, who was outside creation. Similarly, to take Aristotle's first cause was to prove the existence of movement in things, not God's existence. On the other hand, Duns realized that, by man's very nature, his proofs for God could only be from effects – *a posteriori*; accordingly, illumination was no alternative. Thus in his critique of both traditions Duns showed his awareness of the inadequacy of Augustinianism no less than of Thomism.

Secondly, Duns's alternative is notable for the degree to which he restricted the scope of reason. It is *a posteriori* like St Thomas's proofs, but not from sensory experience. The concept of being is the most universal and certain of all human knowledge. But since, through Adam's transgression, man can only know by abstraction and is not able to seize the truth directly, he is dependent upon the senses for his knowledge. He cannot, therefore, attain to the true nature of being as it appears to him in individual things; for these describe only individual contingent beings. Accordingly, Duns has no use for Aristotle's categories of potency and act as a means of describing God, because they bear no analogy to Him. To posit God's attributes from created being is to conceive God in created terms. Similarly, analogy would imply an order of priority in beings, with God's coming first; and this distinction between divine and created being would mean describing God in His own terms – from intuition, not from evidence.

For this reason Duns criticized Henry of Ghent for adopting analogy. He himself took over Avicenna's concept of being as a universal nature which could be applied indifferently to all that existed, including God: 'It extends to all that is not nothing.'* Univocity differs from analogy, firstly, in dealing with the general notion of being and not with concrete individuals actually existing; secondly, it is the most abstract degree of being possible, the same at all levels; thirdly, it is a common nature, the foundation of all other natures; that is, it precedes actual beings and is not derived from them.

This reduction of being to its ultimate degree of abstraction is the only possible means of maintaining a unity which embraces God as well as His creatures and yet transcends sense perception. It applies in one and the same sense to all being. It is the one way by which man can reach a general view; but since it is still at only the lowest reach of being it cannot explain God except in terms of the modes of being: for that is all which the concept of being enables us to deduce.

These modes were infinite being and finite being; and Duns directs his proof of God's existence to showing, (1) that there

*See *Opus Ox.*, 1, 3, 2.

must be a first being (the *Primus* of Avicenna) and (2) that this being must be infinite. Duns proves the first by holding that there must be a first cause, for otherwise there would be a regression to infinity; that, by the same token, this first cause must be the final end of all being; and that it must be ultimate perfection and first being.* Similarly if the idea of a first being is possible, it must exist; otherwise its non-existence would be the result of another cause. But since it is, by definition, it cannot owe its existence to another; therefore to be possible it must also be necessary. As Duns says 'by excluding from being all other cause than itself, intrinsic and extrinsic, it is impossible of itself for it not to be'. That is, the very notion of primacy engenders necessary being. From this it must follow that this first being is infinite, for, as its own justification, it cannot be governed by anything; and, as unrestricted, it is infinite.

The very concept of the first being can tell us a certain amount about God: as first perfection He must be omniscient, containing in Himself the models of all that exists in creation; as infinite His essence must be indivisible, although His attributes can be distinguished formally; each corresponds to an intelligible form which our names – beauty, wisdom, perfection – designate. We shall hear more of the formal distinction later. Nevertheless, through Duns's conceptual demonstration of God, much that was germane to His nature was excluded from reason; the Trinity, many of His attributes (justice, mercy, goodness), His providence become matters only for belief – truths 'which, however, are more certain to Catholics supported not by our unseeing intellect, untrue in so many things, but firmly by God's most certain faith'.

Duns had largely followed Avicenna in his concepts of univocal being and his proofs of God. It was when he came to examine God's relation to what was outside Him that he broke off sharply. Like Henry of Ghent, Duns refused to see any meeting-point between God as necessary being and the contingent being of His creatures, except through God's will. Where Avicenna had made possible being necessary, since

*For the proofs see *Opus Ox.*, 1, 2, 2.

God Himself acted necessarily, Duns and Henry of Ghent made it radically contingent, lacking in itself any *raison d'être*. This conviction that the contingent could not lead back to the necessary had, as we have seen, led Duns to reject any but abstract notions for proof of God. It led him, equally, to make all knowledge of God stop this side of His will. Beyond expressing God's will to create, this world could offer no explanation of His ways; it certainly could not specify the way in which God worked. Consequently, there is a discontinuity between the divine and the created which is absent from the much more precise order of St Thomas. Duns in no way subscribed to the latter's specification of the relation between first and second cause to describe God and His creatures.

Duns's emphasis upon God's will as the creative cause of His actions has often been described as voluntarism; and within clearly defined limits this can be accepted. It does not mean that God's will ran riot in His own nature, or that He acted blindly; it meant simply that, in relation to all that is outside Him, God does as He wills. In God Himself His will is simply the expression of His essence; it acts on the knowledge that His intellect provides. Thus God's knowledge informs His will; and He can know without willing.* When we come to His creatures, the will is supreme because, from all the possible beings that God knows in His essence, the will then chooses those that are to be given existence; in this sense, then, for God to know His creatures is for Him to will them. 'The idea in the divine mind is an eternal reason according to which something can be formed outside this thought . . . ' It is here that Duns breaks off both from Augustinianism and from Thomism, each of which had held that the divine Idea is identical with God's essence; Duns on the other hand insisted that they were posterior to His essence, the result of His knowing Himself; this is not the same as making them created, but it made them the result of divine intellection.

When we come to Duns's theory of knowledge we can see the importance of this difference. With God's will as primary, and creation radically contingent on its workings, Duns could

*For this see *Opus Ox.*, I, 35 & 36.

have no place for the divine Ideas of the Augustinian tradition: these would constitute an unbroken link from God's essence to His creatures, where Duns wanted to emphasize the discontinuity between the necessary and contingent. For the same reason, he rejected divine illumination: it would make knowledge dependent upon the archetype or Idea in God, where Duns made all reality start with His will. In this sense, Duns was far less of a Platonist than St Thomas, while compared with Henry of Ghent he not only went with him in distinguishing essences from the divine Idea, but surpassed him in going on to deny divine illumination. For Duns, the intelligible lay with the essences in things; these were the forms which had originated from the possible Ideas in God and been given actuality by His will. But they were external to His nature. To know them was only to know a created essence, not to be brought any nearer to the divine essence.

Now the means by which Duns marked off these divine Ideas from the essences in things was his famous 'formal distinction'.* The formal distinction denoted the presence of different forms within a being, while not constituting a real distinction which would have broken its unity. Thus it is possible to recognize the humanity in Socrates as a distinct form in Socrates, without making it really separate from him as an individual. This, as we can see, was a modification of the doctrine of the plurality of forms. Its novelty lay in doing for Duns's doctrine what the *esse essentiae* did for Henry of Ghent's: it marked off the created natures from their Ideas in God; but whereas, for Henry, the *being* of the essence distinguished them, for Duns it took the *idea* or the *form* of the essence. This is where Duns's so-called realism is to be found: he identified the individual with its essence or form, as independently recognizable. But, from a strictly technical point of view, this was not realism in the sense of making the universal primary: on the contrary it was another aspect of the primacy of essences or natures which Duns took over from Avicenna and which we have seen in the univocity of being. Because the essence or the nature comes first, it was indifferent to either a

*ibid.

genus or a species; it was first and foremost a nature. As Avicenna had said, 'a horse is simply a horse': it was a horse before anything else. If it were a genus there would be no individuals; if it were an individual, there would be only one horse. Thus, as with so many Augustinians from William of Auvergne to Henry of Ghent, Duns's universe was a universe of essences in contrast to the Thomist universe of actual beings; reality dealt with essences, which contained both individuals and universals. Once more, as with St Thomas, Duns was dealing with metaphysical entities, not logical categories. This is what distinguishes them both from the thinkers of the twelfth century.

Duns's view of individuation is essentially the rider to the formal distinction. Since all universality and individuality was subsumed under essence, there had to be some specific determination which would distinguish the individual. This Duns called the 'thisness' (*haecceitas*) of anything.* It was the most immediate manifestation of the essence it represented – the particular 'thisness' of the general 'thatness'. Every individual was, therefore, 'the ultimate actuality of the form'. 'There is only an ultimate individual difference which determines the specific form.' Duns himself did not employ the term as much as his commentators after him; but it shows us a very different view of individuation from that of St Thomas. In common with all the Augustinians, it looks to forms and not to matter to determine individual being. Duns regarded matter as having its own form, and as able to exist independently. 'Matter has a certain positive reality outside the intellect . . . and it is the virtue of this reality that it can receive substantial forms.'

So far as the human soul was concerned, it had its own substantial form independent of the form of the body. 'Even without the form of the soul, the body endures, and so it is universally necessary to posit that form by which the body is a body separately from that by which it is animated.' There is therefore a plurality of forms in man with the soul as the final act and form of the human being. 'Thus every composition

*See *Opus Ox.*, II, 3.

is divided into two essential parts: on one part, its own act, that is to say, the ultimate form by virtue of which it is what it is; on the other part, the potentiality proper to the act, which includes the first matter with all the preceding forms. In this sense, I agree that this total being (*esse*) takes its complete existence from a single form which confers on everything that which it is; but it does not follow from there that everything contains simply one form, or that several forms are not included in the totality, not as specifically constituting the composition but as included in the total of the composition' (*Opus Ox.*, 1, IV, 16, 3). There could be no more succinct exposition of the foundations of the formal distinction.

Perhaps Duns's strongest Augustinian trait is to be found in his doctrine of the human will. With Henry of Ghent and the Franciscans he emphasizes its primacy in all human actions. 'The will commanding the intellect is the superior cause of its action. The intellect, however, if it is the cause of volition, is a subservient cause to the will' (*Opus Ox.*, IV, 49, 2). The reason for this is that, while the intellect seeks the truth, the will seeks the good – which is superior to truth as charity is superior to wisdom.

In contrast to Godfrey of Fontaines, who pushed to the limit the determination of the will by its object, Duns made the entire cause of willing rest with the will.* 'The total cause of willing in the will is the will.' The will alone is the source of freedom; for, unlike the intellect, whose knowledge is determined by the object known, the will can accept or reject what is brought to its attention. This very freedom is for Duns a sign that the will can only know finite beings: there is no question, as with St Bonaventure, of seeing a necessary connexion between good things and the supreme good which is God. Man, moreover, can know what he must do to reach his true end by following the moral law of doing good and the divine law of the Ten Commandments. Indeed Duns's view of the nobility of human will in its search for the good gives him a more exalted conception of human nature. Even without original sin, the Incarnation would have happened, for God,

Opus Ox., 1, 8.

in His love for His creatures, wished to associate His Son with man. This is further indication of the undetermined way in which God operated; there did not have to be an occasion in order for Him to act.

There is a similar absence of any correlation between divine actions and created forms in Duns's doctrine of grace and merit. Although he accepts the orthodox teaching of the necessity of a supernatural habit for meritorious actions, he adds that God could dispense with such forms if He willed. All that God has ordained He could as well achieve by other means. Already we have here the first glimmerings of the indeterminacy which Ockham was to exploit so ruthlessly.

Duns, then, was first and foremost a theologian determined to restore to God the powers that had been usurped by the philosophers. By making God's will the only law of creation, the unknowability of God became his starting-point. Unlike St Thomas, his concern was the discrepancy between faith and reason as opposed to their harmony. Although this served to rescue God from determinism, it struck, at the same time, a damaging blow at scholasticism. Duns's system is a commentary on the 1277 condemnations; it gave expression to the mounting desire to withdraw theology from the grip of pagan philosophy. Its most striking feature was the discontinuity which it introduced between the natural and the supernatural.

The effects were far-reaching. In the first place, Duns excluded some of the most fundamental questions from the discussion: many of the attributes of God, the Trinity, providence, and the immortality of the soul. This, in the second place, tended to set reason loose from the guidance of authority: with no ascertainable link between God and His creatures, Duns, in effect, diverted reason from discussing matters of faith and restricted it to natural phenomena. Thirdly, in the circumstances of the time, there could be no simple return to a more direct faith. For better or for worse, the full-fledged body of metaphysics and philosophy that had grown up could not be summarily dismissed: to leave it free to follow its own course was ultimately to concede to the natural standards of Averroism. It put theology in the same danger as that constituted by Averroism – of being toppled from its pedestal by those uncommited to its laws.

Although Duns had the opposite intention, his system upset the precarious balance between faith and reason. He had breached their unity too far for others not to widen it. This was not long in happening.

Perhaps the most direct sign of Duns's influence is in the *Theoremata*; they used to be considered the work of Duns, but recent study has tended to deny this. In any case, they adopt Scotist positions, such as univocal being and the formal distinction, to show that there can be no proof of God except as first cause: 'it cannot be proved that God is living'; nor that He is unique; nor that He is the only cause of the universe; nor that He alone is capable of acting without the aid of secondary causes. The great significance of the *Theoremata* is that they carry Duns's principles to their logical conclusions: that is, that to start from philosophy is never to reach a concept of the Christian God. It means becoming enmeshed in necessary causes and secondary causes, because these deal with physical laws and so with natural necessity: natural reason cannot transcend the limitations of secondary causes. But God is unconstrained. Therefore, faith, not reason, can alone describe Him. The scepticism that comes from Scotism is at the opposite pole from that of Ockhamism, but it is scepticism none the less. It was Duns's greatest legacy to the fourteenth century.

The first two decades of the fourteenth century are a confusing welter of doctrines; little is clear-cut, and it is artificial to talk in such terms as Augustinianism, Thomism, or Scotism. It is true that the latter immediately attracted followers and commentators, like Francis of Mayronnes and William of Alnwick; but eclecticism was the rule in an age preoccupied with the scope and limits of reason. Then, with the appearance of Ockham, we can say that a new era really opens.

Two of the most lively and important thinkers before Ockham were Peter Aureole and Durandus of St Pourçain. Aureole (*d.* 1322) a Franciscan, who became Archbishop of

Aix-en-Provence in 1321, was one of the most combative of all medieval thinkers. Despite his Franciscan allegiance he was far more faithful to Aristotle on those points where he followed tradition: he regarded matter as without actuality and form as only existing with matter. But he went further than these in his desire to suppress all superfluities. Only the individual was real; therefore the problem of how to explain individuation did not arise.* 'Everything is singular and nothing else.' Reality was only concerned with the singular; it is the mind that creates universals. Thus all knowledge is appearance, the result of the intellect's assimilation of the thing to itself. 'This appearance is not in the thing but only in the intellect.' What we have in the intellect, then, is a concept; by this means we know all things.

Now this is very different from the intelligible species of St Thomas: firstly, Aureole has in fact made the thing known inseparable from the knowing subject, so that the concept is at once the real thing and the thing as we see it. It is not therefore a species that we are distinguishing, but a nature as it appears in the mind. Secondly, our knowledge deals primarily neither with individuals nor with universals, but with natures in themselves. 'Things themselves are seen to the mind and that which is known is not another reflected form, but the thing itself as it appears, and this is the concept of the mind or an objective notion.' Thus in the case of a rose – an important example as it is taken up by Ockham – the form that we experience is the actual rose so far as we are able to know it; or rather it is our concept of the actual rose. Our knowledge therefore deals with immediate things; but as they appear to us, not in themselves.

As we might expect, Aureole makes a sharp distinction between the value of our different concepts: those which deal with individuals are the most worth while because they come closest to reality; the universal, on the other hand, is a pure figment of the imagination. 'It is more noble to know a thing individually and clearly than to know it in an abstract and universal way.' The differences between these types of

*For what follows, see especially *Sentences*, 1, 9.

knowledge come from the different concepts we have: 'The diversity of concepts . . . is ultimately derived from the diversity of impressions . . . one of which is more perfect, another less, on account of which the same thing in the intellect appears objectively more or less perfect.'

This view has been called pure 'conceptualism', that is, that knowledge is only of concepts, not of real things. But to describe it so is to neglect the very real objective value that Aureole put upon the senses. What in fact he was doing was to simplify the process of cognition, in common with Durandus of St Pourçain. He was trying to arrive at a way of making mental knowledge correspond with external reality, while taking account of the manner in which things were known. In one sense, he was nearer to Duns Scotus than to St Thomas: for he recognized the rose as a rose, as Duns recognized the horse as a horse; he parted company from him in making our concepts sovereign. But he cut away the species as completely unreal, leaving nothing of St Thomas's moderate realism. 'For by seeing a man or a rose, we do not reach the view of this or that rose or this or that man, but simply as rose or man.' It differed from both Scotism and Thomism, in refusing to translate this knowledge into real terms.

Another aspect of Aureole's rejection of all but individuals can be seen in his treatment of God's knowledge of free future actions (future contingents). This was to become a burning question because it raised in a very acute form the relationship of human knowledge to faith. How could God's eternal knowledge be described in temporal terms? The impossibility of doing so had always been recognized by Christian thinkers. Ultimately predestination was a mystery which belonged to God alone. It was Duns Scotus who first raised the question in a new form: in his emphasis upon God's will as a law unto itself he had broken the causal connection between God and His creatures; He was too vast and free to be the object of proof or discussion. Consequently, there could be no enunciated relationship between His willing and free will; God's own freedom made everything else so contingent that it was the guarantee of all freedom and contingency.

Duns's view of the future had rested on two main theses: the first was that all contingency was the result of God's will and could not be simply attributed to the Ideas He had of all possibles. 'The contingent should be sought in the divine will or the divine intellect; not, however, in the divine intellect . . . because whatever the intellect understands in that manner [i.e. without reference to the will], it understands entirely naturally and by natural necessity, and so there can be no contingency in knowing anything that it does not know, or in understanding anything that it does not understand by such primary understanding: therefore the first contingent should be sought in the divine will.' In other words, contingency can only come through the free choice of the will and not from the inherent knowledge of the intellect. This made God's knowledge approbative and active.

The second thesis was the separation of the past, present, and future in God: although God knew all things in His essence, He knew them as they were; for to know them all as eternally present would be to falsify the future and the past. Such a view lent itself either to not committing God to knowledge of what was not already in being, or to harnessing His will to all that was created, allowing it no autonomy. Both applications were employed during the fourteenth century, and for the first time the future came to constitute a real problem.

Hitherto there had been no real difficulty in relating what God knew to what would be, so long as this knowledge was already present in Him: He knew the future not as future but *sub specie aeternitatis* with everything ever-present in Him. There was no conflict between His omniscience and contingency. This, the traditional way of Bonaventure and Thomas, put God beyond all temporal considerations, but once His own knowledge had to correspond to temporal phases He could no longer know the future as present: to know it in advance would be to antedate it and so to rob it of contingency. It was this which largely gave rise to the controversies which broke out.

The problem can be posed as follows: if God knows all things, past, present, and future, how can His creatures be properly said to have freedom of action? Can Socrates enjoy real free choice, if God knows in advance what Socrates will do or not do? Aureole answered the question in the negative:* he refused God eternal knowledge on the ground that if something is really contingent it cannot already exist eternally. He reverts to Aristotle's position of denying God knowledge of individuals. For something to be known with certainty is to make it determined: it cannot be at once true and false; thus if something is known to God, before it takes place, it cannot be contingent; God's knowledge of contingents must therefore be neutral. He cannot know them before they have occurred. Aureole was only the first among many who were to take up this position, so destructive of traditional thinking.

Durandus of St Pourçain (1270/5–1332) also displays a certain unorthodoxy in his thought. He was a Dominican whose main offence was to contravene the doctrine of his order – Thomism. For this he was involved in a running battle with Hervé Nédélec, Peter of Palud, and other Dominicans. Durandus was not the first Dominican to be anti-Thomist: we have only to recall Kilwardby; and his own master James of Metz showed a similar tendency. In Durandus's case, however, it involved a struggle which caused him to rewrite his main work, the *Commentary on the Sentences*, three times: the second edition was after the condemnation of certain of his doctrines at the Dominican chapter-general of 1309. In the third edition, during the 1320s, he reverted to many of his initial positions.

Durandus, like Aureole, was an unquiet spirit in search of new and simpler modes of thought. In common with Aureole he rejected the proliferation of concepts; and both used the very expressions (e.g. 'It is pointless to do by more what can be done by less' or 'More should not be posed where less suffices') that used to be associated with Ockham's so-called 'razor'.

Durandus, though from a very different position, joined Aureole in denying the existence of intelligible species, universals, and hence the need to explain individuation. He recognized the individual as constituted of form and matter,

*See *Sentences*, I, 38.

but denied the latter to be essences in their own right. He therefore paid special attention to the question of the relationship between things. Relation becomes an ever more pressing problem during the fourteenth century because of the breaking down of the metaphysical unity among things. So long as there were essences, forms, genera, species, everything had a place and the problem was not their connexion but their distinctness. Now, however, the need is no longer to account for individuation but to ensure some means of relating what are taken to be separate entities. Thus, as between the thirteenth and fourteenth centuries, matters are reversed.

Durandus's approach* was to follow Henry of Ghent's triple distinction which he made in the modes of being when discussing the Trinity: being in itself (substances), being in another (accident), being in relation to another (relation). Now there are two kinds of relation, a real one between different things, and a logical one, deriving from reason. Real relation is distinct from the reality on which it is founded, not as a thing (*res*), but as a mode of being (*modus essendi*). It therefore does not enter into the composition of that to which it is related. Where real things were involved, relation between them was one of causality; but most relation was only one of reason (difference, similarity, etc.).

So far Durandus had been following Henry of Ghent and James of Metz; it was when he applied his concepts to the soul that the trouble began; for he denied the reality of the active intellect, and the action of intelligible species. He was condemned for holding that 'to feel and understand are immanent actions; therefore they are really the same as feeling and understanding'. In other words, operations were not distinct forms. This cut at the distinctions which had governed so much of thirteenth-century thinking: in this case the faculties in the soul and the need for an active intellect: 'He also said there, that such immanent actions are from the begetter itself and from the object only as a *sine qua non*.' Accordingly, for Durandus, the act of knowing issued from the relationship between the intellect and the object known; this object is the

*See *Sentences*, I, 33.

individual. The universal, therefore, does not exist in reality but only as the outcome of the individual thing's impact upon the understanding: 'it is trifling to say that the universal is in things, for the universal cannot be in things, but only singularity' (*Sentences*, II, 3, 7). The universal, then, exists only in the mind as a logical unity.

Thus, as with Aureole, though by a different psychological process, the truth is directly grasped by the intellect; there is no need to make this understanding into a concept which corresponds with reality; it is a direct contact with reality. The knowledge in the mind is the same as what is known. 'Truth first consists in this, that the thing is thus apprehended as it is in *the nature of a thing* . . . so that truth is only a relation of reason . . . according to the intellectual being which is understood and real being' (*Sentences*, I, 19, 5). All truth, therefore, is objective as opposed to Aureole's view that it is subjective. In each case, the intelligible forms and species of St Thomas and Duns Scotus have been cut away.

In his views on God's relation to His creatures Durandus comes close to a natural determinism when he suggests the efficacy of intermediaries, like the spheres.* He tends to make the created order so autonomous that, unlike Duns, there seems no need to invoke God's will; there is virtually a rupture of the connexion between nature and grace. 'God is not the cause of free will except in so far as free will is from Him and conserved [by Him].' Again: 'It follows that those things which are produced by the action of the creature are not produced immediately from God.' On the contrary, 'Those things which are from God through the medium of secondary causes are not from Him immediately'. This leads Durandus to the conclusion that 'The heavenly body has causality over free will by impeding its action indirectly . . .'. His view on future contingents,† therefore, comes close to Aureole's, though more circumspectly put. God does not know future contingents in their actual existence, but as they will be; moreover, those contingent actions which result from secondary causes are not His immediate concern, and so do not come

Sentences, Bk. II, 1, 14 and 15.　　　†*ibid*, I, 38.

within His purview. 'But of those things which come from God by means of secondary causes there are many which beyond divine knowledge have causes impeding them ... therefore these, notwithstanding God's knowledge, will come to pass contingently.'

At the other extreme, Durandus allies this autonomy of secondary causes with God's absolute power to dispense with created forms: this is particularly apparent in his view of grace, which leads him to absolve men from its necessity, if God so wills: 'A man can be dear to and loved by God before he has grace formally inhering in him' (*Sentences*, 1, 17, 1). On the other hand, man by his own powers is able to initiate the bestowal of grace and is able to avoid mortal sin. These conclusions, although not pressed too far by Durandus, recur among Ockham and his followers. Indeed, the whole of Durandus's system is a reaction against superfluities either in nature or in grace: where he cannot invoke natural reason in his support he seems quite as prepared to call in God.

Another thinker who combated many of the traditional views of the thirteenth century was Henry of Harclay (*c.* 1270–1317), Chancellor of Oxford University in 1312. He upheld God's power to do all that secondary causes could do, while attacking Duns's theory of a common nature to each individual. He moreover wanted to return to Aristotle's view of the universal as another aspect of that which was also individual: a thing is individual (Socrates) when clearly conceived, and universal when the conception is confused (man) – a position similar to Abelard's.

(ii) Ockham and Ockhamism

The advent of William of Ockham (*c.* 1300–1349) was not the bolt from the blue that used to be imagined. His positions had been well-prepared, from most points of view, and it remained for him to weld them into a devastating unity which, for sheer destructive capacity, was unequalled during the thousand years that we have been examining. Yet, as we shall

see, there was also much in Ockham's thought that was positive and of great importance for the future. Different though
he is from St Thomas, he marks a similar turning-point in
medieval thought, though in this case it was to be the
beginning of the end, not its consummation.

Ockham was born at Ockham, in Surrey, shortly before
1300; he joined the Franciscans and studied at Oxford
(1312–18) where he commented the first book of the *Sentences*.
In 1324 he was summoned to the papal court at Avignon to
answer charges of unorthodoxy; and in 1326, fifty-one propositions taken from his writings were condemned. Two
years later, having taken the side of the Spiritual Franciscans
in their controversy with Pope John XXII, he fled from
Avignon with the general of his order, Michael of Cesena.
They joined the Emperor, Louis of Bavaria, at Pisa, and then
accompanied him to Munich. From this time, until his death
there in 1349 or 1350, Ockham was mainly engaged in
combating the temporal claims of the Papacy.

Ockham's main theological works, the *Sentences*, the *Quodlibeta*, and his treatises on predestination, and God's future
knowledge, were probably completed by 1324. In addition to
these, he wrote a series of commentaries on Aristotle's *Physics*
and a number of works on logic. Despite the different points
from which Ockham has been approached, as logician, theologian, or scientist, his outlook is essentially a unity. It combines a radical empiricism with an equally radical contingency. At the immediate point of human experience, only the
individual is real: at the summit of all existence, God's will
is the only arbiter. Consequently, there is in Ockham no
exclusive affinity to any one category, least of all traditional
doctrines. His thought operates at two different levels: at the
natural he is an empiricist, refusing to stretch knowledge
beyond the bounds of ascertainable experience; in things
divine he is both fideist and sceptic, placing all theological
certainty in the tenets of faith and none in reason's power to
elicit them. In one sense, Ockham is destructive of the entire
attempt to synthesize faith and reason; in another, he gives a
new consistency to natural knowledge. He was primarily a

theologian who, in his desire to disengage faith from reason, did not stop until he had reduced their union to absurdity.

It is in his *Commentary on the Sentences* that we find the most comprehensive exposition of Ockham's outlook. Historians have tended to regard it too exclusively as a running dog-fight with Duns Scotus; and while it is true that a great deal of Ockham's attention is directed against Duns' metaphysics, this is far from being the whole story. Ockham shared Duns' desire to disengage God from the toils of Greek necessity; indeed, fundamentally, both Duns and Ockham were prompted by a common aversion to adducing revealed truths from reason. Where they differed was in their points of approach. Duns still maintained a metaphysical framework in which to place a natural theology; Ockham rejected metaphysics and with it natural theology. Duns accepted the traditional concepts, of form, matter, potency, act, cause, effect, to describe being, but refused to apply them to God. Ockham denied that there could be any valid inference beyond that provided by experience. He therefore not only abolished a God adduced from physical laws; he abolished the laws themselves.

Ockham took as his beginning the sovereignty of the individual thing; it alone was real, and therefore it alone corresponded to what could be known. Ockham was not the first to make the individual the sole reality, as we have already seen with Durandus and Aureole. Where he differed was in the radical distinction which he made between things known and the process of knowing. This involved Ockham not simply in matters of logic but psychology as well; and it is worth emphasizing that, to interpret Ockham as a logician who turned metaphysical realities into mental categories, is quite false. It was rather that, because Ockham restricted reality to the individual and knowledge to experience, he had inevitably to reject a host of concepts as mere mental constructions. Unlike Aureole, on the one hand, he did not translate knowledge of real things into concepts of the mind; nor did he follow Durandus, on the other, in making intellectual understanding dependent upon an external object. He held that there were two different types of knowledge, intuitive and abstractive.* Intuitive knowledge involved direct awareness of an object, either in the mind or in reality. 'Intuitive knowledge of a thing is that knowledge by virtue of which can be known if the thing exists or not.' Intuitive knowledge provided demonstrable evidence of the existence of contingent beings – not necessary beings. It was dependent upon a natural object for its cause, though God could by a miracle create such knowledge without the object. The essence of intuitive knowledge, then, is that it provides 'a demonstration of a thing in itself'; it is an awareness of something as opposed to an understanding or judgement of it. It was therefore the foundation of all knowledge: 'Perfect intuitive knowledge is that of which it should be said that it is experimental knowledge, and this knowledge is the cause of universal propositions, the principle of art and science.' Consequently, 'nothing can be naturally known in itself, unless it is known intuitively'.

Abstractive knowledge, in contrast, was not concerned with demonstration but with understanding: 'In opposition to intuitive knowledge, abstractive knowledge does not allow us to know if that which exists is or is not.' It dealt not with facts but with propositions. It had two aspects: 'one in respect of anything abstracted from many individuals; and thus abstractive knowledge is simply knowledge of any universal which can be abstracted from many things . . . secondly, it can be understood according to what it abstracts from existing and non-existing things'. That is to say, it can either refer to abstraction in its accepted sense or to the judgements it makes upon existents or non-existents.

Now two important consequences flow from this division. Firstly, the difference between intuitive knowledge and abstractive knowledge is the difference between evident demonstration and understanding. Although the latter derives from the former, it in no way follows from it. This must be emphasized, because the whole force of Ockham's theory hinges upon the divorce between the thing known and the process of knowing; knowing does not guarantee the truth of that knowledge. Consequently, where Duns Scotus and others

*Sentences, Bk. i, Prologue.

had used intuitive and abstractive knowledge to distinguish experience from intellection, Ockham used it to demarcate truth from speculation. For the former, the object and the intellect alone sufficed. Secondly, it made reasoning the property of terms, or signs, not things. It is here that we see the much greater profundity of Ockham's analysis as compared with Aureole or Durandus.

Ockham distinguished signs as either natural or conventional. Even before the adoption of specific words, spoken or written, the intellect contains notions of things which are the natural effects of its knowing objects. These act as the signs of things, as for example, the idea man, or dog. 'The sign by which I understand man is the natural sign of men, just as groaning is the sign of sickness . . . and such a sign can stand for men in mental propositions, just as a word can stand for things in spoken propositions' (*Sentences*, 1, 2, 7). All concepts were the product of the mind, and the stuff of understanding. Propositions themselves were made up of terms (*suppositiones*); for so soon as the object in the intellect was pondered and no longer directly perceived (intuitive knowledge), it entered the realm of abstractive knowledge. It no longer involved the objects themselves, but the concepts or signs for which they stood. All reasoning lay in the ordering of such signs.

Ockham followed the threefold classification of terms, which had become accepted as part of the new logic of the thirteenth century (*Sentences*, 1, 2, 4). Firstly, there was the material term (*suppositio materialis*) which is the word itself: 'man' as a sound; next, the personal term (*suppositio personalis*) which stands for a particular individual either in the mind or outside it: the clever Socrates; third, there is the simple term (*suppositio simplex*) which, strictly speaking, takes the place of nothing but the notion in the mind: e.g. the species man. Of these three suppositions, only the *suppositio personalis* actually corresponded to something other than itself; although not of itself real knowledge, it could have a foundation in individual things which alone really existed outside the mind. Since the only reality, man, perceived by the senses was the individual Socrates, he alone could be regarded as corresponding to the truth. The *suppositio simplex* offered no equivalent in fact, for no species was to be found in practical experience. The species, then, was a purely mental concept without any extra-mental reality; it was part of the process of knowing – the 'natural sign that can stand for men in mental propositions' – not the thing known.

This is where the great break came; it was a logical consequence of Ockham's metaphysical outlook; for in a universe where the individual constituted reality and experience, universals, species, forms, inferences, concepts, judgements, in short all that which was not individual, belonged only in the intellect. As Ockham said, 'a universal is not anything real existing in a subject either inside or outside the soul',* but 'anything which can be predicted of several things'. Its universality therefore lay 'in predication not for itself but for things it signifies'. The genus 'is not common to several things because of the identity between them, but through a certain common signification by which the same sign is common to several things signified. And so the universal is only a sign'. This sign, as we have already said, is the result of a natural quality in the soul. 'Beyond the act of understanding there is no need to posit anything else' as a cause.

The effects of Ockham's theory of knowledge were revolutionary. Based upon the sole reality of the individual, it provided a purely psychological explanation of universals: as a function of the mind they consisted in a concept of individuals confusedly known. They had no other *raison d'être* than 'nature occultly operating in universals'. Thus for the first time no real correspondence was sought for them: even Abelard with his theory of *status* had sought to relate universals to things; Ockham ruthlessly purges even these. This enabled Ockham not merely to make all species, relations, and formal distinctions logical categories, as opposed to realities, but to introduce a new order of being.

It was marked by two notable features: the first was that, since individuals were the only reality, there could be no

Sentences, I, 2, 7.

inference from cause to effect except as the result of experience. That is to say, to demonstrate the existence of A or the cause of B it was necessary to know these as facts: intuitive knowledge alone was the means of doing so: 'the knowledge of a simple [i.e. real] thing is never the sufficient cause for knowing another simple thing'.* There can be no abstractive knowledge where there has not first been intuitive experience. There is therefore no inherent principle of physical causality. Consequently, all being became made up of discrete entities, sharing no common nature; essence was indistinguishable from existence; substance was no longer to be regarded as a separate category – that which subsists in itself – but could only be known through its qualities, as for example the fire is known by its heat; matter is not Aristotle's potentiality but in act, since it exists as any other nature which exists: therefore it does not change on receiving a form, but, on the contrary, is inseparable from form in every being.

Secondly, Ockham gave a new direction to physics. He turned from qualitative distinctions to quantitative: that is to say, by accepting a thing as complete in its own right, he could only distinguish it from something else as physically separate. Thus extension, which had previously been regarded as an accident of matter (as matter had been regarded as an accident of form), now became the means of marking off one thing from another. Concepts were sacrificed to physical reality, leaving only distinct composite beings: 'Extension or quantity does not designate an absolute or relative reality outside the substance of the quality, but it is a voice or concept which principally designates substance and connotes several other things . . . ' (*Sentences*, IV, 4). Not only does this lead Ockham to jettison the classical metaphysics but also to annex movement to bodies, instead of making it a separate entity.

Aristotle's universe had run on the assumption that it was finite, moved by an external cause. This had been taken up by all the scholastics, not least by Duns Scotus, who had only differed from the Aristotelians in refusing to work back from the physical laws of the world to its creator. All change and

*See *Sentences*, Bk. I, Prologue, 9.

movement were the result of a change from one state to another through an efficient cause. Ockham, true to his principle of making only the individual real, saw no such dependence of an effect upon inner principles: a body fell not because of a separate principle which moved it to realize its nature, but by the attraction of the earth's mass; a body moved not through inner impulsion but from an outer impetus. Above all, there could be no assurance that the world was finite, or that it had a governing unity, or that it was not eternal, or that there were not several worlds. All these beliefs were founded upon Aristotle's assumption that there cannot be a regression to infinity. But this lies outside the range of practical experience, and, moreover, it rests upon distinctions that are inaccessible to natural reason. Thus Ockham did what no one else had yet done: he transposed a metaphysic of individual existence into a new conception of the universe. Destructive though it might be of natural theology, it helped to liberate natural knowledge.

Ockham had arrived at his view of nature and reality by a process of empiricism; at the level of natural causation he denied nothing but what was undemonstrable. His was a reaction in the strongest terms against the luxuriance of classical metaphysics, but it was not scepticism any more than it was pure logic. When we turn to theology, however, we are faced with a different situation, one which, in its effects, bears no direct comparison with Ockham's natural empiricism.

Now there are two main aspects to Ockham's treatment of faith. One is to rule out what cannot be demonstrated; the other is to invoke God's absolute power (*potentia absoluta*) in matters of dogma. In the first case, Ockham rejects any certain proof for God's existence by means of a first cause: we have no intuitive knowledge of Him and so we cannot infer that He exists: 'Nothing can be known naturally in itself, unless it is known intuitively. But God cannot be known by us intuitively from our natural powers.' In the second place, the cosmology of a finite series of causes is invalid: not only is there no evidence that something cannot move itself, but in the case of the soul or a falling heavy body it is palpably clear that there is self-movement. Finally, the possibility of an infinity of cause and effect is suggested if we take as an example the vibrations of a long cord: each part moves the next one, so that an infinite series could be propagated.

For these reasons Ockham feels able to reject Anselm's proofs; indeed since all medieval proofs for God's existence ultimately depend upon a first cause, Ockham has cut the ground from under the central support of scholasticism. It is true that Ockham himself is prepared to prove that there must be a first efficient cause, from the need to conserve secondary causes already in existence: but this is not the same as proving that God is creator of these causes. There is nothing to prevent our positing a plurality of first causes in opposition to monotheism, any more than there is anything to prevent our positing several worlds. God's attributes, likewise, undergo a virtual annihilation: as finite, we cannot prove that God is infinite or omniscient or just or good.

In common with Ockham's rejection of all distinction and relation, except those between real things, he allows no formal diversity in the divine essence. The divine names which are given to God signify Him, but are not God. God's being defies analysis, and so does His mode of operating: Ockham acknowledges that He evidently knows all future contingent actions, 'but I do not know how to explain by what manner' (*Sentences*, 1, 38, 1). Ockham's God, therefore, lacks all the elaborate analysis and ordering of the divine attributes which we find with Duns Scotus. The radical simplicity of Ockham's God identifies His will with His knowledge and both with His essence; for God to be is also to know and to will.

Ockham imposes a similar austerity on the human soul: although there is a sensitive and an intellective soul, the will is inseparable from them. The will has freedom of choice, and the act of willing is a rational one; there is no need to describe the will as primary. It is impossible to prove the soul's immortality or its spiritual nature.* These can only be held on faith. In discussing these questions Ockham has limited himself to what is probable: that is, he has, from the arguments

*See *Quodlibet*, 1, 10.

for and against, refused to accept evident conclusions. To use his own words: 'from this it does not follow that this can be demonstrated . . . but we hold this by faith'.

This reliance upon probable arguments instead of proof positive has been widely taken to be the hall-mark of scepticism in the fourteenth century. But this seems too loose a definition: for although it points to a widespread lack of certainty, this does not necessarily involve scepticism; at worst, it withdraws reason from untenable positions: it does not doubt the reality of what is perceived. In itself to make something probable, rather than certain, can be an added source of strength both to faith and reason, as with St Thomas. Where Ockham made a flagrant departure from precedent was by invoking God's absolute power.

Now God's absolute power (*potentia absoluta*) had been used as far back as Peter Damian's time in the eleventh century to preserve God's freedom of action. It differed from His ordained power (*potentia ordinata*) in denoting God's omnipotence purely and simply. It was outside all space and time in that it was uncommitted to upholding any set order in the universe. Freedom to will was its only *raison d'être*. In contrast, God's ordained power was directed to sustaining this world; it constituted God's law of creation, the eternal ordinance by which everything was governed. As given expression in the Bible and interpreted by the Church, it was immutable and irrevocable. Thus while God's ordained power applied less to His own nature than to His creatures, His absolute power referred to Himself, and so, in the final analysis, it could override His ordinances. The latter were only a particular application of a wider authority: like an ambassador vested with certain rights they could be superseded.

This is exactly what Ockham did. Already, we have mentioned that Duns and Durandus had both employed God's absolute power in discussing God's freedom to reward a man not in a state of grace; and Ockham clearly took this up from Duns whose views on this subject he defends against Peter Aureole. The difference between Duns's and Ockham's views of God's absolute power is the difference that runs through their entire outlooks: where Duns had utilized it to assert the radical contingency of all created forms, Ockham uses it with devastating effect to show the impossibility of discussing matters of faith.* In his hands, not only can grace be dispensed with in a meritorious action, but the established categories of good and evil, cause and effect, are overturned: 'God can, if He wills, dispense with all order in awarding man final glory.' In consequence a habit of grace lost its intrinsic worth; free will alone became the *sine qua non* for reward; God could enable a man to hate Him; beatitude could be inefficacious; grace and sin could coexist.

These positions do more than safeguard God from the necessity of following a constant order; they make a mockery of revealed truth. Where Duns had distinguished an order by which God willed, Ockham in identifying the divine essence and the divine will could regard God as synonymous with His will. If God were to be discussed, it turned the discussion to the sheer unrestricted limits of His omnipotence. It is here, in the use of God's *potentia absoluta*, therefore, that the full impact of scepticism is to be met; for it applied to God and to faith, Ockham's principle of neutrality towards what was unproven. It meant the refusal to be committed to what could not be verified. When applied to faith it led less to probability than to possibility: for in the absence of A to the exclusion of B, either was possible. In God's case, it meant that it was always possible, by His absolute power, for Him to act in one way as opposed to another. This in turn led to a radical indeterminacy, far more extreme than that of Duns: in starting from a neutral position, anything was possible, and so there could be no means of knowing what He might will. Morality for the first time lay simply with God's arbitrary decree; with God and His will synonymous there could be no way of judging right or wrong other than by the decrees of His will. Thus any switch from God's ordained to His absolute power involved throwing all certainty, morality, and indeed probability into the melting-pot: in their place anything could emerge.

With nothing beyond His range, God could be judged by

*For what follows see *Sentences*, I, 17.

the farthest flights of fancy. It was this which made God's *potentia absoluta*, rather than mere probability, the real heart of fourteenth-century scepticism: it served the double end of freeing God from reason and experience from faith. To say that anything is possible for God and to apply this to generally accepted tenets was to dissolve the whole foundation of a natural theology: where probability simply questioned, God's absolute power destroyed. Where reason ended, God's *potentia absoluta* began, taking charge of what was not subject to verification and showing how uncertain and unknown it was. It removed all effective standards of judgement. In that sense, the God of scepticism ceased to be the God of tradition: He was so unknowable that His attributes melted in the blaze of His omnipotence, leaving no certainty.

The doubt that God's absolute power cast was not applied indiscriminately by either Ockham or his followers; we noted its reference to God's ability to create intuitive knowledge of a non-existent, but generally it was directed to those matters where faith and reason were both involved. It was mainly applied to questions of grace, free will, merit, and, in some cases, future contingents, because all these could be interpreted from practical experience in addition to being the subject of revelation. This meant that theology and experience could give two different answers to the same question: accordingly God's absolute power was invoked in an effort to free the natural from a supernatural explanation and to treat it in the light of practical experience. This seems to be confirmed by the conclusions which were drawn: as we have seen, free will and human autonomy were the gainers: they were, in the name of God's absolute power, freed from the necessity of supernatural habits and forms; conversely, habits, forms, standards, a fixed order – all suffer annihilation from God's power to dispense with them: 'whatever God can do by means of an efficient cause, He can do immediately'. This, in effect, is Ockham's text for destroying any mingling between faith and reason: in the name of the contingency in God's will, there can be no certainty in His actions.

Ockham's use of God's absolute power opened a new era;

and until the second half of the fourteenth century all theological discussion was permeated by God's *potentia absoluta*. It gave the final stamp to his outlook in putting theology beyond the reach of reason. This is the dominant tone which Ockhamism set: it was not one of unbelief, so much as doubt over its rational foundations. The constant cry is not that we do not believe, but that belief is a matter of faith. Thus Ockham helped to transform faith as much as reason: while the latter came increasingly to rest upon empirical observation and natural causation, the former was directed increasingly towards a positive theology, with its own independent truths: 'all truths necessary to man in his journey to eternal beatitude are theological truths'. Certainty lay in faith alone without the need of intermediaries. At one and the same time, a growing empiricism was giving rise to a growing fideism. Ockham perhaps did more than anyone else to effect this change.

Ockham's doctrines met with immediate response, and the period until the Black Death, which carried off so many of his generation, is the most extreme and unorthodox in the history of medieval thought. So far it has hardly been examined; it still suffers from a tendency among historians to look for a largely non-existent continuity with the main streams of thirteenth-century thought. Yet it becomes ever more difficult to speak of an Augustinian or Aristotelian tradition the more we consider the thinkers concerned. Robert Holcot (*c.* 1300–1349), the English Dominican, is a good example of how deeply Ockham's scepticism had penetrated even St Thomas's order. Holcot's works include a variety of commentaries on the Bible, and like many of his order, including Thomas of Waleys, he combines his interest in theology and preaching with a fascination for the pagan world of the ancients.

His main theological work, the *Commentary on the Sentences*, shows very forcibly how times had changed since the days of St Thomas, or even Duns Scotus. Firstly, the extent of the Commentary had shrunk severely: its four books together totalled a mere handful of questions. Secondly, these were very largely devoted to God's will, God's knowledge of the future, merit, grace and its relation to free will, sin, and the sacraments.

Holcot follows Ockham in his two main tenets: his theory of knowledge, and the use of God's *potentia absoluta*. With each, however, he goes farther than his master, reducing all objects of knowledge to concepts, and giving God's absolute power such unqualified application that it swallows up any semblance of order. Thus, where Ockham had always made free will a *sine qua non* in an act of merit, Holcot removes even this pre-requisite.* Not only is there no order between grace and glory, but God can love the sinner more than one in grace; there is no need for free will to do anything to gain divine acceptance: 'one loving God less [than another] can be loved the more by God'; a man can merit by false faith, and, conversely, can receive no reward for fulfilling God's precepts. God Himself 'can deceive and lie', and in the case of His knowledge of future contingents God could cause Christ to deceive His disciples. Holcot's discussion of future contingents is notable for the way in which it involves revelation;† he tends to suggest that God, rather than be misled in His knowledge of future contingents, knows only what is necessary: contingents are outside his pur-view. As with Aureole and Durandus, it is largely an alterna-tive between God's knowledge and free will, a further sign of the breakdown in the union of faith and reason.

The audacity of many of Holcot's conclusions, sheltered by the umbrella of God's *potentia absoluta*, is equally striking in two other contemporaries, Thomas Buckingham and Adam of Woodham. Both of these show the same limitation in their range of questions and a similar preoccupation with the rela-tion of free will to God's will. Buckingham (*c.* 1290–1351) besides removing any call for a state of grace in man, is particu-larly concerned with safeguarding the freedom of the human will from necessity, divine or natural. As a free act must be contingent, it cannot be known to God except contingently: that is, as equally able to be or not to be. God's knowledge of future contingents, therefore, cannot be certain. Consequently, what He reveals in the Word of Christ may never come to pass; consequently, Christ Himself can deceive and be deceived. Revelation itself, in so far as it refers to the future, is

Sentences, I, 4.   †*ibid*, II, 2.

reduced from an eternal verity to a mere contingency. God Himself is put at the mercy of events outside His own control.

Adam of Woodham (*d.* 1357), a confrère of Ockham's, is the most extreme of all his followers. He, particularly, is so aware of the magnitude of God's *potentia absoluta* that everything touching the relationship between God and man seems fraught with its consequences. 'It seems to me that the doctors would have in vain distinguished between God's ordained and absolute power were He not able to do and dispose differently than He has in fact [i.e. by His ordained power]' (*Sentences*, I, 17, 3). Grace itself becomes so neutral that it can coexist with mortal sin; more, an angel or a man in a state of grace can have their future damnation revealed to them. On future contingents Adam takes Buckingham's path in allowing God contingent knowledge of contingent actions: any proposition which refers to the future can be true or false; therefore what is revealed in the Word may never take place. Moreover, by His absolute power, God is free from the necessity of accepting His own revelation: He can, therefore, turn against His own knowledge and indeed go so far as to mislead and to sin: 'It can be said that He could lie as He could sin' (*Sentences*, III, 5).

These are only a few of the number who followed Ockham; but their preoccupation with carrying speculation to the farthest realms indicates a deep-seated change in the climate of thought. It can only be described as one of extreme scepticism to all that could only be taken on trust; for it shows an overriding lack of confidence in any attempt to apply reason to faith.

In Paris a similar outlook can be found in John of Mirecourt and Nicholas of Autrecourt. John of Mirecourt, a Cistercian, was condemned in 1347 by the Chancellor of the University for over forty erroneous opinions taken from his *Sentences*. These views derived from a number of different thinkers and show no real unity of outlook. John held that there could be no certainty of external reality since God could make the illusory seem real; God could determine the human will even to sin and to hate Him.

Nicholas of Autrecourt had also to undergo condemnation in 1347 when his letters to Bernard of Arezzo and his *Exigit ordo executionis* were condemned. Nicholas took to extremes Ockham's theory of knowledge. The only order of certainty was experience, and the only evident and certain principle is that of contradiction: that is, a thing cannot be what it is not. Thus he concluded that the predicate must be identical with the subject it describes; or, put another way, knowledge of a thing can only apply to that thing and no other. Accordingly, there was no means of inferring one thing from another, and hence no principle of causality: 'it cannot be inferred from one thing known . . . that another thing exists'. All knowledge is therefore reduced to appearances, and all certitude to probability: 'I say, therefore, if any certainty for us inheres in things that it is probable that all that appears to be is, and all that appears to be true is true.' Only our five senses guarantee certainty.

Nicholas has often been called the Hume of the middle ages; but this is to misunderstand him. Nicholas was an extreme empiricist who took the appearances of individual things to be real, without being prepared to move to general inferences. Hume on the other hand restricted himself to the certainty of our perceptions without accepting their correspondence to an external order of reality. Where Nicholas did show his scepticism was in helping on Ockham's demolition of any fixed essences in the world: substance was unreal; we had no evidence of the faculties in the soul (though we had self-awareness of the soul); God could not be proved. It is hardly surprising that Nicholas, in adhering to the atomic theory of a universe of discrete individuals, with no apparent unity, should come into conflict with dogma.

(iii) Science

In the present state of our knowledge of the fourteenth century we have no clear idea of the lineage of many of its thinkers. It is often held that most of the scientific knowledge of the period was from Ockham's disciples, but this is far from certain. John Buridan (*d.* after 1358), for instance, may have been an Ockhamist, but he also, as rector of Paris University for the second time in 1340, presided over a condemnation of some of Ockham's doctrines. Moreover, while following Ockham's logic, he took a different view of metaphysics, where he accepted the reality of the concept. The essence of a thing – the humanity of Socrates – was as real as the individual; it was but another aspect of the same reality. The so-called ass named after Buridan, and which was supposed to have starved through inability to make a choice between two equally attractive bundles of hay, was probably a parody of his teaching on the will. Buridan held that ultimately the will could not but choose what it judges to be the best, though it could for a time suspend judgement.

When he applied his metaphysics to physics, Buridan reached a strikingly fruitful conclusion on movement. Contrary to Ockham, he rehabilitated movement, as well as quantity, as independent categories. Thus where Ockham had attributed movement solely to that which was moving, Buridan made it the result of an impulse (*impetus*). A body, once set in motion, was not maintained thus by the air, as Aristotle had held, but by the velocity of the initial impulse, itself proportionate to the mass of the body. A heavy body will not travel so far as a lighter body just because it contains more matter; similarly it falls more quickly because an impulse is added to its fall, thereby quickening its descent.

Nicholas of Oresme (*d.* 1382), in addition to his importance in political economy, was an even more outstanding scientist, especially in his theory of falling bodies, where he developed Buridan's theory of *impetus*; astronomy where he upheld the diurnal movement of the earth; and geometry where he used coordinate lines.

Two other important successors to Buridan were Albert of Saxony and Marsilius of Inghen. Albert (1316–1390) began his studies at the newly-founded University of Prague, from where he went to Paris and later to Vienna. Like Buridan, he combated Nicholas of Autrecourt's atomism and also followed his master in his theory of *impetus*, which he applied to the movement of the planets. Marsilius of Inghen (*d.* 1396) gave a more metaphysical interpretation to the problem of *impetus*, regarding it as distinct from movement with its own separate nature. He, too, bears witness to the growing exodus from Paris University, following the Great Schism; he became first rector of Heidelberg in 1386.

Whatever the precise relationship of Ockhamism to science, it is abundantly clear that the latter developed and grew in circumstances where practical experience was increasingly treated in its own right. So long as there was no clear-cut division between natural and supernatural knowledge, there could be little scope for independent investigation of natural phenomena. The emphasis of the sceptics upon verification of all experience helped towards this by making real causality the only yardstick. They dispensed with the final and the formal causes, leaving the field free for the interplay of material and efficient causes. From this point of view, there was no need to explain experience in any but physical terms. Thus if the fourteenth century signalled the breakdown of scholasticism it also ushered in a more genuinely scientific outlook in the West than at any time since ancient Greece.

(iv) The theological reaction and mysticism

The haze that still prevails over our knowledge of the fourteenth century prevents any clear sight of many of its thinkers. The position of important men like Walter Burleigh, Richard FitzRalph, Gregory of Rimini, as yet eludes our grasp, though they all seem to have opposed the 'modern way' (*via moderna*) associated with either Ockham or his followers: Burleigh particularly seems to have directed much of his fire against Ockham's theory of knowledge, while Gregory of Rimini and FitzRalph, in theology at any rate, combated the extreme views which grew up among thinkers like Holcot, Buckingham, and Woodham.

Perhaps the most outstanding of all these anti-sceptics was Thomas Bradwardine (*c.* 1290–1349), proctor of Oxford University, Archbishop of Canterbury, and one of the foremost mathematicians of the day. His *De Causa Dei* is the most remarkable testimony we have to the prevalence of un-orthodox doctrines on grace, free will, merit, and future con-tingents. It consists of a sustained polemic against their upholders, whom he describes as the 'Modern Pelagians' because they were trying to subvert God's grace by free will. In his own words: 'I rarely heard anything of grace said in the lectures of the philosophers . . . but every day I heard them teach that we are masters of our own free acts, and that it stands in our power to do either good or evil, to be either virtuous or vicious.' His *De causa Dei*, which originated in a course of lectures, was designed to rebut the multitude who, in their zeal for free will, even allowed it such liberty over the future that its deeds were put before the voice of the prophets. The work was moulded to the twin questions of grace and future contingents, which, as we have seen, were rife among Ockham's followers.

It is not hard to see why Bradwardine dubbed his opponents Pelagian, for although their views had a very different source from those of Pelagius, they led to many of the same effects. The sceptics, by putting God beyond the terms of human understanding, left no knowledge of His ways or nature to reason; His will, instead of being the constant point of reference, became the source of uncertainty; and the effect on man was to make him virtually self-sufficient, since he could not be discussed in theological terms. It enabled the sceptics to ignore the fallen state of man; grace lost any intrinsic efficacy and could be dispensed with; merit had its origin in free will; the future became its preserve; and revelation when applied to the future had no more certainty than any other contingency.

Bradwardine's reply was to reassert God's grace to the exclusion of all merit and to win back to God all power which he considered to have been usurped to man. His defence of God's cause was essentially the reply of faith to scepticism; it was from one for whom theology came first.

The outstanding feature of *De Causa Dei* was its refusal to concede anything to fact or to natural evidence. Bradwardine, on the contrary, saw all truth as revealed truth, and in this sense his outlook may well be described as the doctrine of authority. He judged everything in divine terms; and the effect of his system was to make all creation merely the extension of the divine will. This he achieved by making God the senior partner in every act of free will. God was not only first cause but the most immediate cause, moving the creature more immediately than it moved itself. This principle of divine participation is something far more extreme than any of the traditional concepts. Where St Thomas had held that every action of a secondary cause was both entirely from itself and entirely from God, Bradwardine virtually disregarded the former. Furthermore, his principle of divine participation was founded on the direct movement of God's will as the cause of all that concerned His creatures. This made God's determinism into an active and immediate control extending as much to future actions as to the present.

From these positions Bradwardine was able to put revealed truth into motion: since God was senior partner in every created act, He must come first in whatever was under discussion; since, equally, He was omnipotent, and had all the attributes enumerated in dogma, neither He nor His creatures needed to be subject to any practical proof. Thus, once having established God's existence, which Bradwardine did by a combination of the unmoved first mover and Anselm's ontological proof, all discussion became merely the enunciation of first principles: in the case of the creation of the world in time, for example, there was no need for hesitation over its probability; it sufficed that God, as creator of all things, must also have created time. Similarly, with grace, merit, free will, future contingents, these problems allowed of equally definitive answers. Because God must be involved in all that His creatures did, His grace must come before a meritorious act of free will; the future was not only known to God but willed by Him: hence contingency far from being outside His knowledge was the product of His willing. By these means Bradwardine was able to regard the whole of creation as the extension of God's will; given His nature as revealed in Scripture, everything else followed.

Now the significance of Bradwardine's outlook is that it did for theology what scepticism was doing for reason: it made it a self-contained body of laws and principles which had no call upon the resources of natural experience. Bradwardine employed the full weight of dialectic and Aristotle to make faith independent of metaphysics or philosophy. Although he used reason, it was to establish his theological standpoint that he did so. Like his opponents, though for different reasons, he regarded God as too absolute to be described in any but His own terms: fact and logic were there only to lend support to what had been divinely ordained; he made everything follow from the premises of God's existence, not from those of reason. Consequently he was full of scorn for reason's attempt to reach God. 'Oh, blush for shame, philosophy and arrogant knowledge, to presume to have the smallest understanding of God.' Thus Bradwardine, as much as the sceptics, destroyed the union between faith and reason. By putting all truth upon a theological plane, he refused to concede to natural considerations. His answer to the challenge of scepticism was the authority of dogma. There is much in Bradwardine's reliance upon Scripture and the irrevocability of the divine will which is to be found in the Reformers of the sixteenth century. It is evidence of the new form that theology was taking in response to the challenge of scepticism.

Although Bradwardine so far remains an isolated figure in his struggle with Ockhamism, mysticism also provided another outlet from the exigencies of a natural theology. Mysticism, at least since the time of St Bernard, had remained part of the medieval scene, often colouring the outlooks of some of the greatest thinkers – such as Bonaventure. But it became a definable movement again towards the end of the thirteenth century, largely under the impulse of Albert the Great's Neoplatonism and with Cologne as its centre. Already Albert's pupils, Hugh of Strasbourg (d. 1268) and Ulrich of Strasbourg (d. 1277), had emphasized the Neoplatonic elements in his doctrine, notably the soul as an independent substance, the need for illumination, and the so-called flow of being from intelligence to intelligence. Ulrich, particularly, gave expression to this resurgent Neoplatonism, most of the main propositions of which are to be found in his thought: a hierarchy of Intelligences which are the bearers of the Ideas inhering in God; universal illumination through the divine light and with it the soul a spiritual substance, receiving its knowledge through illumination; the identification of being with form. With Dietrich of Freiburg (*d.* 1310), another Dominican, the groundwork of a speculative mysticism was laid, when he took this Neoplatonic outlook one stage further and saw the centre of the soul as a divine 'recess', directly illumined by God.

Although not a mystic himself, Dietrich betrayed the pronounced influence of Proclus on his thought. This was due mainly to the series of translations of Proclus's works made by William of Moerbeke in 1281; and henceforth Proclus became one of the main sources of mystical inspiration. In Dietrich's case, the hierarchy of Intelligences which emanated from God, through the Word, meant that the active intelligence of the human soul was in direct contact with Him. It was no longer a faculty in the soul, but a distinct substance bearing the light of God and situated in the recess of the soul; it constituted the soul's essence, not *vice versa*, and therefore all understanding proceeded from turning inwards towards it. It is not hard to see that, in spite of the Aristotelian terminology which Dietrich used (such as the active and possible intelligences), he had, in fact, reverted to the Plotinian doctrine of the soul as an image (*similitudo*) of pure being in God and that all knowledge lies in retracing the path to its source in Him. It led Dietrich to mingle the created and the divine, and to seeing the beatific vision as a created light augmented by grace.

John (Master) Eckhart (1260–1327), a German Dominican of high standing, virtually broke down the accepted order of Christian belief in his concern to make God the source of all intelligibility. The deviations to which this led him caused him to be condemned in 1329, two years after his death.

Eckhart's thought is confusing because he seems to change his terminology between his earlier and his later works; but nevertheless there seems little doubt of its ultimate import. Like Plotinus and Proclus, he tends to view God as the One, the source of being rather than the first being. In his earlier Questions on being, he takes up a position that makes God Intelligence first and foremost; He is being only by virtue of His understanding: 'His understanding is the foundation of His being'. Although Eckhart later modified this, throughout his works there lurks the distinction which Gilbert de la Porrée had made between God as divine being and God as the form divinity; indeed in his discussions on the Trinity, Eckhart reverses the order between the Divine Persons: he makes the Father wisdom under which are subsumed the life of the Son and the being of the Holy Spirit; this is in contrast to the accepted way enunciated by St Augustine, where the Father as being is the foundation of the wisdom of the Son and the life of the Holy Spirit. Its importance is that Eckhart, in positing the soul's return to God, is trying to make it transcend all being to reach its source in the Intelligible nature of the One.

At the other end of the scale, Eckhart regarded creatures as non-being; they only share in being in so far as they have an intellect, thereby participating in the pure being of God. Man's affinity with God lies in the understanding in the soul: it is a divine spark – a direct image of God, containing the same simplicity and purity that the divine intellect contains. Thus to reach God is to turn inwards to this divine element: it is to cast off all desire and aspiration (even those towards sanctity and God Himself), and to attain to a state of sheer abnegation and nothingness. Hence a man's highest attainment is Poverty: to do nothing, to own nothing, to know nothing; thereby he is open to God.

The importance of Eckhart's doctrine lies in his disavowal of the sacraments or prayer or grace as helping directly to this end. Although they have their part as a preparation, they, too, must be cast off if man is to have direct access to God. This rejection of the traditional requirements of the Church shows the danger to authority which such mysticism represented.

John Tauler (1300–1361) and John Ruysbruck (1293–1381) are striking testimony to the influence of Eckhart. Tauler followed him in seeing the depth of the soul as its essence,

in which reigned peace and repose, and through which direct
contact with God could be made. Ruysbruck, on the other
hand, tended, as St Bernard before him, to stress the interaction between God's grace and the human will: he took a
more active view of the soul's ascent to God, in response to
the grace which God infuses. Hence with him, mysticism becomes more a doctrine of movement than rest: contemplation
can only be achieved through a series of necessary stages which
lead to a gradual orientation of the soul to God.

(v) Political theories

By the fourteenth century, the secular state, like reason
itself, was being withdrawn from ecclesiastical jurisdiction.
Dante, Marsilius of Padua, and Ockham all asserted its claim
to independence and, indeed, political hegemony over the
Church. This separation of the two powers is often ascribed to
Averroism. Certainly its influence on a man like John of
Jandun (d. 1328) is not wanting, while Dante himself gave
Siger of Brabant an honoured place in heaven next to
St Thomas. But, once more, it would perhaps be more just
to speak of an Aristotelianism uncommitted to Christian
authority.

Dante Alighieri (1265–1321) was the first to make an all-out
defence of the primacy of a secular Empire, which he regarded
as direct heir to ancient Rome. His main emphasis was upon
the necessity of universal peace as the prerequisite of the good
life of reason. This demanded a universal ruler, to be supreme
arbiter of all other powers – a position which could only rest
with the Emperor, holding his authority directly from God.
Thus Dante, unlike St Thomas, who had accepted a balance
between *regnum* and *sacerdotium*, overthrew the doctrine of the
Two Swords. His main thesis of a supreme universal ruler
independent of the Church became the battle-cry of Marsilius
and Ockham.

Marsilius of Padua (d. between 1336 and 1343) was a com-
panion of the Averroist John of Jandun. In his *Defensor Pacis*
he gave full rein to the separation of the secular from the

spiritual. Throughout the work there is a belief in the self-sufficiency of the natural which enables him to postulate a single ruler, the Legislator, for all earthly society. He denied that the priesthood was a separate body; it was distinguished only by its profession, and in matters of government it came under the jurisdiction of the prince. The Pope himself should be subjected to a General Council, including laymen as well as clerics.

Ockham, likewise, affirmed the independence of the State. Following his flight from Avignon, he especially directed his attacks against the Pope, who, he held, was as liable to error as any other mortal. With Marsilius, he also vested supreme ecclesiastical authority in a General Council of the Church. Thus the progression was complete: the State, which for St Augustine had barely existed, was now all but omnipotent.

Select Bibliography

I. SOURCES

The great majority of medieval philosophical and theological writings can still only be found in Latin, with Migne's *Patrologia Latina*, Paris 1844–64, in 221 vols, the largest single collection.

There are complete English translations of the works of St Augustine (Dodds, Edinburgh 1871–6, 16 vols, and *The Fathers of the Church*, New York, 10 vols so far) and of St Thomas Aquinas (by both the English and the American Dominicans). In addition selections have been made from the writings of each (W. J. Oates, *Basic Writings of St Augustine*, 2 vols, New York 1948; A. C. Pegis (ed.), *Basic Writings of St Thomas Aquinas*, 2 vols, New York 1944) as well as numerous renderings of individual works.

For the works of the majority of medieval thinkers, however, the most accessible and comprehensive collection of texts in English is to be found in R. McKeon, *Selections from Medieval Philosophers*, 2 vols., New York 1923–30.

II. GENERAL WORKS

E. Bréhier: *La Philosophie du Moyen Âge*, Paris 1937.

F. C. Copleston: *A History of Philosophy* (Burns, Oates and Washbourne), vols. 2 and 3, 1950 and 1953.

É. Gilson: *La Philosophie au Moyen Âge*, Paris 1944.

É. Gilson: *A History of Christian Philosophy in the Middle Ages* (Sheed & Ward) 1955.

M. Grabmann: *Die Geschichte der scholastischen Methode*, 2 vols., Freiburg im Breisgau, 1900, 1910.

Ueberweg-Geyer: *Grundriss der Geschichte der Philosophie*, vol. 2, Berlin 1928.

III. REFERENCE WORKS

The *Dictionnaire de Théologie Catholique*, Paris 1903–50, provides important articles and bibliography on all the main medieval thinkers.

H. Rashdall (ed. Powicke and Emden): *Medieval Universities*, Oxford 1936.

P. Duhem: *Le système du monde*, Paris 1913–17.

IV. INDIVIDUAL STUDIES

The following are a few of the works which may serve as an appropriate introduction to some of the more important thinkers and topics.

St Augustine:
   E. Portalié: article in *Dictionnaire de Théologie Catholique*.
John Scotus Erigena:
   M. Cappuyns: *Jean Scot Erigène, sa vie, son œuvre, sa pensée*, Paris 1933.
St Anselm:
   A. Koyré: *L'Idée de Dieu dans la philosophie de S. Anselm*, Paris 1923.
Abelard:
   J. K. Sikes: *Peter Abailard*, Cambridge 1932.
School of Chartres:
   A. Clerval: *Les Écoles de Chartres au moyen âge, du Ve au XVIe siècle*, Paris 1895.
St Bernard:
   É. Gilson: *La Théologie mystique de Saint Bernard*, Paris 1934.
Arabian philosophy:
   Carra de Vaux: *Les Penseurs de l'Islam*, 3 vols, Paris 1921–3.
   S. Munk: *Mélanges de philosophie juive et arabe*, Paris 1927.
Jewish philosophy:
   J. Husik: *A History of Mediaeval Jewish Philosophy*, New York 1936.
Grosseteste:
   A. C. Crombie: *Robert Grosseteste and the Origins of Experimental Science*, Oxford 1952.
Bacon:
   R. Carton: *La Synthèse doctrinale de Roger Bacon*, Paris 1924.
St Bonaventure:
   É. Gilson: *The Philosophy of Saint Bonaventure*, London 1938.
St Thomas Aquinas:
   M. C. D'Arcy: *Thomas Aquinas*, Dublin 1953.
   F. C. Copleston: *Aquinas*, Penguin Books 1955.
   É. Gilson: *Le Thomisme*.
Henry of Ghent:
   J. Paulus: *Henri de Gand, Essai sur les tendances de sa métaphysique*, Paris 1938.

BIBLIOGRAPHY

Duns Scotus:

  E. Longpré: *La philosophie du B. Duns Scot*, Paris 1934.

  É. Gilson: *Jean Duns Scot*, Paris 1952.

Ockham:

  L. Baudry: *Guillaume d'Occam: sa vie, ses œuvres, ses idées*, Paris 1949.

Index

The majority of thinkers have, in accordance with their treatment in the text, been listed under their first name.

Aachen, 59

Abbo, 90

Abelard, Peter, 93, 96, 104, 105, 106, 107–14, 115, 116, 118, 122, 123, 124, 129, 130, 131, 136, 139, 169, 171, 178, 223, 260, 279

Abubacer, 155–6

Academy, the, 125

Adam Marsh, 190, 256

Adam of Petit-Pont, 131

Adam of Woodham, 260, 292–3, 296

Adelard of Bath, 115, 116–17, 118, 121, 122, 173

Adrian IV, Pope, 125

Africa, North, 24, 26, 27, 33, 57, 142

Agobard, 61

Aix-en-Provence, 273

Alacens, 12, 249

Alan of Lille, 132–3, 170, 195

Alaric, 24, 33

al-Askari, 143

Albert, the Great, 127, 169, 186, 206, 207–11, 213, 215, 227, 228, 229, 247, 299

Albert, of Saxony, 261, 295

Albi, 84

Albigensian heresy, 84

Alcuin, 33, 59–61, 87, 130

Alexander of Aphrodisias, 175

Alexander of Hales, 129, 139, 194, 197, 198, 199, 200, 203, 204, 210, 237, 247

Alexander of Neckham, 185

Alfarabi, 12, 146–8, 149, 150, 151, 154, 165, 174, 182, 183

Alfred of Sareshel, 174, 175, 186

Algazali, 155, 156, 174

Alkindi, 145–6, 174

Alps, the, 25, 88, 89

Amaury of Bène, 127, 128, 172, 182

Ambrose, St, 33, 74, 94

Anglo-Saxons, 24, 52

Anselm, of Besate, 95–6, 114

Anselm, of Laon, 106, 131

Anselm, St, 40, 49, 63, 64, 89, 92, 97, 98–103, 104, 105, 106, 107, 112, 114, 115, 130, 131, 133, 138, 139, 170, 187, 191, 198, 200, 201, 205, 216, 223, 234, 236, 237, 239, 287

Apuleius, 126

Aquinas, St Thomas, 11, 12, 19, 64, 66, 88, 111, 127, 141, 142, 147, 151, 156, 157, 164, 165, 166, 175, 176, 180, 193, 194, 197, 198, 199, 200, 201, 205, 206, 207, 208, 209, 211–24, 227, 228, 230, 231, 232, 233, 234, 235, 236, 237, 238, 240, 241, 242, 244, 245, 246, 247, 251, 258, 262, 263, 264, 265, 267, 268, 269, 271, 273, 274, 275, 280, 291, 302

Aquitaine, 82

Arabia, 142; *see* also Islam

Arabian thinkers, 12, 16, 141- 62

Arabic, 115, 143, 144, 171

Archimedes, 143

Arianism, 12, 52

Aristotle, 12, 13, 14–15, 16, 17, 47, 48, 49, 87, 90, 93, 95, 105, 114, 115, 117, 122, 125, 127, 128, 135, 139, 141, 142, 143, 144, 145, 146, 147, 148, 149, 152, 153, 154, 155, 156, 157, 158, 159, 161, 162, 165, 166, 168, 170, 171–6, 177, 179, 181, 182, 183, 186, 187, 188, 190, 191, 193, 195, 196, 197, 199, 202, 204, 205, 206, 207, 208, 209, 210,

211, 213, 214, 215, 216, 217, 218,
220, 221, 225, 226, 227, 228, 229,
230,233, 242, 251, 263, 264, 265,
273, 276, 279, 280, 285, 298

Aristotelians, *see* Averroists, Christian Aristotelians

Arius, 113

Arles, 53, 128

Arras, 126, 236

Athens, 47, 55, 56

Augustine, 58

Augustine, St, 11, 12, 16, 27, 32,
33–46, 47, 52, 53, 61, 66, 68, 71,
73, 80, 92, 94, 98, 99, 100, 102,
103, 113, 116, 129, 134, 135, 136,
138, 170, 183, 184, 185, 187, 188,
191, 192, 193, 195, 196, 198, 199,
200, 201, 202, 203, 204, 205, 212,
214, 216, 232, 234, 235, 236, 237,
238, 251, 301, 303

Augustinian friars, 245

Augustinianism, 16, 162, 170, 185,
187, 188, 190–4, 195, 196, 198,
199, 201, 206, 211, 231–8, 241,
243, 244, 247, 261, 264, 267, 269,
272

Augustinians, *see* Augustinianism

Aureole, Peter, 261, 272–6, 278,
281, 283, 288, 292

Auxerre, 62

Avempace, 155–6

Averroes, 12, 141, 142, 143, 151,
155–62, 164, 165, 166, 173, 174,
182, 188, 208, 218, 221, 226, 227,
228

Averroism, 142, 156, 166, 170, 171,
179, 191, 206, 212, 214, 226–31,
238, 271, 272, 301

Averroists, *see* Averroism

Avicebrol, 12, 141, 143, 162–4, 165,
166, 174, 187, 188, 190, 194, 196,
233

Avicebron, *see* Avicebrol

Avicenna, 12, 17, 141, 143, 148–55,
156, 159, 160, 161, 162, 163, 165,
172, 174, 182, 183, 184, 187, 188,

195, 209, 210, 218, 220, 221, 228,
233, 241, 242, 244, 247, 265, 266,
268, 269

Avignon, 80, 255, 280, 303

Bacon, Roger, 169, 190, 195, 246–9

Bagdad, 155

Beauvais, 183

Bec abbey, 89, 97, 98

Becket, Thomas, 125, 126

Bede, 27, 33, 58–9, 61, 62, 130

Béguines, the, 256

Benedict Biscop, 58

Benedict, St, 27

Benedictine monasticism, 50, 57,
58, 82

Berengarius, 95, 96, 97

Bernard of Arezzo, 294

Bernard of Chartres, 117–18, 120,
121

Bernard, St, 83, 89, 113, 115, 124,
134–5, 136, 139, 169, 195, 198,
299, 302

Bernard Silvestris, 120, 172

Bible, 12, 52, 56, 60, 64, 73, 97, 114,
119, 129, 131, 180, 220, 288, 291

Black Death, 257, 291

Boethius, 16, 32, 47–50, 51, 57, 60,
63, 90, 94, 95, 105, 108, 116, 118,
120, 121, 122, 126, 132, 133, 136,
175, 180, 195, 196, 210, 233

Boethius of Dacia, 227

Bohemia, 256

Bokhara, 148

Bologna, university of, 85, 89, 97,
131, 177, 178

Bonaventure, St, 40, 64, 129, 139,
141, 191, 194, 195, 197–206, 210,
212, 213, 216, 222, 223, 228, 229,
233, 234, 235, 236, 237, 238, 244,
270, 275, 299

Boniface VIII, Pope, 255

Boniface, St, 27

Bourges, 245

Bradwardine, Thomas, 188, 261,
296–9

Britain, 24, 25, 27, 57, 81, 87, 116, 194, 256, 257
Buckingham, Thomas, 260, 292–3, 296
Burchard of Worms, 93
Burgundio of Pisa, 175
Burgundy, 81, 82
Buridan, John, 261, 295
Burleigh, Walter, 296
Byzantium, 25

Calabria, 128
Cambridge, university of, 236
Candidus of Fulda, 62
canon law, 93, 130–1, 250
Canossa, 81
Canterbury, 59, 97, 98, 237, 240, 296
Carolingian Empire, 17, 27–31, 33, 55–73, 74, 78, 87, 115
Carthage, 116
Cassian, John, 53
Cassiodorus, 32, 50–1, 57, 60
Catania, 175
Catharism, 83
Cathars, the, 133
Chalcidius, 115, 126
Champagne, 79
Charlemagne, 27, 28, 29, 30, 31, 55–7, 59, 60, 61, 63, 73, 78, 80
Charles the Bald, 33, 63
Charles Martel, 27
Chartres, 60, 88, 95, 115, 116–26, 127, 139, 170
Christ, 13, 52, 53, 55, 56, 65, 66, 71, 83, 95, 119, 128, 135, 292–3
Christendom, 82, 87, 141, 166, 176, 256, 258
Christian Aristotelians, 206–24
Christianity, 11, 17, 18, 34, 35, 36, 58, 70, 72, 133, 145, 165, 182, 191
Church, 11–12, 25–30, 32, 33, 46, 56, 57, 61, 73–4, 78, 79, 83, 88, 91, 173, 179, 249–50, 256, 302–3

Cicero, 60, 118, 121, 125
Cîteaux, 82, 83, 132
Cistercians, 82–3
Clairvaux, 83, 116, 134
Clarenbaldus of Arras, 126
Clement IV, Pope, 246
Clovis, 27
Cluny, 81
Cologne, 207, 213, 262, 299
Compiègne, 105
Constantine, donation of, 250
Constantinople, 23, 86, 175
Constantinus Africanus, 115, 116, 121, 122, 173
Copernicus, 249
Corbie, 62
Cordova, 164
Corinth, 175
Courçon, Robert, 172, 178
Cousin, Victor, 108n.
Crassus, Peter, 250
Crusades, 83

Damian, Peter, 91, 92, 96–7, 115, 116, 134, 249
Daniel of Morley, 174
Dante, 302
David of Dinant, 127–8, 172, 182
Democritus, 121
Denmark, 27
Denys, the Areopagite, 63–5, 66, 67, 135, 164, 187, 195, 213
Descartes, 11, 211, 213
Didier, Archbishop, 52
Dietrich of Freiburg, 211, 300
Diocletian, 23
Dominic Gundisalvi, 174, 182
Dominican friars, 84, 168, 170, 171, 181–2, 194, 197, 206, 207, 213, 231, 237, 239–40, 261, 276, 300
Donatism, 52
Donatus, 118, 180
Duns Scotus, John, 88, 92, 129, 139, 141, 147, 152, 180, 184, 188, 194, 206, 219, 231, 234, 236, 239,

241, 242, 258, 259, 260, 262–72, 274, 278, 279, 281, 282, 285, 287, 289, 291

Durandus of St Pourçain, 261, 272, 274, 275, 276–9, 281, 283, 287, 292

Eckhart, Master John, 300–1
Edessa, 143
Egbert, 59
Egypt, 116, 142
England, *see* Britain
Erigena, *see* John the Scot
Étienne Tempier, 229
Euclid, 12, 115, 132, 133, 143, 144, 146, 175, 249
Eustace of Arras, 236

False Decretals, the, 130
Faustus of Riez, 12, 16
Ferrières, 62
feudalism, 28, 79
FitzRalph, Richard, 296
Flanders, 79, 81, 85, 256
Fleury, abbey, 60, 90
France, 27, 55, 62, 80, 81, 84, 87, 131, 255, 256, 257
Francis of Mayronnes, 249, 272
Francis, St, 181, 237, 238
Franciscan friars, 84, 128, 168, 170, 181–2, 190, 194–206, 231, 234–9, 240, 246, 256, 261, 262, 263, 270, 280
Franks, 25, 26, 27
Fredegisus, 61
Frederick II of Germany, 257
Fulbert of Chartres, 95, 116, 117
Fulda, 60, 87

Galen, 115, 116, 143
Gaul, 24, 25, 53, 57, 58
Gaunilo, 102, 201
Gelasius II, Pope, 74

General Council of the Church, 302–3
Gerard of Cremona, 174, 175
Gerard of Czanad, 96
Gerbert (Pope Sylvester II), 90–1, 95
Germany, 24, 27, 62, 80, 81, 87, 96, 207, 257
Geyer, Bernard, 108n.
Gilbert de la Porrée, 119, 121–4, 125, 126, 127, 131, 133, 180, 195
Giles of Lessines, 228, 229, 240
Giles of Rome, 229, 232, 242, 245, 262
Gloss (on the Bible), 62, 131
Godfrey of Fontaines, 232, 244–5, 270
Gottschalk, 62, 66
grace, 19, 37–8, 41, 45, 53, 54, 71, 135, 136, 199, 200, 204, 224, 261, 271, 278, 279, 289–92, 296–8, 301, 302
Gratian, 93, 130, 131
Great schism, 256
Greece, 11, 12, 13, 16, 18, 19, 28, 63, 94, 141, 155
Greek, 63, 117, 129, 143, 171, 175, 187, 247
Gregory I, the Great, Pope, 27, 28, 52, 58, 66, 74
Gregory VII, Pope, 91, 250
Gregory IX, Pope, 173, 183
Gregory of Nyssa, 67
Gregory of Rimini, 296
Gregory of Tours, 57
Grosseteste, Robert, 169, 173, 175, 185–90, 191, 192, 193, 194, 199, 201, 246, 248
Guerric of St Quentin, 207

Halifax, Robert, 260
Haréau, 119n.
Haroun-al-Raschid, 142
Hegel, 11
Heidelberg, 296

Henry II of England, 125, 126
Henry IV of Germany, 90, 91
Henry Aristippus, 175
Henry of Ghent, 231, 234, 241–4, 245, 258, 263, 265, 266, 267, 268, 270, 276
Henry of Harclay, 279
Heraclitus, 13, 216
Hermann of Dalmatia, 118, 174
Hermann the German, 174, 175
Hermes Trismegistos, 132
Hervé Nédélec, 276
Hildebrand, see Gregory VII
Hildebert of Tours, 115
Hilduin of St Denis, 66
Hippo, 33
Hippocrates, 115, 116, 143
Holcot, Robert, 260, 261, 291–2, 296
Hugh of St Cher, 207
Hugh of St Victor, 116, 124, 126, 129, 131, 136–8, 139
Hugh of Strasbourg, 211, 299
Humbert, 91
Hume, 294
Hundred Years War, 257
Huns, 24
Hus, John, 256
Hussites, 256
hylomorphism, 163–4, 193, 196, 202, 203, 233, 234, 236, 237, 239, 240, 247

Ibn Gabirol, see Avicebrol
Innocent III, Pope, 84, 127, 178, 256
Innocent IV, Pope, 173
Investiture contest, 80, 91, 130
Iona, 58
Ireland, 27, 57–8, 62, 72
Irish monasticism, 58
Isaac of Stella, 136
Isidore of Seville, St, 33, 51, 59, 61, 62, 66, 130
Islam, 25, 51, 141–62, 196

Italy, 24, 25, 26, 27, 47, 50, 51, 52, 57, 80, 83, 87, 88, 89, 96, 129, 213, 214, 234
Ivo of Chartres, 93, 97, 130

Jacquerie, 258
James of Metz, 276, 277
James of Venice, 175
Jarrow, 58
Jerome, St, 94
Jerusalem, 86
Jewish thinkers, 12, 16, 141n., 162–7
Joachim of Flora, 128, 256
Joachism, 12
John XXI, Pope, see Peter of Spain
John XXII, Pope, 256, 280
John of Damascene, 129
John of Jandun, 302
John of Mirecourt, 293
John of Parma, 128
John Quidort, 240
John de la Rochelle, 195
John of St Giles, 207
John of Salisbury, 117, 118, 123, 124–6, 131, 139, 250
John the Scot (Erigena), 17, 32, 33, 62–72, 95, 98, 112, 119, 127, 128, 164, 242
John of Spain (or Avendeath?), 174
Judaism, 165
Julian of Toledo, 130
Justinian, 26–7, 51, 143

Kant, 11
Kilwardby, Robert, 230, 232, 236, 239, 240, 246, 261, 276
Kinnesrin, 143
Koran, 155, 157, 162

Lambert of Auxerre, 225
Lanfranc, 89, 92, 98, 131

Languedoc, 84, 256
Laon, 60, 88, 106, 116, 130–1
Lateran Council, the fourth, 127, 128
Latin Averroism, *see* Averroism
Leibniz, 238
Lerins, 53, 58
Lincoln, 186
Loches, 105
Loire, 90
Lollards, 256
Lombards, 26–7, 51, 52
Lombardy, 79, 83, 85
Louis IV, of Bavaria, 257, 280
Lull, Raymond, 238
Luther, 134, 256
Lyons, 61, 83

Magyars, 72
Mahommedanism, 142
Maimonides, 12, 141, 162, 164–5, 166, 208
Malaga, 162
Manegold of Lautenbach, 97, 106, 131, 250
Manicheism, 12, 33, 34, 183
Marseilles, 53
Marsilius of Inghen, 295–6
Marsilius of Padua, 256, 302–3
Martianus Capella, 50, 118
Matthew of Aquasparta, 234–6, 237, 244
Maurice of Spain, 172
Mauricourt, Peter of, 248
Maximus, the confessor, 63, 65–6, 67, 120
Maxton, 262
Mediterranean, 25, 26, 27, 72, 79, 85
Michael of Cesena, 256
Michael Scot, 256
Molesme, 82
Monte Cassino, 89, 116, 213
Montpelier, 132, 178
Moses, 17

Motazilites, 143
Munich, 280
Mutakallimin, 143
mysticism, 116, 133–9, 256, 299–302

Naples, 213
Neoplatonism, 12, 15–16, 17, 34, 35–6, 38, 40, 41, 44, 46, 48, 63, 68, 69, 70, 71, 72, 119, 142, 144, 145, 148, 149, 152, 154, 156, 157, 160, 162, 163, 164, 173, 176, 192, 196, 214, 221, 245, 249, 299
Neoplatonists, *see* Neoplatonism
Nestorius, 113
Nicholas of Amiens, 124, 132
Nicholas of Autrecourt, 293–4, 295
Nicholas of Cusa, 127
Nicholas of Oresme, 249, 261, 295
Nominalism, 49, 104–14, 259, 260
Nominalists, *see* Nominalism
Normandy, 89
Normans, 178
Northmen, 27, 33, 72, 83
Northumbria, 57–8
Norway, 27

Ockham, William of, 113, 129, 180, 184, 193, 256, 258, 259, 260, 261, 271, 272, 273, 276 279–91, 292, 293, 294, 295, 297, 302–3
Ockhamism, 259, 272, 279–94, 296, 299
Odovacar, 24
Old Testament, 40, 128, 162
Olivi, Peter John, 236, 237, 239
Orange, 53
Orleans, 61, 88
Ostrogoths, 24
Otloh of St Emmeran, 97
Otto of Freising, 124
Oxford, 85, 169, 180, 181, 186, 187, 190, 192, 194, 230, 236, 240, 246, 261, 262, 279, 286, 296

Pantheism, 36, 72, 121, 127–8, 172
Paris, 19, 60, 88, 106, 118, 121, 127, 129, 131, 132, 134, 172–3, 183, 186, 187, 188, 194, 197, 207, 213, 214, 225, 227, 237, 240, 241, 245, 246, 257, 261, 262, 293, 294, 296
Paris, condemnations by Bishop of, 166, 213, 228, 229–30, 234, 239, 246, 258, 263, 271
Parmenides, 13, 216
Paschasius Radbertus, 62
Patrick, St, 58
Paul, the deacon, 61
Paul, St, 114
Pavia, 97
Peckham, John, 236–7, 246
Pelagianism, 12, 38, 52–4, 59
Pelagius, 38, 52, 113, 297
Persia, 142, 143, 148
Peter Comestor, 131
Peter Lombard, 129–30, 137, 178, 180, 260
Peter of Palud, 276
Peter of Pisa, 61
Peter of Poitiers, 131
Peter of Spain (Pope John XXII), 225
Philip II, of France, 178
Philip IV (the Fair) of France, 225, 262
Philip of Greve, 183
Pisa, 175, 280
Plato, 12, 13–14, 15, 16, 17, 48, 49, 115, 117, 118, 120, 135, 139, 140, 145, 146, 147, 150, 176, 184, 199, 210, 216
Platonism, 16, 40, 46, 47, 62, 114, 115, 117–26, 159, 186, 218, 221
Plotinus, 15, 16, 17, 34, 44, 132, 144, 152, 300
Poitiers, 27, 121
Porphyry, 48, 95, 105, 107, 122, 175
Porretani, 124
Prevostin of Cremona, 131
Priscian, 118

Proclus, 15, 16, 17, 132, 144, 175, 176, 213, 214, 245, 300
Provence, 84
Pseudo-Denys, see Denys the Areopagite
Ptolemy, 119, 143, 174, 175
Pythagoras, 140

Quadrivium, 50, 61, 116, 119, 126, 137, 168, 180, 186
Quintilian, 60, 117

Raban Maur, 61–2, 73, 87
Raoul Ardoul, 124
Ratramnus of Corbie, 62
Raymond of Toledo, 174
Realism, 49, 104–14, 259, 260
Realists, see Realism
Reichenau, 60, 62, 87
Remy of Auxerre, 62
Renaissance, the, 11
Rheims, 60, 90, 124
Rhine, 24
Richard Clapwell, 238, 240.
Richard of Middleton, 234, 239, 240, 246, 261
Richard of St Victor, 116, 138–9, 200, 201
Risaina, 143
Robert of Melun, 124, 131
Robert of Rétines, 118, 174
Roger Marston, 234, 236, 246
Roland of Cremona, 207
Roman Empire, 16, 23–31, 33, 45, 50, 55, 78, 142
Roman Law, 24, 25, 250
Rome, 11, 33, 45, 47, 78, 82, 178, 256
Roscelin, 104–5, 108, 109, 113, 124, 131
Rouen, 250n.
Ruysbruck, John, 301–2

Salerno, 85, 116, 177
St Denis abbey, 66
St Martin abbey, 59, 60
St Victor abbey, 53, 116, 131, 136
Saracens, 72
scepticism, 34, 259, 272-99
scholasticism, 92-4, 129, 141, 170, 212, 260, 262, 271
Scotism, 259, 272, 274
Scotland, 58
Scripture, see Bible
Seine, 131, 178
Seneca, 121
Sens, 113, 134, 172
Sentences, 115, 128-33, 180, 260-1
Servatus Lupus, 62
Sicily, 81, 85, 87, 174
Sidonius Apollinaris, 25
Siger of Brabant, 227, 228-9, 230, 302
Signy, 134, 136
Simon of Tournai, 131
Simplicius, 175
Soissons, 105, 134
Stella abbey, 136
Spain, 24, 25, 27, 52, 57, 72, 81, 85, 87, 90, 142, 162, 164, 175
Stilicho, 24
Stoics, 73, 196
Surrey, 280
Sutri, 82
Switzerland, 80
Sylvester II, Pope, see Gerbert
Syria, 142-3, 155

Tagaste, 33
Tauler, John, 301-2
Tempier, Étienne, 245
Tertullian, 41
Thierry of Chartres, 118-19, 120, 126, 127
Theobald, 125
Theodore of Tarsus, 58
Theodoric, 24, 47, 50, 51
Theodulf, 61

Theoromata, 272
Thomas of York, 190
Thomism, 156, 162, 179, 183, 192, 193, 194, 211-24, 227, 229, 230, 231-4, 236, 239, 240, 244, 260, 262, 263, 264, 267, 272, 274, 275
Toledo, 130, 174
Toulouse, 172, 173
Tournai, 131
Tours, 61, 87, 95, 115, 116, 120
trivium, 50, 61, 63, 126, 137, 168, 169, 186
Turks, 86

Ulrich of Strasbourg, 211, 299-300
Urban IV, Pope, 173
universals, 48, 104-14, 117, 118, 122-4, 125, 149-50, 158, 160, 217, 223, 235, 259
universities, 84, 168, 176-81

Vandals, 24, 33
Varro, 50
Vercelli, 95
Victorines, 170, 198, 249; see also Hugh and Richard of St Victor
Vienne, 52, 237
Vikings, see Northmen
Vincent of Lerins, 53
Visigoths, 24
Viterbo, 197
Vivarium, 50

Walafrid of Strabo, 62, 87, 130
Waldenses, 133
Waleys, Thomas, 261, 291
Walter of Bruges, 236
Wearmouth, 58
William of Alnwick, 272
William of Auvergne, 182-5, 186, 187, 188, 190, 191, 192, 193, 198, 210, 221, 233, 235, 242, 247, 269

William of Auxerre, 183

William of Champeaux, 106–7, 108, 124, 131, 136, 260

William of Conches, 120–1, 123, 126, 127, 140, 172

William de la Mare, 238, 240

William of Meliton, 195

William of Moerbeke, 16, 173, 175–6, 213, 300

William the Pious, 82

William of St Amour, 197, 214

William of St Thierry, 121, 135–6

William of Shireswood, 239

William of Ware, 239

Witelo, 249

Wyclif, John, 256

York, 59

York Anonymous, 250

Zeno, 143

Zoroastrianism, 142, 145

THE PELICAN HISTORY OF THE WORLD

It is often urged that world history is best written without the limitations of frontiers. Nevertheless it is national character, national development, and national power, which incite the curiosity of most of us, and it is these things which seem to be behind most of the international problems with which we are faced today. Therefore, in preparing the plan of *The Pelican History of the World* the Editor, J. E. Morpurgo, has decided that the old familiar emphasis upon national history has meant sufficient to justify its continuance in this series.

Each volume is written by a specialist, and the emphasis given to such matters as trade, religion, politics, foreign relations, intellectual and social life, varies between volume and volume.

A HISTORY OF MODERN CHINA
by Kenneth Scott Latourette

HISTORY OF MODERN FRANCE: I
by J. A. Cobban

HISTORY OF THE UNITED STATES
VOL. I : COLONIES TO NATION
VOL. 2 : NATION TO WORLD POWER
by J. E. Morpurgo and Russel B. Nye

THOMAS À KEMPIS

THE IMITATION OF CHRIST

Translated by Leo Sherley-Price

L27

After the Bible itself probably the best-known and best-loved book in Christendom is *The Imitation of Christ*, Thomas à Kempis's guide towards Christian perfection, which for over five hundred years has continued to exercise a widespread influence over Christians of every age and race. Unfortunately most English translators have tended to misrepresent this book – either by making acknowledged alterations in the text to accord with their personal views, or by presenting it in a pseudo-Jacobean style. Thus many would-be readers have passed it by, and missed the advantage of Thomas's profound wisdom, his clarity of thought and vision, his wide knowledge of the Scriptures and Fathers, and his clear understanding of human nature and its needs. It was time for a new translation, and L. Sherley-Price, a senior Chaplain of the Royal Navy, has provided it for the Penguin Classics series. His, the first unabridged edition in modern English, presents a complete, accurate, and readable version to the public.